Tips

Ideas for Secondary School Librarians & Technology Specialists

Second Edition

Sharron L. McElmeel, Editor

PROFESSIONAL GROWTH SERIES®

A Publication of THE BOOK REPORT & LIBRARY TALK
Professional Growth Series

Linworth Publishing, Inc.
Worthington, Ohio

Library of Congress Cataloging-in-Publication Data

Published by Linworth Publishing, Inc.
480 East Wilson Bridge Road, Suite L
Worthington, Ohio 43085

Series Information:
        From The Professional Growth Series

ISBN 0-938865-93-5
5 4 3 2 1

Table of Contents

About the Editor

S harron L. McElmeel is a veteran educator who has learned much from her peers. She often teaches courses in literature and technology to her professional peers and to undergraduates who are entering the field of education. Much of her own writing is the result of requests made to her for information she has gathered about authors and illustrators. Among her many publications are ABCs of an Author/Illustrator Visit, Research Strategies for Moving Beyond Reporting, and Literature Frameworks: From Apples to Zoos–all published by Linworth Publishing, Inc.

Linworth Publishing, Inc. has also released the 3rd revision of Internet for Schools–a book she co-authored with Carol Simpson; and World Wide Web Almanac: Making Curriculum Connections to Special Days, Weeks, and Months which she co-authored with Carol Smallwood.

Sharron L. McElmeel was born in Cedar Rapids, Iowa, and obtained an undergraduate degree in education and later earned a Master's degree and pursued post-graduate work at the University of Iowa. For the past 25 years she has lived in a rural area of Linn County in Iowa where she shares her home with her husband and more than 10,000 books. When she is not writing she is enjoying her family– four sons, two daughters, and three grandchildren, reading, and her role of community activist. Visit her website at http://www.mcelmeel.com.

Introduction

The first edition of *Tips* was published in 1991. It was a collection of contributions to the "Tips" column published in each edition of THE BOOK REPORT since its first issue. The book proved to be as popular as the column. Now this new compilation is gleaned from contributions that have appeared in the "Tips" column since the publication of that first edition. All of the contributions have been included from THE BOOK REPORT: *The Magazine for Secondary School Library Media & Technology Specialists*. Selected items have been gleaned from the "Tips & Pointers" column that appeared for several years in *Technology Connection*—now a popular section included in THE BOOK REPORT and its sister publication LIBRARY TALK: *The Magazine for Elementary School Library Media & Technology Specialists*.

Sharing with colleagues seems to be a hallmark of the specialists who deal with library media centers and with technology. Testimony to this is the heavy traffic on LM_NET <ericir.syr.edu/lm_net/>, which is a virtual sharing forum for school library media specialists. That listserv and the many contributions to the "Tips" column are ample evidence that we are a sharing group.

This compilation contains almost 800 ideas. Not all of the ideas will be new to all readers. But each item will be new to someone. Some of the ideas are similar—but with a slightly different twist or focus. Many of them are bound to be just the idea you can use or the idea that sparks a great new adaptation appropriate to your situation.

This was the case of one library media specialist who was inspired by the tip, "Bring History to Life." She located a historical expert to portray Harry

S. Truman in her school. It was such a success that she established weekly forums. The forums were rotated through the noon hours, on Fridays, in her high school. Sometimes the forums were instructional, sometimes entertaining, and sometimes social. Over 200 students came to hear a costumed telling of *Beowulf*. Dozens of parents and students displayed arts and crafts for sale before the holidays. On another Friday, the principal was available for a round table discussion about school policies. There are explanations of the technical aspects of the next school play, coffeehouse days, and readings. Students assist in suggesting topics and guests. They volunteer their talents. Harry S. Truman's life seemed a long way from the rock and roll band that performed one day. But in terms of inspiration, the source was the same.

Sometimes you may not be able to use the hint because of the equipment available to you, and a comparable hint is not included for the equipment you do have. However, even in those situations, the hint may lead you to ask others who are more experienced with your particular equipment whether that function is available to you. For example, in one hint the keystrokes are given to capture a screen shot using a Macintosh computer. Similar information is not included for the PC, but certainly there is a way an image of the screen can be captured to print in handouts or manuals to use with your students. A little checking with others may give you the answer. Without the hint you might not have ever asked the question—and would not have ever known that it could be done.

This book is divided into nine sections. Just as it is difficult to catalog a book when it is equally appropriate in two distinct areas, so too was it difficult to categorize many of the hints. We were able to identify nine basic strands:... And They Will Come; Computers—Easing the Curriculum; Curriculum Involvement; Managing the Library; Library Skills; Odds and Ends; Public Relations; Read, Read, Read; and Volunteers—Students and Community. Each of the contributions fits in one of the strands quite nicely. Some could easily have been placed in two and sometimes three sections; however, they appear only once.

When an idea sparks an adaptation that fits your situation better, keep in mind that your variation on a good idea may spark yet another variation for someone else. It's worth sharing. Consider sending your idea to be published in *THE BOOK REPORT: The Magazine for Secondary School Library Media & Technology Specialists*. Contributions may be sent by e-mail to linworth@linworth.com or via U.S. mail to Linworth Publishing, Inc., 480 East Wilson Bridge Road, Suite L, Worthington, Ohio 43085

Sharron L. McElmeel, Editor

SECTION 1

...And They Will Come

> **There are really only two objectives the library has:
> to get children to come to the library and to keep them coming.**
>
> *Phyliss R. Fenner, 1939*

Creating an attractive center with enticing displays will help bring students and staff to the library–that is the first objective. In secondary schools the library seems to be more-and sometimes less–of an option then it was at the elementary level. Students are generally scheduled into classes at specific hours, and unless their class is scheduled into the library for research, they are seldom released from the classroom "just to go to the LMC." Students are expected to use the library during their study hall or before or after school. Some students seldom have an opportunity to use the resources of the library media center during class time. That makes it especially important that students are aware of the resources and services available in the school's LMC. In many instances the displays will be an outgrowth of specific activities, contests, public relations activities, and so forth. Good old-fashioned advertising will acquaint students and staff with what you can offer. Here are some ideas contributed by readers.

Student Art in the Library

Each month, the library and the art department in our high school spotlight the student "Artist of the Month," who sets up a mini show in the library conference room. We also receive donations of student artwork for display. When our county librarians' meeting was held at our school, the elementary school librarians admired our display of pâpier-mâché and remarked that the items would be excellent in displays at their schools. Because of this interest, we now circulate student artwork to other schools in the county.

— *Carolyn Davis, C. D. Hylton High School, Woodbridge, Virginia*

Kids Who Read Succeed

To celebrate National Library Week, we sent out a snappy form letter to local and national celebrities asking them to fill out a questionnaire telling us why they like to read and the title of their favorite book. We also requested a photo for our display. Response was overwhelming. Locally, we heard from business leaders, the chancellor of the university, authors, and artists. We heard from our state's governor and the President and Vice-President of the United States. Students were amazed that these people were once junior high schoolers who liked to read. Weeks later, students were still stopping by our bulletin board display of the replies, and they stayed to check out books.

— *Dede Atkinson, Woodland Junior High School, Fayetteville, Arkansas*

See You In September

At the end of each school year, the advisor of our school yearbook gives me all the photos taken during the year that were not used. I choose action shots depicting life at our school and display these in my September "welcome back" bulletin board. Although the display is simple to make, it is the most popular one of the year.

— *Anita Jump, Sacajawea Junior High, Federal Way, Washington*

A Stellar Welcome

To welcome students back last fall, we captioned our library display case "Here's to a Stellar Year—Welcome." Under the caption, we displayed photocopies of the previous fall's yearbook pictures of each student and listed the names of new ones. Shiny silver stars completed the display, which drew crowds of students eager to find their faces and those of their friends.

— *Kathy Frederick, Chamberlin High School, Twinsburg, Ohio*

Authors' Photos on Walls and Shelves

After several author visits, I hung framed photos of the authors under a banner reading "Authors We Have Known." The display created so much attention that we put other photos, taken at state conferences, in acrylic frames and set them on the shelves near the authors' books. On the fiction shelves, there is a photo of William Sleator among the S's. In the 811's, students find a photo of Jack Prelutsky.

— *Wendy Braddock, Indian Hill Middle School, Cincinnati, Ohio*

Banned Books

To get ready for Banned Book Week in September, I begin planning in the spring. I use the ALA list to gather books that have been censored. In each book pocket, I place a 3 x 5 card with the reasons the book was banned. The books make an effective display during Banned Book Week.

— *Patricia Jackson, Baldwin County High School, Bay Minette, Alabama*

Editor's Note: The American Library Association has a Web site at <www.ala. org/bbooks/> that provides background about Banned Book Week, lists of most frequently banned books, and information for public relations during the week. smc

Banners

Put *Print Shop* or any other banner-making program to good use. Make banners promoting special or frequently used URLs. The banners can then be used to decorate your lab or media center.

— *Mary Alice Anderson, Media Specialist, Winona (Minnesota) Middle School*

Bulletin Board for School News

One of the four bulletin boards in the library is reserved for school news. I display any news article mentioning the school, students, faculty and alumni. Students and teachers alike enjoy seeing their pictures and news stories displayed in a prominent place.

— *Lee Anne Kendall, James Buchanan High School, Mercersburg, Pennsylvania*

Bulletin Boards on Video

The costs of film and development discouraged us from taking photos of bulletin boards so we could recycle materials and remember designs from year to year. Our solution was to video-tape all new bulletin boards. We labeled a tape "Bulletin Boards" and simply add new footage to it whenever we put up a new display.

— *Carole Bell, Brown Middle School, McAllen, Texas*

Bulletin Boards: 3-D

Each time I put up a bulletin board with a theme, I include paperback books that reflect that theme. For example, the Halloween bulletin board displays horror and supernatural titles, the Valentine's Day board shows romances, and so on. I hang the books on the board by looping strong string around the bindings and tying knots. The knotted ends are tacked to the bulletin board. Doing this not only creates interest in the books, but adds color and a three-dimensional effect to the display. Students have often asked me to remove books from the bulletin board so they can read them.

— *Shelley Glantz, Arlington (Massachusetts) High School*

Career Week

We use library resources to help promote our school-wide career week. A computerized banner taped around the circulation desk reads "Career Information to Go," while book jackets and pamphlets are showcased. Also on display are career reference books, tapes and film-strips. Classes are invited to career lessons that help students use the available resources. The school administration appreciates the library's support in making career week a success.

— *Carolyn Samuels, Fallstaff Middle School, Baltimore, Maryland*

Catalog Card Recycling

When we automated, we recycled the catalog cards as Christmas decorations. Garland ropes were strung with cards and wooden beads. Cards spelled out "joy" and "Ho, Ho, Ho!" on the door and the bulletin board. During the year, we used the garlands and cards to celebrate Valentine's Day, St. Patrick's Day, and graduation.

— *Janet Kirk, Parsons (Kansas) High School*

CD-ROM Border

Back "issues" of CD-ROMS make a nice border for a bulletin board or other display. Just string them together with yarn and they become a 90s-style border. And they are attention getting.

— *Mary Alice Anderson, Media Specialist, Winona (Minnesota) Middle School*

Celebrating the Bard's Birthday

On April 23rd every year, our library staff and the English department celebrate Shakespeare's birthday with a traditional English tea. The entire staff is invited for tea, crumpets, jam, watercress sandwiches, and the like. One English class makes birthday cards to decorate the library conference room.

— *Gloria Fulghum, Avondale High School, Avondale Estates, Georgia*

Classroom and Library Displays

To help make a connection between the classroom and the library, borrow items from teachers and students to use in a display. For example, sports equipment could be combined with a display of sports books, finished craft items from home economics classes with craft and hobby books, and so forth. Be sure to include the teachers' and students' names in the display. Teachers enjoy a chance to highlight classroom projects, and both students and teachers get new ideas from the books.

— *Linda A. Hensley, Clinton-Massie High School, Clarksville, Ohio*

Displaying Personal Favorites

During National Library Week, we have a special display of favorite books and records. The name of the teacher or student who claims a particular item as a favorite is penned in handsome calligraphy in a bookmark and tucked inside the item. This display has generated positive comments and encouraged reading.

— *Anonymous*

Easy Bulletin Board Lettering

We now use the computer to make bulletin board lettering. Using banner/poster software, we print the large words on a laser printer. Then we run the printed pages through the thermal transparency maker. The transparencies (uncut or trimmed) are attached to the bulletin board. Since the unprinted portions are transparent, background pictures and colors are still visible.

— *Edna Boardman and Joan Varty, Minot (North Dakota) High School, Magic City Campus*

Recognizing Library Users

To encourage use of the library, I make a large poster on *Print Shop* that says, "I am a frequent user of the library." Students who come in often autograph the poster, and it is displayed outside the library door. The idea is

even more fun at the holidays when I make a giant card for each period that offers greetings such as "Happy Holidays from First Period Library Users" and "Seasons Greetings from Second Period Library Users." Signed cards are displayed in the hall.

— *Patricia Kolencik, North Clarion High School, Tionesta, Pennsylvania*

February Book Lovers

Our annual February bulletin board catches everyone's eye, and students now ask about it ahead of time. The display is titled "Books We Love." On large red hearts, we arrange pictures of students and staff along with the title of their favorite book. Pictures are borrowed from yearbook files and so are of good quality. We try to interview a variety of people, including athletes and musicians. Sometimes book choices break down stereotypes—students were impressed that the custodian's favorite book was *The Last of the Mohicans*. For some participants, this is the first time anyone has asked them to name a book they like.

— *Cheri Ricker, Phoenix (Arizona) Christian Junior/Senior High School*

Foreign Language Gourmets

As a display for foreign language week, we "set" a table using different colors of construction paper as placemats and plastic tableware. Cookbooks of various nationalities were opened to colorful double-page spreads that served as "entrees." Placecards named the country of origin. The centerpiece could be a standup cookbook display. Copies of recipes from around the world or a bibliography of ethnic cookbooks could be included.

— *Rosmond Douglass, Nathan B. Forrest High School, Jacksonville, Florida*

Good Day for Displays

So many interesting projects were produced during library research classes, for example, three-dimensional castles, that we created a special display of these projects. To ensure a large audience, the display was scheduled for the day that the community voted for the school budget.

— *Anne Ozog, Waterloo (New York) Middle School*

Graduation Bulletin Board

A popular display that continues to generate student interest is the annual graduation bulletin board. An appropriate motif is selected to symbolize graduation (diploma, mortarboard figure of a graduate), and all prospective graduates come to the library to sign their motifs. Once all signatures are collected, motifs are cut out, mounted on card stock in school colors, and then laminated. Top ranking graduates are placed on the bulletin board, while other graduates are displayed on the glass wall above our library's reference section. Often, I include a display of books about college and career choice underneath the bulletin board names. At the final graduation practice, motifs are given to graduates to place in their senior memory books.

— *Susan E. Couvillon, North Vermilion High School, Maurice, Louisiana*

Having Fun with Dewey

When seventh graders are reviewing the Dewey decimal system, one project involves writing fictional titles for books in each general category. Wacky ideas abound! This year I used the students' titles in a bulletin board display. Here are some examples: "Mrs. Zimmerman's Encyclopedia of 'Do It Right'" from the 000s; "'Just Between You and Me' by Newt Gingrich's Mom"; "Martian Math Made Easy" from the 500s; "Forces from Beyond the Cosmos: How A Microwave Really Works" from the 600s.

— *Sherry Hoy, Tuscarora Junior High School, Mifflintown, Pennsylvania*

Highlighting Books

I always admired the colorful round highlighters that are available from book promotional companies such as Upstart, but such luxuries are beyond my budget. Now I make my own out of heavy poster board, decorate them, and place them on books displayed on tables. Some of the more successful highlighters promote books featured on the instructional television series. After students view a lesson from one of the series, I pull the featured books and insert highlighters that say "Seen on Cover-to-Cover" or "Seen on Storybound." Recently I have tried different shapes such as a ghost and jack-o'-lantern for Halloween books.

— *Marcia Bethea, Maple Junior High School, Dillon, South Carolina*

Homemade READ Posters

We've borrowed an idea from the American Library Association's series of posters that feature celebrities reading. The popular posters now share space in our library with our own posters of students. We make our posters by photocopying and enlarging a 4 x 6 photo of a reading student. (The original photo is given to the student.) On the library wall, Michael J. Fox is gripped by The Skeleton Crew. Beside him, our own Becky reads The Island of Blue Dolphins in front of the science room aquarium. A classically coifed Glenn Close hugs *Pride and Prejudice*. Next to her, our Jarret reads *Of Mice and Men* to his stuffed toy mouse. Another poster is captioned, "Read. It's cool." It shows the entire ninth-grade class reading with their shades on, in the shade.

— *Miji Campbell, St. Thomas Aquinas School, Red Deer, Alberta, Canada*

Homemade Reading Posters

Take photos of teachers and others in the building reading their favorite books. Then make these photos into posters to promote reading. There will be many double takes as students recognize people from the school in the posters.

— *Linda A. Vretos, West Springfield High School, Springfield, Virginia*

Honoring Seniors

In May we feature graduating seniors in displays. A favorite bulletin board is titled "And They're Off." We begin with a map of the United States and of our state (Texas). Seniors are invited to add their name and their college choice with its school colors to the list in the library. Student names are written on pennants cut from construction paper of the appropriate color. Pennants are placed around the maps with lines pointing to the location of the school. Another popular display for May involves saving newspaper clippings, athletic and theater programs, and anything else featuring student names all through the year. The title of the display, "It Was a Very Good Year," is surrounded by a collage of the items collected.

— *Susan Rhoads, Highland Park High School, Dallas, Texas*

Inspiration from the Alumni

Every year for open house, I put up a display of books written by graduates of our school. We hang a letterman sweater, photos of the author from old yearbooks, and a current photo, if available, next to the books. The display now takes two glass cases outside the library door. The teachers love the display so much that they remind me to put it up. They also give me the titles of more books since they have taught here longer than I have and are more familiar with graduates' careers. Students are inspired by the display.

— *Laura J. Viau, McQuaid Jesuit High School, Rochester, New York*

Library Quilt

The faculty, staff, and students of our high school worked together to tell the story of our school in quilt squares. We started one autumn by giving out squares of fabric. We hoped to get the squares in by Christmas but actually got them ready to piece one year later. Students, teachers, cafeteria workers, and secretaries did squares in cross-stitch, embroidery, and paint. Parent volunteers were drafted to finish up 24 of the squares. The squares were then quilted by the members of a local church. The project created a frenzy of people working together and enjoying the library. Now hanging on the wall of the library, the quilt is a treasure that fulfills our school motto: "The Tradition Continues."

— *Joellen G. Cullison, Deer Park Senior High School, South Campus, Pasadena, Texas*

Name the Author

To encourage interest in authors, I made a "Name the Author" bulletin board for the middle school library. Pictures of popular authors were posted with their names concealed below. Students could test their ability to recognize the authors before they checked the names.

— *Allison Trent Bernstein, Blake Middle School, Medfield, Massachusetts*

Name the Top 10

Remember when radio stations made a show of playing the top 10 hits? I do the same, but with books. Under the rubric "Strope's Top 10," each month I display the 10 books and post summaries of those I liked best, ranked 1-10. During National Library Week, I read through my summaries and choose my 10 favorites for the year. "Strope's Top 10" promotes my own reading as well as students' reading.

— *Carol Strope, Fairmont Junior High, Boise, Idaho*

National Hobby Month

After all the excitement of the holidays, returning to school in January can be a letdown. Since January is National Hobby Month, a hobby-matching contest perks everyone up and promotes the library as well. Before the holidays, ask staff members to bring in an icon representative of their hobby. To make an entry blank, list participating staff members alphabetically on one side of the sheet, on the other list all icons. The object, of course, is to match the staff member to the correct hobby. A brightly colored display case complete with computer generated signs holds all the paraphernalia. In our contest, several announcements on the PA

system brought students to the library; many entered more than once. Winners received a paperback book of their choice.

— *Cheryl Mason, Munster (Indiana) High School*

Post Office Posters

A good source for huge posters is your local post office. My post office saves all out-dated posters for me, and by trimming off or covering the date, I have a poster that will last forever.

— *Evelyn Hammeran, Randolf (New Jersey) High School*

Preserving Letters

Pre-cut commercial alphabet letters make great signs, but the letters are expensive and damage easily. To preserve them, I photocopy individual letters or whole words. My signs are as clear as the originals and can be enlarged or reduced to suit my needs. Best of all, my purchased letters last forever.

— *Barbara Resnick, Queens Vocational High School, Long Island City, New York*

Projection Bulbs as Decorations

Don't throw out used projector bulbs. Use the hot glue gun to attach ribbons and bows. Hang them on a Christmas tree in the library. They make a great conversation piece.

— *Gina Drifmeyer, Jefferson Davis Middle School, Hampton, Virginia*

Recognizing Successful Alumni

A display of books and articles published by alumni of the school proved so popular that the teachers asked if I could do a display of alumni who were active in music. The teachers and staff provided compact discs, cassettes, and musical instruments for the display. Students helped find yearbook photos and copied them. We included current photos of the musicians if available and newspaper articles about them. Photographs of the display were sent to the musicians. We hope to build a circulating collection of alumni recordings.

— *Laura J. Viau, McQuaid Jesuit High School, Rochester, New York*

Recycle the Card Catalog

I love antiques and could not bring myself to dispose of the solid oak card catalog when we computerized circulation. So I moved it to a place of honor by the entrance to the library, crowned it with plants, and displayed books on its open drawers.

— *Patricia Jackson-Jones, Baldwin County High School, Bay Minette, Alabama*

Recycled Store Displays

I often ask stores for promotional items they no longer display. I use the items to promote library activities. For example, a three-foot-long inflatable airplane was displayed with the slogan "See the World, Visit Your Library," and a life-size figure of Jim Carrey "held" a book and instructions for a seasonal reading program.

— *Leslie Lacika, Kingman-Delaware Middle School, Dingman's Ferry, Pennsylvania*

Retailing the Library

Store managers are sometimes willing to give or sell (at a reasonable cost) display items that can be used in the library. For example, a video store donated a large cutout of the stars of the movie *My Girl*. I added a sign saying "My girl loves to read" and placed the display in the hall outside the library. A life-size display of the movie star Christian Slater is used to announce the cut-off date for our reading contests. Giant happy faces that once hung in a sporting goods store now greet students entering the library.

— *Carole Bell, Brown Middle School, McAllen, Texas*

Senior Survey

The librarians surveyed seniors working in the library during April and May, asking each of them the same two questions:
1. What are your plans for fall?
2. If you could do high school over again, what would you do differently?

Responses were printed out with each senior's name and their answers to the questions and posted colorfully on large display boards in the library. We called the display "Senior Choices." We learned which colleges students had been accepted to, scholarships and awards given, jobs they planned to apply for, or military service plans. Responses to question two were frank, often mentioning courses they wish they had taken, better grades, or AP courses they should have taken. Their answers proved to be interesting and valuable for both younger students and the faculty! School administrators, parents, and board of education members came to read and enjoy the display. Our simple survey turned into a powerful and valuable lesson for the whole school.

— *Sandra Brady, Churchville-Chili High School, Churchville, New York*

Soar into Spring Display

During the last days of April and the beginning weeks of May, we make and display kites that feature the names of students who have received awards during the year-in academics, sports, and contests. We make a kite for each student or winning team and list their accomplishments. Kites that are displayed on the bulletin boards are printed on one side only, but kites that can be hung from the ceiling are printed on both sides. Students like to see their names flying high in the library.

— *Janet Wartman, West Liberty Salem School, Powell, Ohio*

Soccer Stars & Other Players

Soccer is popular at our school so we used that motif to publicize the fall media program. We purchased the "Read" poster (American Library Association) that shows actor Andrew Shue (*Melrose Place*) in soccer attire. We centered this poster on a display board and surrounded it with individual photos of students who played on our teams. The players chose the books as well as the setting and posed for their photographs. They had a great time hamming it up for the library. A hint for others who use this idea: since the photographs are popular, offer to get reprints at cost for anyone who wants a copy.

— *Patsy H. Troutman, Providence High School, Charlotte, North Carolina*

Stick with It

Do you put posters up with masking tape rolled in two and stuck behind each corner? If so, the tape probably comes loose from the wall before the school year is over. Here's a trick I've discovered: at each corner, attach the tape at a different angle. I've found posters stay up much longer this way.

— *Carol Burbridge, Jardine Middle School, Topeka, Kansas*

Summer Travel

I ask teachers to bring in photographs of their summer activities, such as vacations or working around the house, for display at the beginning of the school years. Students huddle around the display case, intrigued and amused to learn that their teachers actually have a life outside the school building. Since many teachers travel to foreign countries, we all travel vicariously.

— *Jan Hembree, Central High School, Carrollton, Georgia*

Summer Travels Highlighted

Each fall the library stages a display based on the summer travels of our teachers. I send the teachers and other staff members a memo explaining the display and asking for photographs and a description of the vacation sites. Along with the photos, I display a map with locations pinpointed and books related to the places visited.

— *Ann Yawornitsky, Wilson Southern Junior High Library, West Lawn, Pennsylvania*

Teacher Features

We like to feature teachers in our library display case. One of our most popular displays was the "Mr. Legs Contest." Polaroid photos of our male teachers' legs were placed on view, and votes were cast at five cents each to choose the best looking. Voting became heated (and profitable for us) as teachers encouraged their students to stuff the ballot box. The winner received a T-shirt designed and painted by one of the art teachers. "Mr. Legs" wore shorts with his T-shirt the day after the contest ended. We have also featured faculty baby pictures, pets, and souvenirs of trips. In the future, we plan to highlight other jobs our teachers have had. In February, a display of faculty wedding pictures brought crowds to the library.

— *LaMae Strange and Jean Power, Georgetown (South Carolina) High School*

Teacher Silhouettes

Part of our celebration of National Library Week was a display of silhouettes of teachers who read. An overhead projector was used to produce the outlines of the teachers on black paper. Each silhouette was displayed holding a construction paper 'book" with the title of a book the teacher had read recently. The teachers were good reading role models-and good sports to be viewed so prominently and be the subject of so much discussion. Some teachers incorporated this idea into their own lesson plans.

— *Bev Wright, Hendrix Junior High School, Chandler, Arizona*

Teachers' Favorite Book Contest

Our school recently began a school-wide sustained reading program. To help get it off the ground and to convey the idea that teachers read for fun, we sponsored a Teachers' Favorite Book Contest. All teachers were asked to submit their favorite book title, author, or genre. We then used desktop publishing to print signs so teachers could post their favorite title beside their classroom

door. Students could pick up a contest entry form in the library. They had to match selected teachers and books by reading the posted signs. We also had a display of teachers' favorites in the library.

— *Cindy Walters, Nimitz High School, Houston, Texas*

Teachers' Pets

One of our most popular display cases featured the pets owned by the teachers. Staff members brought in photos of their pets and listed name, breed, owner, and any anecdotes. The case was soon crowded with photos of dogs, cats, horses, calves, and one bird.

— *Jean E. Miller, Western High School, Russiaville, Indiana*

Teachers' Toys

"Toys from the Past" was the theme for our library showcases during December. We asked high school teachers and other employees to share a toy from their childhood. Teddy bears, Lincoln logs, metal airplanes, and dolls were labeled with the contributor's name and displayed around a Christmas tree. The display of over 40 toys was a conversation piece and seemed to bring students and staff together in discussions about the toys.

— *Joy Hays, Raytown (Missouri) High School*

Technology Bulletin Board

I designed a technology bulletin board for my classroom. Among the items I found for the board were a border that pictured computers and two magazine articles, "Teaching with Technology in the Classroom" and "Jobs in 2000." The item that has generated the most interest is a card on which students can write a favorite Internet address, show a printout of a page from the site, and add other information. Students come to class early on Monday morning in hopes that their favorite site will be selected for the bulletin board.

— *Lynn Kimberlin, Alan C. Pope High School, Marietta, Georgia*

Too Much Display Space?

To cope with a display wall measuring 31 x 11 feet, I cover the wall with bright paper and add a standing caption, "An Up Close Look At..." Then I post student work from major projects. For example, each year the sixth grade does research on endangered species, producing reports illustrated with maps and sketches of animals and plants. In this case, I add to the standing caption the words "Endangered Species" and fill the wall with their work. Students in every grade enjoy seeing what others have done and reminisce about or anticipate similar projects. A related idea is to provide bright circles of construction paper and markers to older students so that they can write notes congratulating younger students on their work. These circular notes form the borders of the display, making a bright spot that everyone contributes to with very little work for me.

— *Ginger Williams, Williston-Elko Middle & High Schools, Williston, South Carolina*

Unsticking Posters

To protect posters being taped to the wall, stick pieces of tape in strategic locations on the back of the poster. Then roll more tape, sticky side out, and place the roll on top of the tape already on the back of the poster. The poster is ready to attach to the wall. When you take down the poster, you can remove the rolled tape and no damage is done to the poster.

— *Edna Earl Rouse, Marion (South Carolina) High School*

Who's Who & Who's New

Using a digital camera and the computer, I took pictures of all teachers new to our school and created a "Who's New" display. A second display called "Who's Who," featured photographs of administrators, counselors, and the office staff. These displays not only match names to faces but also draw attention to the new technology.

— *Doris Fox, Aldine Senior High School, Houston, Texas*

Your Move

During the chess tournament between Russia and India, a teacher who is a chess fan and I collaborated on a display in the library. The teacher set up the chessboard showing the position of the pieces each day the tournament was played. We had pictures of the two players and small flags representing their countries. Newspaper articles were attached to the table, and books on chess completed the display. I was amazed at how many of the middle school students knew how to play chess. Even non-players came in each day to see the progress. During lunch periods, students may play chess, checkers, or dominoes in the library.

— *Diane C. Pozar, Wallkill (New York) Middle School*

Computers – Easing the Curriculum

Libraries were among some of the first departments in the school environment to utilize computers. Automated library catalogs and circulation systems have made the handling of clerical duties in a library more efficient. Many computers in the school now have Internet access and provide full online resources to the school's and library's patrons—students and staff. Maintaining these systems and organizing the software has become part of the challenge of providing resource services in many libraries—another duty for many library media specialists. There are many "tricks to the trade"—tricks that will help keep the computer management time to a minimum and the utilization of the technology to a maximum. Secondary students who are proficient with computers may be of assistance with some of the configuration and management activities; thus, suggestions for both managing the computer systems and in using the library's computers are included here.

'At Ease' Advice from Online Colleagues

Recently, a student in our lab was bypassing the *At Ease* (1.0) security system on a Macintosh (System 7.01) in our lab. He also gave *At Ease* a new password. To find a solution to this problem, I posted a question to LM_NET asking how this malefactor could have been pulled off.

How the *At Ease* security could have been breached:

▶ Restarting the computer with a startup disk from home

▶ Holding down the shift and! or control key while rebooting the computer and therefore bypassing extensions

▶ Bringing in a Disk Tools disk and erasing the *At Ease* preference folder

Preventing a repeat in the future:

▶ The newer version of *At Ease* is not so easy to bypass. Advice: Get the upgrade.

▶ Make sure the Control Panel alias is not in the Apple Menu.

▶ Make sure the password has a numeral in it so a student cannot run a dictionary program against it.

— *Floyd C. Pentlin, Lee's Summit (Missouri) High School*

A History of Problems

One way to keep track of problems when you have a number of computers is to compile a notebook with a separate section for each computer. In each section, keep the serial number, model number, and sources of funds used to purchase the computer. Whenever there is a problem, note it in the section for that computer. In the future, if you have problems with that same computer, you can provide the technician with the computer's repair history. You also may be able to solve some problems yourself by referring to the binder to see what has been done previously by the technician.

— *Kimberly M. Casleton, South Columbus Elementary School, Columbus, Georgia*

A Tent on a Computer

We have two computer reference stations in the media center. Although several of the resources are available on both stations, some of the lesser-used or more expensive resources are available only on one. To assist students, we put a tri-fold sign, or information "tent," on top of each reference station indicating the resources available on each computer.

— *Sharron L. McElmeel*

After School Taping

When you share a VCR with other class-rooms, conflicts can arise in taping public TV shows after school hours. One solution is to ask parents to tape specific programs. Be sure to check the legality of each taping before making a request. Most public television shows carry specific rights for educational use.

— *Sharron L. McElmeel*

Alias Name

Many people who use Macintosh computers pull the application program icon on the desktop to easily locate and start a program. Another method is to create an alias of the application program icon and place it in the Apple Menu items folder inside the Systems folder. This will allow users to easily start a program while keeping the desktop area clean and uncluttered. If you place an asterisk at the beginning of the alias name, the Apple Menu item program alias will move to the top of the menu.

— *Matthew Clay, Carrollton, Georgia*

An Address Book for URLs

Avoid URL overload and address errors by creating a file to save and organize information on promising Web sites. Simply set up a word processor (or Notepad) file named "URL." Create a blank page to receive addresses you will copy and paste in. If you are collecting URLs on several topics, you may want a page for each topic. Before opening your browser, open the appropriate URL page in your word processor and run it minimized. It takes just a second to copy and paste a URL onto your page and then continue browsing. Be sure to save before closing.

— *Kathy Tobiason, The American School, Japan*

Avoiding Computer Mix-ups

Our library is online, but we keep a spiral notebook to check out books manually when the computer is set in a different directory, for power interruptions, and so forth. This worked fine, but we felt that we were spending too much time trying to decide which method we had used to check out each book and that we were not clearing all the fines.

The solution was to color code our date due stamps. A green due date means the item was checked out by computer; a red date means it's in the notebook. Now we have less wasted time and fewer students receive an overdue notice in error.

— *Vickye Drury, Diamond Hill-Jarvis High School, Fort Worth, Texas*

Editor's Note: An option is to keep the notebook only as a temporary check-out procedure. Once the power is back on, or the directory is returned to the check-out screen, simply type in the student ID number and the barcode for the book. The checkouts then, are all in the computer and there is no quandary as to where the check-out record is or isn't. smc

Bigger Print for All to See

At a workshop where two to three teachers were working at one computer, I enlarged the font on the Internet workstation. This is easy to do with *Netscape*. In the Options menu, choose General Preferences, then Fonts. Click on Choose Font and then Change Size. I found that 18 was a good size for small group viewing.

— *Shelley Glantz, Arlington (Massachusetts) High School*

Bigger Type

When using an LCD computer projection panel or a large-screen monitor and Netscape to show an Internet site, make the document's text more readable by increasing the size of the font. In *Netscape 3.0* go to the Options menu on the main menu bar, choose General Preferences and then Fonts. Select a larger number to increase the font size. In *Netscape Communicator 4.0* one may access the preferences file through the Edit menu. Similar procedures are available for other Web browsers. Enlarging the font size is also a helpful option to use with individuals who read larger print more easily.

— *Sharron L. McElmeel*

Bookmarks for Bookmarks

I have created paper bookmarks with a list of "bookmarks" for World Wide Web sites related to curriculum areas. Not only are the paper bookmarks handy for students at school but the information can also be used at home.

— *Bev Oliver, Indian Hill High School, Cincinnati, Ohio*

Building Independence

Even if you are supervising students accessing the online resources, you may not always have time to immediately help each student to get online. So that no one is kept waiting, we worked out simple, step-by-step directions, printed them on a tag board, laminated it, and put the directions beside each access computer. Now, instead of waiting for us to do it for them, students feel a sense of accomplishment when they log on all by themselves.

— *Carol Burbridge, Jardine Middle School, Topeka, Kansas*

Built-in Screen Saver

If you do not have a screen saver program on your Macintosh or if you want to remove a program that slows down your computer, use the built-in screen saver. From the Control Panel, scroll down to Screen, slide the time bar to the desired setting, and make sure there is not an x in the box indicating that you want the screen saver feature turned off. With this feature on, the screen is darkened after the selected amount of time.

— *Tricia Tucker, Elm Street School, Newnan, Georgia*

Bumpered Computer Carts

Several computers in our library are kept on mobile carts. The monitors extend beyond the back of the carts, and passing kids accidentally shove the carts into the wall, shifting the monitors to the edge of the cart. We solved the problem by screwing two sturdy doorstops to the back of each cart.

— *Katherine Clinesmith, Ed W. Clark High School, Las Vegas, Nevada*

Cache Sites

If you use a network browser such as Netscape and connect to the Internet via a modem connection, you may wish to cache the site ahead of time so that you are not at the mercy of the connection. Simply open the Web site you wish the students to use and make the connections to all the links that you plan to use. As you go, the pages will be cached onto your hard drive and will be accessible from the Go menu. This is particularly helpful if you are paying for online time, have unreliable connections, or simply want to focus on a finite group of Internet Web pages.

— *Sharron L. McElmeel*

Card Catalog Forms Useful for URLs

Even in the day of electronic wizardry, we still use the old fashioned subject card catalog form to keep all our Internet site URLs. This way, regardless of which computer is being used to do a search, and without having to rely on an interminable list of bookmarks, the user can type in and go to the precise location. Our subject cards include "see" and "see also" references as well.

— *Barb Cutler, Lakeside School, Seattle, Washington*

CD-ROM Information Window

I create a window on our computer desktop that calls attention to the CD-ROM programs that will run on a particular computer, but the CD-ROM itself must be requested from the desk. Patrons may quickly glance at the "Ask for CD-ROM" group screen to check which CD-ROM programs are ready to run on that particular multimedia computer. We have about 25 such standalone programs installed only once on three multimedia computers in the library; therefore, each computer offers eight or nine programs. A list of the programs available on each of the three computers is also posted nearby for easier reading without going to the actual computer screen.

— *Janet Hofstetter, California (Missouri) High School*

Checking Parental Permission

Our school board requires that students have parental permission to use e-mail and the Internet. We give each student a single sheet with the full text of the Acceptable Use Policy on one side and a form for parent and student to sign on the other. We file the sheets and compile a computerized list for ready reference. We require students to display their school picture ID cards near the keyboard every time they log on. We can easily check the ID against our alphabetized permission list.

— *Edna Boardman, Minot (North Dakota) High School, Magic City Campus*

Cleaning CD-ROMs

Recently a CD-ROM that would not open kept flashing a "15" error message. I called the company that produced the program, but no one seemed to know what the message meant. One company representative said she had heard technicians talk about cleaning discs with a glass cleaner. She emphasized that I should not use a circular motion, but that I should clean it from the center to the outer edge. It worked!

— *Janis V. Isenberg, Middlebrook School, Trumbull, Connecticut*

Code for Every CD-ROM

If computers in a building vary in size and capabilities, it is difficult to know if a specific CD-ROM will work properly on the borrower's computer. To facilitate teacher and student checkout and use of CD-ROMs, give each computer unit in the school a number. Similar units can be given numbers in the same range. Put these numbers on each computer. As you buy CD-ROMs, code them with the numbers of the computer units. For example, a CD-ROM that requires a 14-inch monitor would be coded "Use on #13, 15, 100-199." That means computer units #13 and #15 and all units in the 100 series have at least a 14-inch monitor. Those checking out the CD-ROM must remember only their computer's unit number rather than knowing details such as memory capacity, monitor size, and so forth.

— *Sharron L. McElmeel*

Color-Coded Task Badges

The popularity of electronic encyclopedias, atlases, and the Internet has created unique supervision issues for the practicing media specialist. I have devised a system of colored badges for each electronic resource in the media center. Students pick up the badges from the circulation desk to show which resource they will be using. The use of bright fluorescent colors—pink for the Internet, green for multimedia encyclopedias, and so forth—has helped me to determine if students are staying on task and using the resource correctly. I can see these brightly colored badges easily from across the media center. The task of supervising students has become less time-consuming as well as result-oriented.

— *Jill Davidson, Eagle's Landing Middle School, McDonough, Georgia*

Comfortable with CD-ROMs

At a recent workshop for teachers who are novices on using electronic resources, I felt that they needed to have their comfort level raised. Since the workshop took place just before Halloween, I bought "silly" prizes related to the holiday. Each participant won a prize for answering a question or finding some information on a CD-ROM or the Internet.

— *Shelley Glantz, Arlington (Massachusetts) High School*

Commands on the Caddies

One of our standalone computers has an external CD-ROM drive that requires a carrier for the disc. For each CD-ROM we buy, we also purchase a plastic caddy for it and label the caddy with the command words to access the program. We find this makes the students more self-sufficient starting the programs themselves.

— *Caroline C. Bennett, Creekside High School, Fairburn, Georgia*

Computer Check-Out Poster

Our library is responsible for keeping track of the computers on rolling carts that circulate through the school. We have always had the machines on our computerized library circulation system, but we have found that keeping a poster-size computer check-out chart on the wall has been a lifesaver. It allows us to make instant computer reservations based on hardware configuration, since every computer setup is slightly different. The chart also shows which teacher has used a particular machine and when. We recently were able to help a teacher who had misplaced her grade disks because the chart showed us exactly which computer she had used and who got it next.

— *Joellen G. Cullison, Deer Park Senior High School, South Campus, Pasadena, Texas*

Computer Club

In order to fully benefit from the technological knowledge that our students have, our school started a computer club. The students in the club have helped train other students and teachers to use word processing, e-mail, and the Internet. They also update our Web site and help research new technology.

— *Michelle N. Rich, Archbishop Wood High School, Warminster, Pennsylvania*

Computer Journals

Since I have a music theory class and only one computer, I ask that students keep a computer journal for noting directions about how to use our music computer program (*Music Lab*). Whenever they use the computer, they document which program they performed, their score, and what they need to work on. I check the journals weekly to see where I can help each student. By keeping journals, the students become more self-reliant when using the computer, and I am able to work with other individuals in the class.

— *Cynthia A. Wilson, Sprayberry High School, Marietta, Georgia*

Computer Named Benjie

When you overhear students at our middle school talking about Cassie, they could be discussing the well-known book character or one of our computers. Each of the 30 computers in the library media center is named for a book character. The computers are identified by a nametag at the top of the monitor. Another label at the bottom of the CPU gives the title of the book, the author's name, and the call number. We chose books that celebrate our cultural and ethnic diversity or show characters overcoming challenges. In addition to Cassie from Mildred Taylor's *Roll of Thunder Hear My Cry*, we have Yingtao from *Yan, the Youngest and His Terrible Ear* by Namiokai, and Simon from *See Ya, Simon* by Hill. The names help everyone, including the technical support workers. It's easier to find Benjie than to "look for the second computer on the left."

— *Suzanne Carson, Northside-Blodgett Middle School, Corning, New York*

Computer Trouble-Shooting

When using the phone to talk through a computer problem with a media specialist or a teacher from another building, always sit at your own computer as you help them walk through the difficulty. You'll be able see their problem firsthand and try out a solution before offering advice.

— *Steve Baule, Glenbrook South High School, Glenview, Illinois*

A 'Reel-y' Neat Idea

Looking for a way to recycle your old 16mm empty take-up reels? I wrap coaxial cables around mine. Wrapping keeps the cables from tangling. Another bonus—the wrapped reels require minimum storage space. Microphone cables can also be stored this way.

— *Judi Furman, Hoech Middle School, St. Ann, Missouri*

Success Hangs by a Peripheral

In a graphical environment, the difference between success and failure depends on peripherals. I'm referring to the computer input devices—keyboard and mouse. Taking care of your keyboard is a simple matter. To remove the dust, use a flathead screwdriver or dull knife to gently pop the keys out of the keyboard. Then, use a blow dryer to blow the dust out or wipe it away with a clean cloth. Usually, a dirty mouse will cause the pointer on the screen to move jerkily or not at all. If you have never opened a mouse, follow the Boy Scout motto and be prepared. While it is not a complicated task, it's wise to avoid getting carried away. Here are the tools you will need:

▶ Clean cotton swab
▶ A capful of isopropyl alcohol
▶ Carpet

Gently unscrew the bottom of the mouse with your thumb (there's a circular opening on the bottom of the mouse), allowing the mouse ball to drop into your hand. Rub the ball on the carpet, or a similar surface, until it is clean. Then, moisten the cotton swab with alcohol and carefully wipe the plastic rollers inside. Don't press down too hard.

— *Miguel Guhlin, Mt. Pleasant (Texas) Independent School District*

Computers to Go

Encouraging teachers to take school computers home over the summer is an excellent way for them to gain valuable hands-on experience on their own terms and on their own time. If your school doesn't have a "computers to go" policy, suggest it to your principal. To prevent misunderstandings, write up a simple contract between the school and each teacher about the condition of the computer, responsibility for repairs, and return date.

— *Mary Hauge, Head Librarian, West Aurora (Illinois) High School*

Editor's Note: One caveat—computer labs probably won't be dismantled to facilitate the summer home use, but many classrooms have computers on teacher's desktops or in the room for student use during the school year. If these computers are also connected to the network, be aware that unhooking them and restarting them as a non-networked machine will automatically cause some of the communication settings to be changed. Be sure to check with your district's technical experts to avoid problems once the computers are taken home and again when they are returned to the classroom. smc

Controlling Remote Controls

The new technology has confronted librarians with new problems, among them how to keep track of remote controls for TVs, VCRs, and videodisk players. Fortunately, this particular problem can be solved with a 20-ft coiled telephone cord that can be purchased at a hardware store for $5. I taped both VCR and TV controls together with black electrician's tape, then attached them to the cord, which is long enough to allow the teacher to view the screen from a distance. This is not a foolproof method for keeping equipment and their remote controls together, but for a nominal price it does help.

— *Barbara McDermid, Kromrey Middle School, Middleton, Wisconsin*

Copy Web Addresses

Whenever you see a recommended Web site listed in a mail message or on a listserv and you want to take a look at the site, highlight or select the address. Then use your copy function to copy and paste the address to your Web browser. This procedure saves time and prevents typing errors.

— *Peter Milbury, Chico (California) Senior High School*

Editor's note: Many e-mail software programs now have a feature that delivers Internet addresses as hot links, which will take the user directly to the Internet site, assuming that an appropriate browser is also located on the computer hosting the e-mail software. One caveat—the sender must remember to include the entire URL in their message. Those URLs that are sent without the "http:" portion of the address will not be a hot link in the delivered message. smc

Create a Nifty Database

I set up a database in *Microsoft Works* for different Internet sites that includes the site, address, curriculum area, and any special notes such as login commands. I have it open when I am on the Internet (particularly when I am on LM_NET). This way I can easily cut and paste any interesting sites mentioned into the database. I am getting quite a collection that I can easily sort for reference and share with staff.

— *Rosemary Knapp, Camas (Washington) High School*

Creating a Graphics Library

You can create interesting and informative educational multimedia presentations using graphics from the Internet. First, decide on the types of graphics you will need for present and future presentations. Next, create a new folder on your hard drive and add subfolders for each of your categories, such as "History: Ancient." If hard drive space is a problem, label a floppy disk for each category. Browse the Web using popular search engines. When you find a desired graphic, save it to the appropriate sub-folder or floppy disk by clicking Save As and naming the graphic. When you are ready to create your multimedia presentation, simply use the Insert menu in your software to insert the desired graphic. You can then resize the graphic as needed. ***Important Note:*** *Be sure to follow the Educational Fair Use provisions of the U.S. copyright laws.*

— *Gregg Farmer, Wheeler High School, Marietta, Georgia*

Creating Lists of URLs

When students do independent Internet research, teach them to open Notepad and use copy and paste to create a list of useful URLs. This ensures correct addresses for use at home or at another time and allows the student to annotate each address for use in a bibliography to turn in with the assignment. The advantage of using Notepad is that students can print their lists rather than saving them with Bookmarks, thus using less hard drive capacity.

— *Sherry Sack, Alan C. Pope High School, Marietta, Georgia*

Disappearing Icons

Do you have problems with icons in Windows 3.x disappearing or being misplaced by the students? This tip will allow you to invoke some basic security restrictions in the Windows program manager that will put an end to these types of problems. First, arrange the icons exactly the way you want them to appear from now on. Second, hold down the shift key and from File, choose "Exit Windows." You should hear the hard drive working. This saves the Windows configuration and writes it to memory. Next, exit Windows and get into the Windows directory, then type *edit program.ini*. Add the following lines to the end of the file, save, and exit.

[Restrictions]

EditLevel=4

NoSaveSettings=1

When you next open Windows you will notice that the Delete, in the File menu, and Save Settings on Exit, in the Options menu, will be faded out. The effects of these two are obvious. However, when you try to drag an icon and put it in another group, you will find that this privilege is no longer allowed. Since the user cannot save the settings, every time Windows is restarted, whatever changes were made during the previous session will be completely forgotten and the window will appear just the way you left it before the security restrictions.

— *Cameron Walton, Carroll County Schools, Carrollton, Georgia*

Modem Madness

Those of us still using modems for our connections at home—and sometimes still in the schools—will no doubt have been annoyed when a program being set up does not list the modem being used. Here's how to avoid the frustration. Go to a program that you have that works with the modem and copy the modem initialization string. Now go back to the new program, select "custom" as your modem choice, and paste the string you copied into the modem initialization location. The program should now work. Also note that most programs work with eight data bits, one stop bit, and no parity

— *Joe Huber, Greenwood (Indiana) Middle School*

Disks for Teachers

As our teachers became more interested in using computers as an instructional aid, they were saving all their work to the hard drive, which was filling up fast. To resolve this, I gave them disks labeled with their names, and I conducted training on saving files to and retrieving information from the disks. Once teachers had their work saved to disks, I was able to clean out the hard drive.

— *Teri Besch, Oak Grove Elementary School, Peachtree City, Georgia*

Domain Alerts

When you are teaching students how to be selective and evaluate information from the Internet, tell them how to check URL addresses for the identity of the sources. If the domain ends in .gov or .edu it is probably reliable information from a government agency or an educational institution. If it ends in .com, warn the students that the source is probably a business or special interest group. If any other domain appears in the address, students should look at the information closely.

— *Shelley Glantz, Arlington (Massachusetts) High School*

Editor's Note: The last three-letter segment, such as "com," "gov," and "net" certainly did indicate the type of host, when the structure of the Internet was first developed. For example, "edu" indicated the address belonged to an educational entity, "net" indicated a networked computer, "com" indicated the address was associated with a company, and "org" indicated the owner was a non-profit organization. In the late 1990s this structure was abandoned, and anyone or any type of group was allowed to purchase and register any domain name. Thus, while many of the addresses still conform to the previous convention of domain names, it is not always true that an "org" domain, for example, would necessarily be a non-profit entity. smc

E-mail Troubleshooter

The district technology coordinator oversees nearly 300 computers and three network servers in the two hours daily that he does not teach classes. To be fair, he asks teachers to e-mail their problems that need his attention. He uses the date and time of the message to decide who gets his attention next. Teachers have quickly learned to send their requests as soon as they discover a problem, so they will be higher on the priority list. If their computer is down, they can usually find one in an adjoining room to report the problem.

— *Janet Hofstetter, California (Missouri) High School*

E-mail Message for Students

We send a message via e-mail to all students who have an e-mail address explaining the basics of our acceptable use policy. We also remind them of the policy when we sign them up.

— *Edna Boardman, Minot (North Dakota) High School, Magic City Campus*

Editor's Note: A global mailing list of all students who have e-mail addresses may prove valuable for other school sponsored messages. smc

E-mail Names

When assigning user names to an e-mail system, use a standard formula. Our schools, for example, use the person's first initial, the first five letters of his or her last name, and a number. Under our system, Becky Johnson would be *bjohns1*. If there were a Bruce Johnson, he would be *bjohns2*. This nearly eliminates the need for a published directory of e-mail addresses in the district.

— *Doug Johnson, Mankato (Minnesota) Public Schools*

E-mail Practice

Find a friend or coworker with whom you can practice sending and receiving e-mail until you feel comfortable with the system. Don't join too many listservs because there will be too much mail to read, but joining those dealing with topics of importance to you can be helpful!

— *Peter Milbury, Chico (California) Senior High School*

Easy Access to Your Mail

Many e-mail packages will allow multiple accounts (configurations for settings) using their software. Save those settings on a disk and create an icon for "starting mail." You do not need to save the e-mail application itself if you can regularly access a machine with the e-mail application installed. By inserting that disk and using the "starting mail" icon to activate the e-mail application, you will be able to use your personal settings to access your mail. If you wish to have the e-mail remain on your mail server, be sure to check the "leave on server" option in your mail package. As a general rule, you should "remove mail from server" to avoid overloading your provider, so be sure to access it from your "normal" site where you will have checked the "remove the mail from server" option.

— *Sharron L. McElmeel*

Eject Disks the Tidy Way

As an alternative to having students eject disks through the trash can, ask them to use the "Put Away" option under the File menu. Tell them to make sure the disk icon is highlighted, then pull down the file menu and select "Put Away" to eject the disk. The icon will clear off the screen.

— *Phyllis Schicker, IMC Director, Purdy Elementary School, Fort Atkinson, Wisconsin.*

Editor's Note: Those Macintoshs with systems of 6.0 or above allow users to eject the disk by merely using the command (apple) + Y keys after the user has quit by using the command (apple) + Q keys. smc

Electronic Tutorials

One way to overcome giving repetitive and time-consuming instruction is to utilize presentation software programs (i.e., *PowerPoint*) to instruct students, faculty, and staff in using the search databases available in the media center. Instead of taking the time to explain over and over the distinctions of using each database, use presentation software to set up tutorials that will take over this task for you. Your patrons need only call up a particular tutorial for self-guided instruction.

— *Michael J. Roth, Lithia Springs High School, Douglasville, Georgia*

Enough Is Enough

Don't sign on to too many listservs when you first begin. Try out a couple at a time and choose the one or two most suited to your needs.

— *Peter Milbury, Chico (California) Senior High School*

Equipment Database

A database of your school's equipment is a quick way to determine if equipment is still under warranty, and it provides a simple way to keep track of equipment purchased with special funding. It also furnishes necessary information for insurance purposes in the event of fire, theft, or other disaster. The following fields are included in our school's equipment inventory: room number, teacher's name, model of the equipment, serial number, purchase order number, date of purchase, and funding source.

— *Sue Dalelio, Downtown Elementary School, Columbus, Georgia*

Exploring the Internet & Magazines

To provide teachers with ready access to new information, we put technology magazines near the computer they use to explore the Internet.

— *Edna Boardman, Minot (North Dakota) High School, Magic City Campus*

Facilitating Repairs

If you do not have adequate technical support in your district, try using part of your repair budget to hire technical support. A local computer company provides us lower hourly rates in return for a guaranteed number of hours of work. They repair what they can on site and keep *File-Maker Pro* repair records on our computer. Additionally, they also figure out things for us and teach us a lot about our equipment.

▶ Prepare equipment troubleshooting and repair forms that teachers can use; keep them in handy locations.
▶ Keep a traveling tool box of cables, batteries, adapters and other odds and ends of things you frequently have to work with if you're called to a classroom.

▶ Develop easy-to-follow, brief directions for things that students and teachers frequently need help with. For example, we created "how to" sheets for common *ClarisWorks* procedures, "help" guides for copying and printing materials from multimedia CD-ROMs, and directions for hooking up various pieces of equipment.
▶ Empower teachers to be self-sufficient users of technology so they can help empower students.

— *Mary Alice Anderson, Media Specialist, Winona (Minnesota) Middle School*

Saving Mice

I use small screws taken from my model railroad to "lock" the track ball-retaining ring into the mouse while still allowing the mouse to move smoothly on the mouse pad. To implement my method, you'll need a flat-headed 0-80 brass screw, 3/16 of an inch long; a #55 drill bit; an 0-80 tap to cut the threads in the drilled hole; and a pin vise—a hand-held device that holds the small drill bit. Once you've assembled the materials, here's how to proceed:

1. Remove the track ball retaining ring and the track ball.
2. Examine the rim of the track ball retaining ring hole to find a spot where the screw can be inserted in the retaining ring at its edge and thread into the mouse body at the rim of the track ball hole.
3. Mark the spot with a felt tip pen.
4. Replace the retaining ring and carefully drill a hole with the #55 drill bit about 1/16 to 1/8 of an inch from the edge. (Get close enough to hit the plastic around the edge of the retaining ring hole.) Be careful not to go too deep with the drill—you don't want to drill into the mouse's electronic guts!

5. After the pilot hole is drilled, use the tap to slowly and carefully cut the threads for the screw. You may find it helpful to remove the retaining ring and cut the threads in the ring and the mouse separately.

6. Use a 3/16- or 1/4-inch drill bit, turned by hand, to countersink the retaining ring so the screw head will be out of the way and not affect the movement of the mouse.

7. Reassemble the mouse and screw in the 0-80 screw. Do not over tighten.

An alternate and simpler method for securing track balls is to use a dab of super glue on the retaining rings. When it's time to remove the track balls to clean the rollers, use a small amount of fingernail polish remover to dissolve the glue.

— *Robin Harris, Yorktown Middle School, Columbus, Ohio*

FAQs for Students

How do I quit the program? How do I save my work? Can I print this? Laminate the answers to these and other simple questions and put them next to each computer.

— *Steve Baule, Glenbrook South High School, Glenview, Illinois*

Long on Ingenuity, Short on Cash

Too few computers? Too many students? No money for an expensive LCD panel? A cheap way to give more students a view of a computer screen is to spend $10 or $15 on two extension cables—one for your monitor and one for the keyboard. Set your monitor with its long cable on a high table and ask the student operating the keyboard to scoot the chair several feet back from the table. Let as many students gather around—kneeling, sitting, standing—as can comfortably see the screen. This works well for small group instruction and collaboration.

Janet McElroy, Central High School, West Campus, Tuscaloosa, Alabama

Fast Netscape Searching

Set your *Netscape* browser (*Netscape 3.0*—go to the Options menu, general preferences) to open with a blank screen. This saves a lot of time and gets students started searching sooner since you do not have to wait for graphics and a gratuitous home page screen to load. Bookmark search engines so students can just click on them without using the *Netscape* "Netsearch."

— *Kristine Cole, Grace Church School, New York, New York*

Finding Your E-mail

If you use *Eudora* on the Macintosh, you can use the find command (found under the Edit menu) to locate messages containing your e-mail name. Once all of your personal messages are found, you can start at the beginning of the mail list, scanning the subject line only. It will save time handling a lot of mail from listservs.

— *Joan Kimball, Hart's Hill Elementary School, Whitesboro, New York*

Five-Minute Trainer

With everyone's busy schedule, it is hard to find time for training on new software. I handle this problem by meeting with the teachers for five minutes at their weekly grade-level meetings. I take a couple of examples of completed work and spend five minutes showing them how the work was done with the new software. If there are no new computer programs, you could show them shortcuts within existing programs or Windows. Remember to keep it to less than five minutes.

— *Kimberly M. Casleton, South Columbus Elementary School, Columbus, Georgia*

Foolproof Stymies Computer Surprises

The Macintosh computer's friendly interface invites lots of free exploration. Some student explorers are just curious. Others are mischievous and looking for ways to rearrange the desktop. In an elementary school, any rearranging often occurs by accident. How can computers be protected from student maneuvers? We use a product called *Foolproof* by SmartStuff Software. The program locks out the control panel, chooser, and other areas of the system that students might rearrange accidentally or intentionally. It is available for both Macintosh computers and those running Windows. To find out more information about this security program go to <www.smartstuff.com/fpsinfo.html>.

— *Catie Somers, DePortola Middle School, San Diego, California*

Free Way to Prevent Free Access

If your school is networked, you can use the power of the network to limit students' access to computer programs, files, and directories. You can "hide" those you don't want students to use and show only the files and programs they need. In my previous assignment at a high school, rather than giving carte blanche to all student programs at one time, we asked our students to log in as the application they wish to use. Students doing word processing, for example, have access only to the word processor files, and not the CD-ROM utilities or the telecommunications software that also reside on the server. Consequently, a student who accidentally or intentionally escapes from a program and lands at a system prompt can wreak havoc only on one application-not an entire server. This approach may not be as foolproof as some of the commercial security programs, but it's free!

— *Carol Simpson, University of North Texas, Denton, Texas*

Go Right to the Top

Getting the most frequently used programs at the top of the list in the Apple menu (on Macintoshes with System 7.0 or above) is as simple as renaming the aliases with a numeral preceding the actual name. The most frequently used item on most of our Macintoshes appears in our Apple menus as "01-Microsoft Works" and is at the very top of the list.

— *Sharron L. McElmeel*

Grading Search Skills

To introduce English classes to our electronic resources, the teachers and I split the classes when they come to the library. The teacher explains how to do the assignment (narrow topics, outline ideas, show examples) while I teach search skills and show how the electronic systems work. After training for two or three class periods, all the ninth graders are ready to do their research. I grade the students' proficiency in search skills, and the teacher records these grades as a homework grade.

— *Lois McNicol, Garney Valley High School, Glen Mills, Pennsylvania*

Handling pkzip

I've often been asked how to get pkzip, how to install it on both Windows and DOS, and how to use it. Well, I don't use the winzip program too much (although I do like the advanced features), but I do use the DOS version, which will unzip any zipped file you obtain (Windows and DOS zipped files).

These are the files you need: pktmzip.exe; pkzip.exe; pkzipfix.exe; and zip2exe.exe—all from the pkz2o4g.exe version program. This program is available at ftp site oak.oakland.edu in this path: /SimTel/ msdos/zip/pkz2o4g.exe. Or you may go directly to their Web site page at <oak.oakland.edu/>. Maneuver to the simtel.net portion of this site and locate the programs you need. This is a self-extracting program, which means you need to make a directory (\ZIP is good) on your PC and then copy the downloaded pkz2o4g.exe into that directory. Then just execute that file by being in that directory and typing: pkz2o4g <enter key>. That .exe file will then decompress into a number of .exe files and other files (.doc files, etc.).

For ease of use I recommend moving or copying the .exe files to your \DOS directory. Then you can execute them from anywhere in DOS at the command line prompt.

What are the functions of the .exe files? They are compression and decompression programs that allow you to save space on disks and transport compressed programs easier. Pkzip will compress the programs, pkunzip makes them whole again, and pkzipfix can fix

some problems that very rarely arise with the compression process. Zip2exe is a new feature that lets you make a self-extracting file in case you need to send it to someone who doesn't have or know how to use pkunzip.

The most common usage for people downloading programs is going to be pkunzip.exe file.

Here's an easy example: Let's say I downloaded the file from SimTel in the education directory called aalpha.zip. To digress just an instant, let me explain what the directory listing at an ftp site means by using the following example: aalpha.zip B 450893 941216 animated alphabet for preschool to first grader. Translation:

aalpha.zip: DOS file name for that program

B: binary program (has actual machine language like a formatted word processor file or an actual software program; its opposite is an unformatted text file—also called an ASCII file)

450893: file size in bytes—450,893 for this one

941216:date when it was placed on that ftp sit —Dec. 16, 1994

last entry (text):the program description

Now to continue the pkunzip tutorial:

1) ALWAYS make a directory in DOS for the zipped file you just downloaded. Do not unzip it in the root directory please! It may have many, many files when it decompresses and you need to keep them separate from your other programs.

2) Now make a directory for animated alphabet called \ANIMAT or whatever you wish. Now copy or move aalpha.zip into that directory.

3) Change directory to that new directory and then issue this command:

pkunzip aalpha <enter key>

(Extension letters .zip are not needed for the command.)

4) Now it will self-extract and you can look for the readme file or .doc file to see which file will activate the new program. The aalpha.zip file has now done its work and may be deleted or moved to storage elsewhere. (I keep important zip files in a \ZIP directory.)

Now we know how to "unzip" a program (using pkunzip.exe). But how about going the other way—compressing files with pkzip.exe? Why would you want to do that? Well, let's say your hard drive is getting filled up and you need to gain some space. You might want to compress some seldom-used programs and just save them on the hard drive as a zipped file. (You'd delete all the regular files and just save the one zipped file that will be much smaller in size.)

Or maybe a program is too large to fit on a disk for easy transporting to another machine, so you need to compress it into a zipped file so that it will fit on the disk. Here's how to do it:

An example: I have a directory called \Splash that is a paint program 2 MB in size. I rarely use it and I want to compress it.

1) Change to that directory.

2) Issue this command: pkzip splash C: ~ splash\ ~ <enter key>.

This is telling the computer to make a file called splash.zip and put in it all the files from the \Splash directory.

3) Now I can delete all the other files and save the zipped file (splash.zip). I will gain savings in space. Now to reverse the process I can type: pkunzip splash <enter key>.

Another example: I want to zip up all my .doc files in my word processor program so I can store them for safety. (.doc files will usually achieve the best performance in zipped files as far as size goes. The smallest performance gain is found with .exe files.) So I change directory to my word processor, \WINWORD, and issue this command: pkzip windocs C:\Winword\ *.doc <enter key>. Now I will have a copy of all my .doc files in a compressed file called windocs.zip.

Well, I hope this helped. It takes practice and experimentation to get good at pkware utilities. They can do many more sophisticated things that you can learn in time.
Good Luck!

— *Russell Smith, Educational Technology Consultant, Region XIV Education Service Center, Abilene, Texas*

Handy Computer Instructions

At each workstation, we put instructions for using the programs installed on the computer. The instructions are inserted in inexpensive acrylic frames.

— *Elisa Baker, Ursuline High School, Santa Rosa, California*

Handy Web Sites

As I compile lists of Web sites, I put the lists in a three-ring binder. The binder is kept near the Internet-access computers.

— *Jody Newton, Rochester (Indiana) Community High School*

Hard Copy Is Handy

It's great to work online, but those old–standbys–pencil and paper–still come in handy. When exploring the Internet, keep a small notepad or tablet at your fingertips for writing notes about the places you visit and the people you meet.

— *Linda Joseph, Library Media Specialist, Columbus (Ohio) Public Schools*

He Who Hesitates...

Check listserv mail daily. Realize that e-mail is so fast that you need to reply immediately to participate. Save the information on setting "nomail" and sending messages.

— *Peter Milbury, Chico (California) Senior High School*

Hypermedia with PowerPoint

Often, *PowerPoint* (Microsoft) is classified as a presentation program, not a hypermedia program. However, using *PowerPoint 95* (for Windows 95), you can use it as a nonlinear, multimedia application. Using the "interactive settings," you can define clickable areas on a slide, which may link to another slide or program or even a URL! If you download the *PowerPoint* Internet Assistant from <www.microsoft.com> and export your *PowerPoint* slideshow as HTML, all of the clickable areas and URLs remain. The slides can be saved as GIFs or JPEGs and essentially become image maps.

— *Harold Doran, Harelson Elementary School*

ID Computers Instead of Students

I have simplified the need for individual passwords in our building by placing an ID number on each of the computers. Students can log in, type in the ID number, and got to basic programming and CD-ROM programs, as well as the card catalog. Using an ID number for each computer rather than a password for each student eliminates the need to save a lot of unnecessary files on the file server.

— *Katrinka S. Major, Media Specialist, Fairplay Middle School, Douglasville, Georgia*

ID for the AUP-Certified

As part of our school district's acceptable use policy, students who are "certified" to use the Internet are issued an ID card. To easily identify these students at the media center computers, I require the students to place their card in a clothespin attached to the top of the computers. I've attached the clothespins with Velcro®.

— *Joy M. Harrison, Buffalo (Missouri) High School*

Important Reference Sources Window

In Windows, I set up a "false window" with icons for important reference sources that we have linked from our school home page. We call the window "Go to HOME PAGE for:" and leave this window open at all times. Students can easily see the names of the icons, which remind them to go to the school home page to find the resource. If they forget and click on the dummy icons, they get a "File not found" error message which generally brings them to the library staff for assistance. We point them in the right direction. Here's how I set up such "false windows":

▶ Go to "File" from the main Windows screen and choose New. (You may have to unrestrict the file menu if you use desktop security.)

- Create a New Program Group. Under "Description," name it something that will reveal the window's purpose, such as "Go to HOME PAGE for:" and save by clicking OK. The "name" you chose will appear across the top of the new group window.
- Create a New Item in the group.
- In the Program Item Properties under "Description," name the item the same as the name that appears on your home page for the link. For instance, I have an icon labeled "CIA World Fact Book" because that is listed as a link on our school's home page.
- Type "C:\" for the command line (still in Item Properties). This won't be a valid path when you've finished your creation, but it will do what you intend—send a student to the desk for assistance. For the working directory (still in Item Properties), just type "C:\" again.
- Choose an appropriate icon. I used the open-palmed hand for everything in the "Go to HOME PAGE for:" group to suggest "stop and think."
- Save by clicking OK.

Since four of my fourteen computers do not have access to the Internet, I created a "false window" on each of their screens, which is named "No INTERNET Access." This reminds everyone who has Internet permission not to choose those computers to use.

— *Janet Hofstetter, California (Missouri) High School*

Internet Address Bank

I placed a 500-card Rolodex next to our telecommunications station to hold Internet addresses. I encourage teachers and students to add to our address bank. I've received everything from addresses for the president at <www.whitehouse.gov> to a Web site for specialized interests, such as <www.eaglecars.com>. Everyone seems to enjoy the hunt. Even more important, the address bank is being used.

— *Cecelia L. Solomon, Powell Middle School, Brooksville, Florida*

Internet Plan Pass

Students are required to have an Internet Plan Pass when they are sent to the library to use the Internet. This pass requires the student's name, date, topic, list of Web site addresses or search engines, and the searcher's signature. Printed on orange paper, this pass is posted next to the computer so that I can see at a glance who is searching the Internet.

— *Pat Hare, Northwest High School, Cincinnati, Ohio*

Internet Tool Box Book

I have compiled a book called "The Internet Tool Box," which sits by the computer with Internet access. The colorful, laminated book contains tips on search engines, navigation of *Netscape*, e-mail, short cuts, and valuable Web sites for teachers and students.

— *Kristen Graham, Ashland (Maine) Central School & Community High School*

Keeping Track of Computer Changes

Updating your computer can improve productivity—or it can bring you and your computer to your knees! One method for ensuring that you remember every change or update is to keep a file in the computer. Create a directory called "Notes," with a file named "CompNote."

The first items in the file should be the computer's location, the history of its purchase, and system configuration information. How much memory does the computer have? How large is the hard drive? Where and when was the computer purchased? What were the purchase order and invoice numbers? Include the sales person's name, if applicable.

Other information to include in the file is: the length of the warranty period; exactly what date does the warranty expire; how to contact technical support; what are the charges; what software and what releases were installed on the computer; and what manuals came with the software and the computer. This is the easy part.

Now, the harder part: Every time you load a new program, backup the system, or make changes to any significant operating files, note the changes in the CompNote file. Skip a line between each entry, so there is always a visual break between entries.

Type the date as the first item in the new note, and then describe any changes you have made. For example: *8/17/01 Upgraded to DOS 6.2.* or *12/5/01 Added a 56k fax/modem card and installed Delrina's Win Fax.*

If you must keep up with changes to multiple computers, name the files anything that describes each computer in eight characters. (This is DOS's requirement.) And keep these notes on the computer in question and also on an administrative computer.

The files must be backed up regularly as well as stored on a disk. These files will become crucial to the smooth organization of a technologically rich school.

— *Melanie J. Angle, Kennesaw State College, Marietta, Georgia*

List-Serv/Subscription Organization

Shortly after subscribing to a listserv or online service, subscribers receive acknowledgments and instructions. Those initial messages contain important information about posting to the list, posting to individuals, signing off, and unsubscribing. With your first subscription to an online service, file copies of the instructions. Then when you need to unsubscribe or have questions, you can go to your "listserv" file for the information you need.

— *Sharron L. McElmeel*

Listserv Tip

On a listserv, if you're going to do something you're not sure about, send it to an individual rather than to the whole list, and then send immediate, individual responses to anyone who helps you.

— *Peter Milbury, Chico (California) Senior High School*

Lunch on the Net

Internet access at our school is restricted to school assignments except for "Lunch on the Net" in the media center. Although students are closely monitored, they are free to surf the Net on topics of their choice. Students choosing unsuitable topics are encouraged in a lighthearted way to choose again. Cars, comics, sports, and music are popular topics. This is a great way for the Internet novice to learn good search techniques without the pressure of completing an assignment.

— *Patricia Stewart, Westlake High School, Atlanta, Georgia*

Mail Folders

Create folders for mail. Don't keep everything in one big "I'll-get-to-it-later" pile.

— *Peter Milbury, Chico (California) Senior High School*

Identifying Computers and Software

I use clear plastic library pockets with adhesive on the back and library book cards to identify each computer. Stick the pocket on the CPU. On the book card I write the make, model, serial number, and county ID number as well as the software that has been loaded and the date.

— *Kate Stirk, Annunciation Catholic Academy*

Making Teachers Look Good

We offered a free *PowerPoint* (Microsoft) class to the first 25 teachers and staff members who registered. The head of the computer science department at a junior college came to our lab to teach the class. Everyone agreed it was great to be able to take a class on site. Many of the participants used *PowerPoint* presentations the next week at back-to-school night and impressed parents with their use of technology in the classrooms.

— *Elisa Baker, Ursuline High School, Santa Rosa, California*

Making Use of Free Cable Programming

A great way to increase the videotape collection at minimal charge is through the Cable in the Classroom program. Most programs have a one-year use permit. The free teacher guides have lesson plans and other support material. During that year there is no limit as to the number of times the program can be shown or by how many teachers. We have been able to increase our holdings by taping from Discovery Channel and the offerings on A&E. Just make sure it is a program designated as a Cable in the Classroom offering.

— *Cecelia L. Solomon, Powell Middle School, Brooksville, Florida*

Messages on Screen Savers

Using the marquee screen saver on the Windows computers in the lab, I leave my students messages, trivia questions, or instructions for the day. Sometimes I continue messages from one computer to the next. The students love it. They are always curious to see what message will be there when they enter the lab.

— *Teri Besch, Oak Grove Elementary School, Peachtree City, Georgia*

Messages to Me

Eudora will let you transfer messages to files known as mailboxes. You can either answer a message immediately or transfer it to one of several mailboxes that you have set up. I call my mailboxes "Reply To This Message, Personal Mail To Me," and "My Target-hits." Set up mailboxes by clicking on the menu bar and choosing Mailboxes.

— *Joan Kimball, Hart's Hill Elementary School, Whitesboro, New York*

Messages to Myself

Our school Internet account requires us to remove any mail downloaded from the server immediately. Sometimes when I access my mail at my school site, I find that there is a message I really want on my home computer. I forward the message to myself either at the same address or at my personal address. Either way I can download the message when I access my mail account from my home computer.

— *Sharron L. McElmeel*

Model the Use of Technology

It's always a good practice to model the use of technology as you teach others to use it. One way to model a digital or paperless classroom concept is to put agendas, outcomes, and teaching materials for technology staff development workshops on the World Wide Web. This saves paper and demonstrates to teachers a way they can implement this in their instruction. This model works especially well for workshops about the Internet. Another good model uses classroom technology in an actual classroom. One of our teachers took a staff development group to her classroom for "show and tell" so that other teachers could see how she uses her scan converter, computer, and monitor.

— *Mary Alice Anderson, Media Specialist, Winona (Minnesota) Middle School*

Monitoring Computer Time

To reduce lines at online catalogs and CD-ROM search stations, we instituted a card timing system. Each search station has a wooden card holder in which students place cards showing their start and end times. Cards are color-coded on each station. We limit the time to 10 to 15 minutes (two minutes for online catalogs). The student turns in the card, and the next student takes over the search station.

— *Joan Enders, Monticello Middle School, Longview, Washington*

Mozart for Learning

Standard system software for Macintosh computers (System 7.5 and above) includes an Apple Extras folder in which there is an AppleCD Audio Player. For convenience in playing compact disks in the classroom (research has shown that classical music enhances learning in most students), make an alias for the AppleCD Audio Player and put it in your Apple menu. The application will allow specific tracks to be played, and you can adjust the volume.

— *Sharron L. McElmeel*

Name Each Computer

Keep a record for each computer and printer listing the type of monitor, hard drive space, RAM, extended memory, type of CD-ROM drive, and the types of different printers your printer is set to emulate. Frequently a new program will require that information when installing it. Naming the computers makes it easier to keep track of repairs, location, and the contents on their hard drives. Naming them 1, 2, 3 or A, B, C tends to be confusing if they do not remain in numerical or alphabetical order. This is the time to be corny (as we were) or literary (authors' names). If students need to find a particular program and you don't have a network, they can look for the name of the computer listed by the program name on a master list of locations. We named each computer and printer. Since our mascot is the Pinto and the media center is somewhat like a Pinto stable, our computers and printers have horse food names such as Bran, Corn, Oats, Lespedeza, Hay, Timothy, Clover, Prairie Grass, and Alfalfa. Each named component has a separate file card with the pertinent information. When installing a program, we pull the cards for the equipment to be used and have them handy for answering equipment questions.

— *Janet Hofstetter, California (Missouri) High School*

Name That Document

When allowing students to save their documents into a student data folder on the class computer, require students to save the document using their name and the date (mm/yy) as the title. They don't forget their own name but often forget the name they have used to save a project. Whenever they go back to the document to revise or edit, it is simply resaved under the same title. When a new piece of writing is begun, it is saved under the student's name with a new date. The teacher can clean up the hard drive by transferring the older documents to a portfolio disk for the individual student or to a class portfolio disk. With the student's name as a title and the date, a document doesn't have to be opened to identify the author and determine which document is the newer of the two. -Sharron L. McElmeel
Netscape Settings for Works Cited
Students using the Internet for research need to know site locations, dates accessed, and URLs for their works cited pages. You can set Netscape to print these features automatically by using the header and footer settings in Page Setup under File on the menu bar.

— *Karen Grant, Moorhead (Minnesota) High School*

Newsgroup Responses

If you use e-mail to respond to a newsgroup, make sure that you know when you are responding to an individual and when to the whole group. Double-check your addresses every time you send an e-mail message.

— *Peter Milbury, Chico (California) Senior High School*

No Address for Junk Mail

Troubled by junk e-mail? Many Web sites collect e-mail addresses of those who visit and resell the names to bulk mailers. One way to forestall the onslaught of junk e-mail is to spoof or eliminate entirely your address on the Web browser. In *Netscape*, choose Options, Mail and News Preferences, Identity. Look at the addresses in the fields on the screen. If any of those are your e-mail address, every Web site you visited could have collected your e-mail address. Blanking those fields can help stem the tide of unwanted e-mail.

— *Carol Simpson, University of North Texas, Denton, Texas*

No More https

You may never have to type *http://* again because *Netscape* and *Explorer* both assume that part of the URL. For example, to get to the University of Illinois Web site, just type *www.uiuc.edu*. On *Netscape*, it is not necessary to type the entire domain name if the URL ends in *.com*. For example, to visit the CNN Interactive site, you don't need to type *http://www.cnn.com* or even *www.cnn.com*. Simply type *cnn* and press Enter.

— *Gabriel R. Gancarz, University of Illinois, Champaign, Illinois*

Editor's Note: Two caveats: Those sending URL citations in e-mail messages will want to include the http:// portion of the URL as many e-mail software programs automatically create a hot link for the receiver, but only if the http:// is included. Also, those typing in white-house, for example will be taken to http://www.whitehouse.com—a far different site than the site one probably intends to reach at http://www.whitehouse.gov. Use this feature with caution. smc

Novell Applications Meter

Our media center has a *Novell* network with 10 computers. Included in the *Novell* software is an applications meter. By setting the application meter to register CD-ROM products each time they are used, we have been able to gather valuable usage statistics. A history report of file server activity shows us which products are most in demand. Renewal of CD-ROM network licenses can be quite expensive, and using the applications meter has enabled us to select products wisely. An added benefit has been the ability to apply for grants that require documentation of computer use.

— *Elaine Chambless, Kendrick High School, Columbus, Georgia*

Ordering Videos from the Teacher's Edition

Our district media center houses hundreds of instructional items, and although the media catalog is curriculum specific, teachers in our 11 schools often overlook videotapes and materials that might be useful for a unit they are teaching. Using a Macintosh computer, an ImageWriter printer, and continuous computer labels, we designed a system that matches the district media collection with particular lessons in textbooks and brings the appropriate media to teachers' attention. First, I page through new textbooks, noting items in the collection that could be used with information on a particular page. I also note areas for which we have nothing in the collection, so we can begin searching for new items to meet those needs. Labels are made with the title of the media and page number of the textbook on line one and the ordering code for the media on line two. Our staff puts the labels in the teacher's editions of the textbooks on the page listed on the first line of the label. When teachers see the label in their texts, they can call the media center and order "right out of the book."

— *Peggy Rabideau, Sylvania (Ohio) City Schools*

Posting Computer Directions

We had trouble keeping directions posted near the computer workstations until I bought Curtis Clips (available where computer aids are sold.) They allow us to clip instructions next to the computer screen by attaching them to the corner of the monitor.

— *Patt Moser, Concord-Carlisle High School, Concord, Massachusetts*

Printed Handouts

When appropriate, introduce students to new software programs or concepts by giving them printed handouts showing the screens they'll be working with. This works to familiarize staff members with new programs as well.

— *Steve Baule, Glenbrook South High School, Glenview, Illinois*

Printing from the Internet Made Simple

If one is still accessing the Internet via a modem, printing may be a problem if the printer does not have a large enough buffer. Simply e-mail the document to yourself to print later or send it, with a request to print, to a coworker who has a laser printer.

— *Peg Weidemann, Horseheads (New York) High School*

Quick Tip for Listservs

Many Internet beginners make the mistake of using UNSUB instead of the correct SIGNOFF command or by writing to the list address instead of the listserv address. This creates problems when an Internet provider changes an address. Those who have used UNSUB find they are receiving forwards of the list postings at their new e-mail address, but they can't sign off because the listserv doesn't recognize the new address. Catch 22, Internet style! What to do? Subscribe to the list again and then send the REVIEW Listname command to the listserv address so the old address can be deleted.

— *Russell Smith, Educational Technology Consultant, Region XIV Education Service Center, Abilene, Texas*

Read Subject Lines

If you subscribe to a listserv, learn to read subject lines and use the delete key. It will make the amount of mail more manageable. Also check your disk space often. E-mail saved in folders can use a lot of space.

— *Peter Milbury, Chico (California) Senior High School*

Record Discovery Channel Documentaries for School Use

Taping programs from Project Discovery on The Discovery Channel and using them in school is legal for one year. They cover science and technology (Monday), social studies and history (Tuesday), natural science (Wednesday), arts and humanities (Thursday), and contemporary issues (Friday). These 25-minute commercial-free documentaries are suitable for both elementary and secondary students. For a free educators' guide to using programs you have legally taped from the

Discovery Channel, go to <www.discover.com> to download lesson plans for the programs. There are also online resources linked to a resource page for each of the programs. One may also order permanent copies of the programs from this site.

— *Anitra Gordon, Lincoln High School, Ypsilanti, Michigan.*

Recording Network IP Numbers

Record network IP numbers for all computers on your network in a database and keep it current. The information is invaluable for avoiding duplicate IP numbers and to track any problems. You can also print labels from the database to put a sticker on the computer.

— *Mary Alice Anderson, Winona (Minnesota) Middle School*

Recycling Disks

Delete all files on demo disks or other computer program disks no longer in use. Number the disks and make available near computers for students to use when saving data for a short time. Saves time deleting data from hard drives. We have enough available that students can even take the disk with them to insure they won't disappear before they need them again. We also sell inexpensive disks; students label the disks with their names and return them to the librarian for safe filing. Journalism students save all their articles, adding to their disks weekly.

— *Janet Hofstetter, California (Missouri) High School*

Rename Print Queues to Make Life Easier

The first year we had our Novell network, I assigned print queues, 1-20, to teachers and kept a record of which print queue matched which teacher. This made it difficult for both the teacher and me to clear print queues. The next year, when teachers changed rooms but the computers did not, the print queue assignments became even more confusing. That is when I discovered how to rename print queues and used the knowledge to rename the print queue to the room number. This made it easy for anyone to clear the print queue. To rename print queues (in v 3.12), go to Printer Console. Highlight Print Queue Information. Highlight the print queue you want to rename. Press F3. A pop-up box will appear that asks you to rename the print queue. Then press Escape. The print queue has now been renamed. You may have to reassign the print station after renaming the print queue. You will not have to reassign the printer assignment, however.

— *Patsy Spinks, Paulding County School System, Dallas, Georgia*

Make a New Print Queue

When we added 11 classrooms to our school, the existing print queues were not enough to accommodate all the new print stations. To make a new print queue, I follow this procedure for Novell 3.12: Go to Printer Console. Highlight Print Queue Information. Press Insert. Type the name of the new print queue. Press Escape. Highlight the new print queue and press Enter. Highlight Queue Operators. Press Enter. Press Insert. Choose the group (in my case teachers) that you wish to give rights to clear print queues. Press Escape. Next, highlight Queue Servers. Press Enter. Press Insert. Choose the print server that needs to be assigned to this print queue.

Press Enter. Press Escape. If you're not sure which print server to assign, look at another print queue and use the same one it is assigned. Press Escape. Your new print queue is now available to be assigned.

— *Patsy Spinks, Paulding County School System, Dallas, Georgia*

Rebuilding Desktop Files

To rebuild the desktop file and improve the performance of a Macintosh, every month or so restart the machine while holding down the option and command (Apple) keys. On a Windows or DOS machine, go to the DOS sub-directory and run SCANDISK to accomplish the same thing.

— *Joe Huber, Greenwood (Indiana) Middle School*

Renaming a Bookmark Folder

When creating a bookmark file home page for students to access the Internet, I had a problem with the name on the root folder. It said "Mary Woodard's Bookmarks," and I did not want that to appear on the home page the students would use. To solve this problem, I went to the Options menu, selected Mail and News Preferences, and clicked on the Identity tab. In the first box, which asks for your name, is the information that *Netscape* uses to create the default name for the bookmark folder. I changed the name from "Mary Woodard" to "Kimbrough Library." I then went into the bookmark folder Properties and changed the name there. Now the bookmark home page says "Kimbrough Library's Bookmarks." Problem solved!

— *Mary Woodard, Kimbrough Middle School, Mesquite, Texas*

Reorganizing Files

After three years of saving files in chronological order on a series of disks, I reorganized files. This was the fastest method:

▶ Using new disks, label each like a file folder (e.g. Forms, Lists, Signs, Purchase Orders/Supplies, Newsletters).

▶ Insert one of the old disks and copy the entire contents to the C: drive.

▶ Change to the C: directory and display the list of files.

▶ Insert one of the new disks. Move the appropriate files to the A: drive one file at a time. Change disks to accommodate the different types of files you are moving.

▶ Delete junk files from the C: directory.

▶ Repeat the process for each of the old disks.

▶ Store all of the old disks in a box marked "originals."

▶ Copy each of the new disks in its entirety to create orderly backups.

— *Jeanne Minetree, Dinwiddie (Virginia) High School*

Verify Before You Reply

When replying to a message that was sent to a group of people, check the "To:" area to make sure your reply is going to the intended person or persons.

— *Peter Milbury, Chico (California) Senior High School*

Saving Time & Trips

In their e-mail messages reporting problems, teachers are asked to quote error messages from the screens and be specific about what led up to the problem. With this information, the technician will have the proper equipment on arrival to solve the problem.

Sometimes the coordinator can e-mail back within minutes a suggestion for solving the problem.

— *Janet Hofstetter, California (Missouri) High School*

Screen Saver Encouragement

Messages can be placed on the screen saver program to promote library activities. For example, put up a message such as, "Turn on to reading!" These directions are for Windows 3.1. Go to Program Manager. Double click on Main. Next, double click on the control panel. Then, double click on the desktop icon. In the screen saver box, click arrow, highlight Marquee and click again. Then, click Setup. Under Setup, you can type your message and change the color and style of the lettering. When finished, click OK and you're done.

— *Frances Tripka, Flynn School, Perth Amboy, New Jersey*

Search Engine Rules

For optimum search accuracy, always check the "help files" or "tips" of each search engine for specific search rules that apply. I have printed each set of search rules and used tab dividers for quick reference in finding rules for each search engine. This allows the students to prepare searches offline without tying up the terminal while they try to figure out how to construct an efficient search. There are too many individual quirks to keep them all straight.

— *Alice Trussell, Manhattan, Kansas*

Search Engines vs. Directories

Search engines and directories are different! A search engine index, such as Alta Vista, Webcrawler, Lycos, and HotBot, is created by a computer program (called a robot or spider) that goes out onto the Internet and indexes information found on servers according to a set of criteria set up by the programmer. The information in the index is then searchable by keywords. A directory, such as Yahoo and Magellan, is created by human beings adding sites to a database. The compilers may use a search engine, but someone still made a conscious decision to add a site to a directory. I have created a slide show about this topic "The Mystery Solved : Differences Between Search Engines and Directories" at <discoveryschool.com/schrock guide/mystery/mystery1.html>.

— *Kathleen Schrock, Technology Coordinator, Dennis-Yarmouth Regional School District, South Yarmouth, Massachusetts*

Self-Tutorials for Make-up Work

For students who need to "make up" library research work, prepare detailed, self-tutorial instruction sheets for each CD-ROM database. Ask some students to proof the sheets to ensure that directions are easy to read and that no steps have been omitted. Print sheets for each database on a different colored paper and then laminate the sheets. Store the color-coded sheets in labeled stacking trays near the computers, and encourage students to use the computers independently. Following these guides should reduce the need for staff assistance.

— *Jeanne Minetree, Dinwiddie (Virginia) High School*

Share Your Feelings

When teaching students to send e-mail messages, I always include examples of "emoticons"—symbols used to express emotions. Better known as "smileys," emoticons provide a creative, shorthand way to share feelings. Once they get the hang of it, students enjoy inventing their own smileys-a practice I encourage. Here are some examples of emoticons students enjoy using.

Emoticon	Meaning
: >)	original smiley face
: > (	frown
8-)	smiley face wearing glasses
:-0	oh no!
;-)	wink
:-D	big smile, laughing

— *Patricia Kolencik, North Clarion High School, Tionesta, Pennsylvania*

Sharing Disks

In a school district that contains both Macintosh and Wintel machines, I have found it beneficial to supply all users with PC-formatted disks for saving their work. The Macintosh OS can read and save to PC-formatted disks. The Macintosh-using teachers and students have to remember to use the 8.3 (8-character file name, 3-character extension) file-naming convention and include no spaces in the file names because some of the Wintel machines run under Windows 3.1, which cannot use long file names.

— *Kathleen Schrock, Technology Coordinator, Dennis-Yarmouth Regional School District, South Yarmouth, Massachusetts*

Sharing Sites on the Internet

When I'm scanning professional journals, I keep recycled catalog cards at hand to jot down Web sites. When I find information about a site with potential for my colleagues, I write the subject at the top of the card, then the name of the site and the address. In the lower right corner I abbreviate the source and date. I e-mail newfound addresses to colleagues. This has caused several teachers to ask how to use the Internet in the library, and they are beginning to surf on their own after seeing some interesting home pages. If a teacher reports that a site has changed or no longer exists, I change the card in my file or throw it away. Teachers and students are given a site card to use at the computer if they want a particular address; this is much easier than using a notebook.

— *Janet Hofstetter, California (Missouri) High School*

Signing Up for the Internet

As more and more students want to use the Internet terminal in the media center, I devised a daily sign-up sheet. School periods are 50 minutes long. Students can sign up for one 25-minute session per day. If no one signs up for the other half of that period, the student can stay online. Students doing classroom research have priority over those who are just exploring. Each student must have a signed parental permission slip on file before he or she is allowed to use the Internet. Students over 18 can sign their own permission slip.

— *Nancy D. Swider, Goodrich High School, Fond du Lac, Wisconsin*

Some Rules for E-mail

A good rule for using listservs is read it, reply to it, and delete it! Only keep those messages of importance. Keep truly personal messages personal. Talk to friends in person, write a note, or use the phone!

— *Peter Milbury, Chico (California) Senior High School*

Static Electricity

Where winter brings snow, the school computer specialist knows it also brings anguished cries from students and staff: Help!! I get an I/O error whenever I try to access a file from my disk or my computer (or my mouse) has just frozen again. If these statements sound familiar, you've probably experienced the effects of static electricity on a computer user's environment. Static electricity is a familiar phenomenon. Remember walking across a floor and giving or receiving a shock just before you touched someone or something? These shocking experiences seem relatively harmless to you, but to computer equipment these small jolts are like a lightning bolt.

Nearly everything in our universe contains tiny particles of negative electricity called electrons. Materials that contain more electrons than others are said to have a negative electrical charge. Electrons travel from the surface of one material to another until the charges on both are equal. This electron rush causes the spark between the two surfaces, an electric current. Static electricity refers to an electrical charge remaining on a surface for a time before it jumps to another material.

Static electricity occurs most frequently as the humidity drops. During cold snowy winters the air is dry. Heating systems remove even more moisture from the air and pass it throughout buildings. In some buildings humidity levels drop as low as 5%. Dry air and static electricity cause several common problems when humans contact the computer. For example:

Statement 1. *I have an I/O error whenever I try to access a file.*

Probable cause: This is caused by a discharge of static from you to your disk. The jolt hits the disk with enough energy to reorient the small metal particles on the surface of the disk whose alignment constitutes your data. Imagine the disk surface as a road. You travel on the road looking for your data. As you approach the section where the "lightning bolt" hit, you see a scrambled mess. You slam on the brakes and stall your transportation (I/O error).

Statement 2. The stored file on my hard disk worked fine yesterday, but now I get an error message every time I try to open it.

Probable cause: *Here, the static discharge passed from you through the computer, scrambling the data in the hard drive file.*

Statement 3. My computer (or my mouse) has frozen again.

Probable cause: The static discharge passed from you to the computer, scrambling information flow and causing your mouse, keyboard, or both to lock up.

Statement 4. *The printer freezes in the middle of my print job.*

Probable cause: The static discharge scrambled the data flow from the computer to the printer. The printer expects a steady, linear flow of information and cannot interpret this scrambled data. It sits waiting until it gets what it wants.

Statement 5. *The printer has a paper jam every hour.*

Probable cause: Paper is also susceptible to dry air. Below a certain humidity level, static sticks pages together, causing more than one sheet to be pulled through the printer at once. Highly charged paper may also cling to surfaces inside the printer, jamming it.

Statement 6. *The laser printer copies have black streaks on some pages.*

Probable cause: Toner in a laser printer is also susceptible to dry air. At low humidity, static buildup between toner particles sticks them together, creating blotches on the paper. A static charge between the paper and toner can cause similar problems.

So what can you do to reduce static charges? If possible, add moisture to the work area with a humidifier. In the work area, consider adding an antistatic mat or grounding strip to the computer or printer. Place an antistatic mat under the chair. Suggest that individuals who carry disks in their pockets purchase a small antistatic carrying case for transporting their disks with minimal risk.

— *Keith Thomas, Lindsay Thurber High School, Red Deer, Alberta, Canada*

Stop-and-Go in the Computer Lab

The computer lab attached to our library contains 26 stations that are used by study hall students and individual classes for word processing. One of the teachers came up with this idea to more efficiently aid students working in the lab. We glued red and green construction paper back-to-back, laminated it, and cut it into 3 x 4 inch pieces. One piece was placed on the top of each monitor, green side up. When students need help, they turn the red side up. They can continue typing and need not sit with an arm in the air waiting for a teacher to help them. -Thelma Seevers, Blair (Nebraska) Community High School Student Disks & Virus Protection

When our computer network was installed, we asked students to save reports and term papers to their personal disks. However, the virus detection system in the network is so sensitive that it often blocks disk use. Now we allow students to save their work on the hard drives. To ensure there will always be space for new files, we remove all student work from the hard drive before school opens in the fall.

— *Jacqueline Seewald, Red Bank Regional High School, Little Silver, New Jersey*

Teachers' Assignments on the Library Web

On our library Web site we post teachers' assignments and link information sites, researched by the library aides. From home or in the library, the students can call up the site and click on their teachers' names to receive the assignment as well as links to more information about the subjects.

— *Roberta C. Rice, Central Valley High School, Veradale, Washington*

Technology Buddies for Teachers

Team with a fellow teacher to pursue your technological endeavors. It can be scary out there in cyberspace. A teammate is valuable in ways that are too numerous to count. You can practice sending e-mail to one another, help each other troubleshoot problems, and in general be each other's "first responder."

— *Pat Southerland, Holley-Navarre Middle School, Gulf Breeze, Florida*

Technology on Wheels

A mobile, multimedia cart is an efficient use of technology. Include a high-power computer, color inkjet printer, color scanner, and digital camera. This cart can go anywhere in the building and be used in the media center when not scheduled for classroom use.

— *Gloria Curdy, Big Sky High School, Missoula, Montana*

Timesaving Trick with Windows

Our school purchased a site-license to install *Print Shop Deluxe* on 75 computers. A network version did not exist for this program when we purchased it. Instead of taking the disks around to each computer and installing the program on each hard drive, I installed the program on one hard drive, set the printer, and then copied the program to the network using Microsoft Windows. I then went to each computer and copied the program to the hard drive from the network using Windows. This saved a tremendous amount of time. I also made a batch file so that teachers could choose to run *Print Shop Deluxe* by pressing P. I copied this batch file at the same time. It can then be deleted from the network and the work is done!

— *Patsy Spinks, Paulding County School System, Dallas, Georgia*

Tried-and-True Timesavers

You can save time by asking teachers to provide responsible student volunteers during study halls and noon hours to format and label computer disks for the school.

— *Steve Baule, Glenbrook South High School, Glenview, Illinois*

Trouble Remembering Passwords?

Having trouble remembering passwords that look like a random selection of letters? Try this trick. Select a short proverb or a saying such as, "When in the course of human events," or "Don't kill the goose that laid the golden egg," and just use the first letter of each word in the saying: "WITCOHE" or "DKT-GTLTGE." It's better than putting the password on a sticky note on your monitor!

— *Doug Johnson, Mankato (Minnesota) Public Schools*

Two-Way Disk Labels

The problem with disk labels is that if you can read the label in the storage box, it's upside down when you insert the disk in the drive. Avoid the aggravation of reading upside down by using *WordPerfect* and 1 x 2-$\frac{5}{8}$ address labels to generate "playing card" disk stickers that read either way. Go to Layout, then Labels. Use center justification and a large type size. After typing all the label titles, copy and paste to get a set of duplicate labels. Adhere each pair to a disk facing up and down so that the reading orientation is correct however you hold the disk.

— *Jeanne Minetree, Dinwiddie (Virginia) High School*

Keep E-mail Copies... Just in Case

Keep an electronic copy of e-mail you send; you may want to forward it later to another person. Creating folders for topics you are interested in is better than printing and filing hard copies.

— *Peter Milbury, Chico (California) Senior High School*

CD-ROM Lists

On the side of each multimedia station, we tape a list of the installed CD-ROMs.

— *Bill Sweeney, Uxbridge (Massachusetts) High School*

Typing URLs

When you highlight a URL line to type in a new URL, don't bother pressing the backspace or delete button before proceeding to type the URL. Once the line is highlighted, it will automatically erase and overwrite as soon as you type the first key.

— *Gabriel R. Gancarz, University of Illinois, Champaign, Illinois*

Update URL Listing

Every two weeks I update a list of interesting URLs for the seventh and eighth graders and for teachers. I keep about 35 copies of the list—enough for a class coming into the Macintosh lab—on the counter. The students can use them while they are in the lab and return them at the end of the hour. When I find a new URL, I try it out to see if the address is accurate and if the material is appropriate for middle schoolers.

— *Virjean Griensewic, Dakota Meadows Middle School, North Mankato, Minnesota*

URL Lists on Word Processing Documents

If you are like me and keep a lot of lists of fabulous URLs for visiting classes but find your bookmark list is overflowing, try this: keep those lists on word processing documents and keep them open while running *Netscape*. Instead of typing the tediously long URLs, cut and paste them into the "open box" from your word processing documents. You might have a document setup for every class if you are really conscientious.

— *Joyce Valenza, Wissahickon High School, Ambler, Pennsylvania*

URLs on File

As I learn of different Web sites, I put them in a word processing file in subject order. The file is on the network so the students can open it in Word Pad, use the Find command, highlight the URL, and paste it into the Web browser.

— *Linda Strauss, Tottenville High School, Staten Island, New York*

Use the Right Disk

Apple's Macintosh Superdrives require a double-sided, high-density disk. The use of other disks may result in error messages that ask for the disk to be reformatted.

— *Barbara Camp, Klein (Texas) Independent School District*

Video Output Converter

We did not have funds to purchase an LCD panel to enlarge the images on our monitors, but we were able to purchase a video output converter. The little box costs about $200 and runs across platforms. In addition to projecting the screen for class viewing, it allows you to transfer a search, interface, or student multimedia project onto videotape (with an understanding of copyright limitations, of course).

— *Joyce Valenza, Wissahickon High School, Ambler, Pennsylvania*

Web Site of the Month

Each month we select a particularly appropriate site to feature on the "Web Site of the Month" banner.

— *Patricia Kolencik, North Clarion High School, Tionesta, Pennsylvania*

What's That Address on the Internet?

Having a tough time keeping track of all those addresses on the World Wide Web? Keep an uncovered Rolodex next to the computer. When visiting a site, users can fill in a blank card with the following information:

▶ Name of Web site
▶ Address of Web site
▶ Subject (curriculum area) of Web site
▶ Brief description of what is available at this site
▶ Evaluation (excellent, good, fair, unacceptable, or waste of time)

Information on the card can then be entered into a database and sorted as needed. File the cards in the Rolodex for future reference. Extra cards can be carried in the user's wallet or purse to jot down addresses of sources to be visited at a later date.

— *Janice Hetzler, Fayette Middle School, Fayetteville, Georgia*

Windows 3.x DOS Prompt Icon

If Windows ever fails to start a DOS window after you have clicked on the MS-DOS icon, begin to troubleshoot the problem by looking for the file DOSPRMPT.PIF in the Windows directory. If the file is where it is supposed to be, go back to the MS-DOS icon and select it with a single mouse click. Pull down the File menu and select Properties. Does the command line contain the full path to where you found the DOSPRMPT.PIF file? If not, type it in. Choose OK to save the changes, and test the icon.

If DOSPRMPT.PJF wasn't in the Windows directory (or anywhere else on your hard drive), you can create one with the Windows PIF editor. The PIF editor is usually in the Main window, and its icon looks like a tag, complete with string. Double click on the icon, and a dialog box will open. Depending on what mode your Windows is using, the box may be arranged differently, but you can find the following text boxes and fill them in like this:

BOX NAME
Program filename:
STATEMENT
COMMAND.COM
PURPOSE
Name a file that starts DOS session in Windows
BOX NAME
Start up directory
STATEMENT
C:/
PURPOSE
Tells the DOS session to start in the root directory
BOX NAME
Video mode/memory
STATEMENT
Text
PURPOSE
Specifies memory for text mode display

BOX NAME
Memory requirements
STATEMENT
128
PURPOSE
Specifies minimum amount of memory required to start the DOS session

Check the "Close window on exit" and "PrtScr" boxes. Save the file as DOSPRMPT.PJF. Then edit the properties for the DOS prompt icon as described above. Double-check the command line in the Properties box to make sure that it accurately reflects where you saved that file. That should fix the problem!

— *Mario Guajardo, Austin (Texas) Independent School District*

Word Process Your Envelopes

Make mail chores easier by learning to use the print envelope function of a high-end word processor. For *Word for Windows*, access the Tools drop-down menu and select Create Envelope (Alt, Tools, Create Envelope). To create an address bank of vendors, enter an alphabetical list into *Word for Windows* just as you would type them on an envelope. When you need to address an envelope, open the file and use Alt, Edit, Find, and type in the addressee's name. The computer will locate the name and address for you. Then use Alt, Tools, Create Envelope to print an addressed envelope.

— *Melanie J. Angle, Kennesaw State College, Marietta, Georgia*

Editor's Note: Macintosh users will find that creating a database of vendors with an accompanying "form" will allow the printing of envelopes as well. smc

Working with Microsoft Works

I use the header/footer field of my *Microsoft Works* word processing program to save the telephone and fax numbers of the company to whom the letter is addressed. I check off the space marked "Don't print the header/footer on the first page," and the information does not appear on my one-page letters. The phone numbers are saved with my files and are available whenever I have a problem. If I want a version for a hard copy file, I can run a second copy with the "Print on page 1," turned on. If a hard copy is saved, the file name and date last updated can be added to the header/footer area so the matching computer file can be easily retrieved later. *The Microsoft Works Reference Manual* gives details on how to create headers and footers and how to use the special codes for file names (&F) and date (&D).

— *Melanie J. Angle, Kennesaw State College, Marietta, Georgia*

Workstation Frames

I purchased inexpensive 8 x 10 acrylic photo frames to use to display directions for our online catalog and CD-ROM workstations. The direction sheets are easy to read and stay fresh and professional looking.

— *Jacqueline Ridings, Greenwood (South Carolina) High School*

Curriculum Involvement

The collaboration between library media specialist and classroom teacher will serve to make the course of study much richer and complete. While some of the following suggestions may not fit your situation exactly, perhaps they will stimulate some adaptations that will. For example, we took the tip, "Advertising Authors," one step forward by formulating a plan for an author visit, which we culminated with an e-mail visit with the author. We translated the suggestion for "Seating Charts with Names and Faces" to create a banner for display. Using the faces of our library assistants, we formed the letters "Welcome" and posted the banner in the library media center. See what you can do with the following.

"Amnesty Night" for Student Researchers

Taking the anguish out of research has been a goal for our library this year. One technique we have tried is making the last afternoon before the due date of a big research paper "amnesty night" in the library. Students who have not completed their assignment, regardless of the reason, may stay in the library as long as they need to. I serve popcorn and allow the students to blow off steam as long as they are attempting to do the work. Since the number of students is relatively small, they get more personal attention, better access to the materials, and more room to work. The teacher and I make no judgments about why these students did not get their work done earlier, and we refrain from lectures about using time more wisely. We try to accentuate the positive: the students realized they had more work to do and took responsibility for it. The lighter after-school atmosphere results in special relationships being formed between staff and students.

— *R. J. Pasco, Irving Junior High School, Lincoln, Nebraska*

Preparing for Banned Book Week

When we received a copy of the Banned Book Week kit from ALA, a social studies teacher joined the library staff in sponsoring a program to make our students aware of the problem of censorship. Students were involved in the planning and had many ideas for posters, displays, bookmarks, and possible speakers. Our program consisted of a panel discussion featuring a magazine publisher, publisher of our local newspaper, a school district administrator, and a school board member. A student acted as moderator. Each speaker gave an opening statement, and then students were allowed to ask questions. Students were interested in censorship not only of books but also of how it affects their lives in what they can wear to school or listen to on the radio. Our district administrator really got a workout answering student challenges to the school's right to decide what is appropriate or not appropriate for individual students. The newspaper publisher was asked to defend his belief that all speech, even hate speech, should not be censored. The program was 50 minutes long and could have gone on longer. Teachers reported that their class period following the seminar was spent on further discussion of censorship. The seminar was open to the public and became front-page news in two local papers.

— *Amy Christianson, Williams Bay (Wisconsin) School*

"Hot" Topics

Our students are encouraged to research and write position papers on controversial topics, but sometimes it seems as if the same topics are used over and over. To provide fresh ideas, I compile a list of "hot" topics as I read the newspaper each day. Every now and then, I provide teachers with the list. We all keep up with the news and no longer are stuck with the same old topics.

— *Patricia Hare, Northwest High School, Cincinnati, Ohio*

"Kiddie Lit" in High School

Our school's English department offers a short fiction course for seniors who are not planning to go on to college. Realizing that some of these 18-year-olds may become parents in just a few years, we have incorporated a "Kiddie Lit" unit into the course. We use *The Read-Aloud Handbook* by Jim Trelease as the text, and I have developed a collection of picture books for our library. Our district's elementary buildings loan us books, our area education agency provides Caldecott titles, and several teachers donate books their children have outgrown. The class reads books out loud, makes book cards, talks about Caldecott and Newbery, and reminisces about favorite books. In the future, we plan to ask an elementary school librarian to come in as a guest speaker and to take a field trip to the children's section of our public library. The display of children's books in our high school library attracts quite a bit of attention. Students ask about the books, sit down with a favorite, or even check one out.

— *Nancy Geiken, Washington High School, Vinton, Iowa*

"Kiddie Lit" in Middle School

To help our middle schoolers understand the importance of reading to young children, we have developed a special collection of read-alouds. The collection is advertised with a big sign that says, "Take home a book to read to a child." We are constantly adding new and used books, including donations from the teachers. The shelf is popular with students who babysit or have younger siblings.

— *Kathy Batkin, Hunt Junior High School, Portsmouth, Virginia*

Live Poets' Society

Each spring our library sponsors an all-school poetry contest in cooperation with the language arts classes. Each student may submit up to three original poems, and the school secretaries and one faculty member serve as judges. Prizes are awarded at a "Live Poets' Society" breakfast for all participants. First, second, and third place and honorable mention winners receive poetry books as prizes, but every student is given a certificate. The local daily newspaper prints the winning poems along with photos of the authors.

— *Virginia Leipprandt, North Huron High School, Kinde, Michigan*

"We Didn't Start the Fire" Worksheet

I listed the 119 people, places, and things in Billy Joel's song "We Didn't Start the Fire" in order to develop a research project. Students look up *who, what, when*, and *where* using reference sources in the library. Each student gets a copy of the lyrics and a corresponding nine-page worksheet that they fill out over a six-week grading period. If you would like a copy of this worksheet, please send a self-addressed stamped envelope to my attention at the East Rutherford Library, P.O. Box 668, Forest City, NC 28043.

— *Pamela K. Childers, East Rutherford High School, Forest City, North Carolina*

Student Slide Shows

Our eighth-grade students who take a foreign language are required to do a report on a country that speaks that language. Slide show presentations have become popular for this assignment. After researching, students prepare a worksheet plan of the show. We emphasize to students that in a slide show

every picture should illustrate a fact. The students work on blank slides. The first slide usually says "Hello" in the foreign language. Following slides might show the flag of the country, map, products, holidays, and places to visit. The last slide gives credit to the producers of the show. Students soon learn that when giving an oral report, it is better to have visual aids. That way the audience is looking at the pictures and not at the student!

— *Elizabeth Garbarino, Riverhead (New York) Middle School*

Editor's Note: With the use of LCD projectors or large screen monitors for projecting images from a computer, an excellent technique for creating slide shows is to utilize the "slide show" function on ClarisWorks *or* Microsoft Works. *smc*

AAA Tour Books on File

The geography and business classes have a yearly assignment to research a state and plan a trip, including places of interest and costs of hotels and entertainment. We asked the local office of the American Automobile Association to donate outdated tour books. We now have all 50 states in our tour book collection and check the books out as vertical file materials.

— *Deborah Dick & Deborah Davis, Kickapoo High School, Springfield, Missouri*

Advertising Authors

After students have read and reported on a novel by a contemporary author, we extend the assignment by asking them to pretend the author is coming to visit our school. Students must promote their authors to make fellow students want to attend. The promotion might take the form of a one-minute television commercial, a poster, a collage, or other idea. The promotion must include some biographical information, something interesting about the author personally, and something about the book. Students have performed raps and written poems. Videotaping the presentations adds interest.

— *Marilyn Teague, Bonham Junior High, Odessa, Texas*

African Arts Festival

A team of teachers worked with library staff to create an African Arts Festival to celebrate Black History Month last February. We set up craft stations and a tasting station. Students could also watch videotapes of dance and singing. Students spent about 15 minutes at each station and left the library with African printed paper, a mask, and a taste treat. African artifacts were on display, and a drum demonstration was performed.

— *Alena Napohitaro, Bellport (New York) Middle School*

Art Class Connection

We are always trying to involve the library in classroom activities. The art teacher, bemoaning how dry the skin on her hands became after a clay unit using the wheel, wondered how she could alter the unit. We suggested that instead of using the wheel, which requires a lot of water and therefore dries her skin, she should have the children make clay slab bookends. After making the slabs using one horizontal and one vertical piece of clay, the children come to the library and check out a favorite book. To finish the project, they sculpt a character from the book or its author and add it to the bookend. This way they involve the library, the book, and the clay.

— *LaDuska Adriance, Cooper Middle School, McLean, Virginia*

Arts for National Library Week

For National Library Week, I invite the performing arts teachers to plan activities in the media center during the four lunch periods. Art teachers display student work; dance, piano and band concerts are given; and the drama students do monologues and improvisations. My favorite activity is the poetry reading by the creative writing classes. I join the students by reading my own poetry. These activities always draw sizable audiences.

— *Jacqueline Seewald, Red Bank Regional High School, Little Silver, New Jersey*

Bibliography Help

As an English teacher-turned-librarian, I know how easily students lose bibliography forms. One of my first tasks in my new position was to compile a comprehensive bibliography form, which was approved by the language arts department. It is now a permanent page in the school's daily planner.

— *Robyn L. Matthews, Thomas E. Harrington Middle School, Mt. Laurel, New Jersey*

Bibliography Style Sheets for All

For students who are working on papers in the media center, I keep multiple copies of a bibliography style sheet at the circulation desk. The language arts teachers have approved the examples, which include electronic sources.

— *Janet Hofstetter, California (Missouri) High School*

Biography Cards

A whole language card set titled "Meeting of the Minds" (J. Weston Walch, 321 Valley Street, Portland, ME 04104) has proved to be an entertaining way for secondary reading classes to use their research skills. The set consists of 65 pairs of biographies that link individuals who have something in common but lived in different times, such as Anne Frank and Maya Angelou or Amelia Earhart and Sally Ride. The cards are categorized by athletes, inventors, entertainers, and so forth. The cards give a brief biographical sketch and a series of questions that can be researched in a media center. Once the questions are answered, students choose a method of reporting their findings, for example, writing letters the individuals might have exchanged or conducting interviews. Students must list their sources for both written and oral reporting. We are considering writing our own biography cards.

— *Nancy Fahner, Charlotte (Michigan) High School*

Birds across the Curriculum

For an across-the-curriculum project, I asked a shop class to build a bird feeder, which was placed in the courtyard outside the library windows. The science class provides the birdseed. Library books are nearby for those who want to identify birds.

— *Susan Moser, Clarion (Pennsylvania) Area Junior-Senior High School*

Black History Month Guests

In honor of Black History Month, our library sponsored a brown bag lunch lecture series featuring prominent African Americans in our community. Students brought their lunch to the library, and we provided the drinks. Response has been so positive that we have been asked to continue it for career talks and Women's History Month.

— *Betty Smith & Charleen Morgan, Jeffersonville (Indiana) High School*

Bookmarks for Bookmarks

I have created paper bookmarks with a list of "bookmarks" for World Wide Web sites related to curriculum areas. Not only are the paper bookmarks handy for students at school but the information can also be used at home.

— *Bev Oliver, Indian Hill High School, Cincinnati, Ohio*

Booktalks by Theme

To reach the 2,500 students in our urban high school with a reading motivation program, we stage booktalks in the media center once a week. The theme of the booktalk is published in the school's weekly bulletin. Personal invitations are extended to teachers whose classes meet during the lunch period in which the talks are given. We have three lunch periods and rotate the talks among them. Last year the theme was related to a multicultural calendar published by the district. This year the themes are the eight career clusters identified in our "school-to-work" initiative. Teachers of English-as-a-second-language and dropout prevention classes were the first to bring their classes regularly. Attendance by other groups and individuals increased throughout the school year.

— *Andrea Angelucci, Ely High School, Coral Springs, Florida*

Bring History to Life

To mark the 30th anniversary of the death of President John F. Kennedy, we asked teachers and outside speakers to share their remembrances of November 22, 1963. One outside speaker had been at the Trade Mart luncheon in Dallas—the President's destination—on the day of the shooting. Another had interviewed President Kennedy prior to his campaign. To complement the oral presentations, we displayed banners, photographs, books, magazines, and newspapers about the event. We also showed videotapes and transparencies featuring the President, and played selections from "The First Family," a comedy album about the first family. Although it required a lot of planning, this event was well worth the effort. Another similarly-organized program on World War II, which featured veterans as speakers, was also very successful.

— *Hildegard Pleva, Linden Avenue Middle School, Red Hook, New York*

Editor's Note: To my surprise, during a teachers' lounge conversation about "where we were when J.F.K. was assassinated," several teachers indicated that they had not yet been born. A program such as this might also help teachers develop a schema for the event so they are better able to share information about it with their students. Great background for literature teachers who might be involved with historical fiction; social studies and humanities teachers who deal with the topic directly; art teachers who might study advertising and posters of the period; and even science teachers who may deal with scientific developments that were involved in investigating the events or in helping the cause, such as immunizations developed to protect soldiers. smc

Calendar Art for the Curriculum

About four months into each year, I purchase reduced-price gift calendars that feature artists, baseball, horses, and other themes related to the curriculum or young people's interests. I put the prints in the library vertical files for teachers and students to use. For instance, if art teachers need extra prints of the Impressionists' work, we are able to supply them. The prints are also great for bulletin boards.

— *Emily F. Castine, Chazy (New York) Central Rural School*

Closed Caption

Since the early 1990s, television sets, 13 inches and larger, have included a decoder for closed captions. Activate the decoder by accessing the menu with the remote control and following directions. Take advantage of closed captions to provide easier access to hearing impaired, ESOL, and visual. Providing both audio and visual presentations may enhance the presentation for all the learners in your classroom, especially when new vocabulary is included in the video. Many video and television programs are closed captioned, often denoted with a "cc" symbol in a box or a statement. Resources to help you bring captioned materials to your classroom include your media specialist, your local television stations, and local organizations for the deaf and hard of hearing.

— *Rebecca McDaniel, Wheeler High School, Marietta, Georgia*

Clues to American Decades

Our tenth-grade class in American Cultures does reports on American decades. To spark interest, I placed a "Clue Board" decorated with a huge paper magnifying glass outside the library. The board is divided into decades starting with 1900. Pictures of persons related to the decade as well as five or six clues about the person are displayed. A candy bar is awarded to the first student who can answer the clues and supply the correct name of the famous person. Correct answers and winners are announced on the intercom. This activity has brought to the library students who formerly had shown little interest.

— *Helen Shaw, Clarion-Limestone High School, Strattanville, Pennsylvania*

Coffeehouse-Poetry Readings & Bongo Drums

When the eighth-grade social studies classes are studying the 1950s and 1960s, I turn the back room of the library into a "beatnik coffeehouse." Students are invited to get a pass for lunch on a designated day, and we take turns reading poetry, either published or original, while they eat in the dimly lit room. I dress all in black, don a long black wig, and borrow a bongo drum from the music department. Of course, we all snap our fingers to show our appreciation for the poetry!

— *Patty Barr, Roosevelt Middle School, Decatur, Illinois*

Coffeehouse

Our high school library sponsors a coffeehouse about twice a year for students to read their original poems or short writings. The creative writing course faculty gives us names of students to contact, and we advertise widely for volunteer student authors. The coffeehouse is held during advisement block, allowing other students to sign up to attend. Decaf coffee, hot cocoa mix, and supplies are purchased through the library budget, and large pots of both are prepared that day. For atmosphere, we close the window curtains, arrange the tables close together, put a battery-operated candle on each, and turn on background music from the 1950s. We also put out copies of the school's literary magazine from past years and chessboards. A sound system with handheld microphone, a tall stool, and a podium are all that's needed for the readers. The librarians "set the stage" for students at the opening, telling students to talk softly, to respond to the readings by snapping their fingers or applauding, and that it's OK to refill their coffee cup. We make the point that each reader's work and point of view should be respected. Students look forward to our coffeehouse gatherings, and we have discovered some outstanding writing that previously only teachers got to read! Warning: Make sure you read and approve each poem or piece of writing before it is publicly read.

— *Sandra Brady, Churchville-Chili High School, Churchville, New York*

Collaborating for Best Results

Before introducing a new idea or reference skill to students, go over the lesson in advance with the classroom teacher. The teacher will understand what is going on and will be able to help answer students' questions when the lesson is presented.

— *Steve Baule, Glenbrook South High School, Glenview, Illinois*

Color Coding Books on Reading Lists

We placed color labels on Perma Bound and paperback books listed on the English department's required reading list: orange for freshmen, blue for sophomores, yellow for juniors, and red for seniors. These books are kept on a separate rack—easy for students to find.

— *Earline Thigpen, Riverdale High School*

Consumer Education

We invited consumer math classes to the library to learn to shop using Consumer Reports. The teacher and I teamed up to develop information sheets that the students filled in to compare products so they could determine which would be the best buy. Students who might have felt that the library has little to offer them got hands-on experience and some skills that they could use in making their real-life purchasing decisions.

— *Mary Pat Lemmons, Edneyville (North Carolina) High School*

Conversations and Collaborations

I collaborated with the science teachers on a project called "Conversations with Famous International Scientists." Students researched and portrayed scientists, using costumes, flags, and props of their countries. We produced a video of the project. I repeated the project with elementary, junior high, and high school students.

— *Madeleine M. Hoss, Metcalf Laboratory School, Illinois State University, Normal, Illinois*

Cooperative Approach to Vertical Files

To increase the information in our pamphlet file on Pennsylvania counties, I asked the eighth-grade social studies and English teachers to do a cooperative project. Students wrote to a chamber of commerce in each Pennsylvania county for information. Later in the year, students gave social studies reports on each county. This project was an opportunity for the English teachers to review addressing envelopes and writing business letters. Letters and reports were completed in the computer lab. The students were delighted to receive mail and add resources to the library.

— *Susan Moser, Clarion (Pennsylvania) Area Junior-Senior High School*

Copycat Buster

Physical education students who are unable to participate in class are sent to the library to write reports. Many of these "reports" were being copied verbatim from encyclopedias. Our solution was to create question sheets about a variety of sports. Each sheet requires answers from several reference books, which has lead to good results. Now, students actually learn something about the activity they are missing.

— *Sylvia Feicht, Kankakee Valley Middle School, Wheatfield, Indiana*

Create an Internet Projects Notebook

I created an Internet Projects notebook for keeping track of the ideas for using it that come over the listservs. I arrange projects alphabetically by title, with the subject line highlighted for easy identification, and notify teachers of new project ideas through the media center newsletter. As projects expire, or I see no interest, I remove them from the notebook.

— *Shelley Glantz, Arlington (Massachusetts) High School*

Technology Pathfinder

We devised a pathfinder to encourage student researchers to use the new technology as well as traditional sources in our library. The pathfinder is a simple list of all computer stations where students can use databases or online services. It provides information about what is available at each station and what the resource is best used for. Here is a sample listing: "MAS (located in the magazine room)—an index to current magazine articles. Includes Magill's Book Reviews." Even though our students are now familiar with automation and technology resources, they seem satisfied to be able to retrieve information from one database, perhaps overlooking other databases or services with additional material.

— *Sally J. Martin, Westlake High School, Austin, Texas*

Cross Curricular Enrichment Activities

In our school, the library staff worked with faculty members to plan cross-curricular enrichment activities. Among the special events was a Spanish Festival that introduced the talents of students taking Spanish. The program also included talks on Picasso and Ernest Hemingway. Another program revolved around the guest appearance of a best-selling author who happened to be in the area in honor of his nephew's 18th birthday. Several weeks later, a returning veteran from the Persian Gulf War held over 350 students spellbound as he spoke of his experiences. The culmination was a fine arts festival featuring the talents of students enrolled in agriculture, journalism, creative writing, speech, art, and music classes. The programs promoted not only the library but also students who had received little recognition in the past.

— *Lorna C. Vogt, Sycamore (Illinois) Senior High School*

Current Events in the Library

One way to get teachers and students into the library is to plan special lessons that enhance the study of current events. For example, when news of the Soviet Union and the situation in that country was prominent in the media, I invited classes studying the situation to spend a period in the library. When students entered, *Overture of 1812* was playing. The library staff served students Russian tea and cookies and gave them the opportunity to taste caviar. When students were seated, I turned down the music and explained that *Overture of 1812* was the musical story of the Napoleonic invasion of Russia. I then presented very brief booktalks on *War and Peace* and *Dr. Zhivago*. As they listened to the finale of the overture, the students were free to browse among books on the Soviet Union. A similar type of activity could be done for any area of the world that is in the news.

— *Judy Higgins, Palisades School District, Perkasie, Pennsylvania*

Customized Style Sheets

When our English department decided to change style sheets, the budget did not include enough funds to provide an MLA pamphlet for everyone. Though reference copies were available in the library, we thought we could do better. Our staff had a great time summarizing the style sheet on one page. All sample citations listed teachers or administrators from our school as authors. Book titles joked about the personal habits or interests of the staff. For example, since I am never seen without a can of my favorite soft drink, our "book with an editor" sample looks like this: Valenza, Joyce, ed. 101 Diet Coke Recipes. New York: Brooklyn Press, 1991. All listed "authors" were good sports. The document looks so matter-of-fact that it takes a few minutes for students to notice the jokes.

— *Joyce Valenza, Wissahickon High School, Ambler, Pennsylvania*

Earthsea in a Day

During School Library Media Month, I organized a day of reading a single book aloud from start to finish. The book was *The Wizard of Earthsea* by Ursula LeGuin. Teachers, administrators, and community leaders (including the public librarian) were invited to read aloud a specific number of pages. In advance, I gave each reader a copy of the book, with the section they would read marked. We began at 8 A.M. and finished with the last bell at 2:03 P.M. Although no student could hear the whole book, many returned during the day to hear another few pages.

— *Linda Wood, South Kingstown High School, Wakefield, Rhode Island*

Equipment at a Glance

To make it easier to locate AV equipment around the school, we have created "Sign-Out Alley," where we have hung a large laminated map of the school with all the room numbers marked on it. Strips of Velcro® are attached to each room, and each piece of equipment has circular key tags, marked with the equipment name and number and attached with Velcro. We have found the best place to attach the tags is near the electric cord at the back. When teachers borrow a piece of equipment, they peel off the key tag and put it on the map to show where the equipment will be.

— *Judy Taylor, Ryerson Middle School, Hamilton, Ontario, Canada*

Facts on Sticky Notes

When students hunt for facts, they write the facts on sticky notes and attach these notes to their worksheets. The colorful sticky notes seem to make the assignment fun.

— *Gayle Schmuhl, Ford Middle School, Brook Park, Ohio*

Fall Preview of Books

In late September or early October, we hold a "fall preview" of new books for the faculty. To draw teachers to the library, we serve refreshments (I provide homemade sticky buns). Books are arranged by subject area, and teachers are encouraged to browse. This has been so popular that we have added another "sticky bun day" in the late spring so teachers can select books to read over the summer.

— *Beth Rearick, West Snyder High School, Beaver Springs, Pennsylvania*

Fanning Interest

If you are looking for new ways to generate interest in reports, you may want to try an idea from our geography teacher who remembered the old funeral home fans that kept us from withering in church on a hot Sunday morning. After researching the Caribbean Islands, geography students constructed a fan to present what they had learned. Materials needed: tag board, a tongue depressor, colored paper, and markers. The front of each fan was decorated with a scene from the island, while the back contained information about its history, culture, and tourist attractions. The finished products were displayed hanging by fishing line from the school library ceiling.

— *Sheila Oliver, Boiling Springs Junior High School, Spartanburg, South Carolina*

Far Away Places

Magazines such as *Southern Living* and *Good Housekeeping*, as well as travel magazines, have check-off lists that may be sent in for tourist information on places in this country and around the world. The items are placed in a popular "Travel Information" file that students use for reports, and teachers use to plan their vacations. I also pick up outdated brochures from a favorite travel agency. The information is used for reports that can be illustrated with the pictures. Art classes also enjoy using the pictures.

— *Alice Lucas, Desoto (Missouri) Secondary Library*

Focus on Resources

An announcement of audiovisuals and pamphlets available from the electric company prompted me to think of the resources available in our own collection. I planned a year-long project, called Focus on Resources, to acquaint teachers and students with resources in the library and the community. I determined to devote a week to each department in which the focus would be on the media available to it. For example, I assembled or organized these daily offerings for a six-day focus on resources for the English Department.

▶ Creative writing resources from a grant-funded arts program
▶ A trivia contest with prizes
▶ Showings of videotapes of special interest to English classes
▶ Storytelling by public librarians and members of an arts council
▶ Instruction in computer networking, online services, and software programs for English classes

I discovered that planning for each subject focus took several weeks. As a result I have revised my goals for the year, expecting to focus on one department every two months.

— *Edna Cogdell, South View Senior High School, Hope Mills, North Carolina*

Geographic Sources

We posted a large hand-drawn map of the United States and asked students and staff to write and attach cards with their names and the names of out-of-state towns where they had lived. Students studying regions of the country could consult these "resident experts," and everyone enjoyed learning who had lived where.

— *Sally Mortier, Peoples Academy, Morrisville, Vermont*

Geography Puzzle Corner

We noticed that bored, restless students—many of whom could not distinguish states from countries—would often visit the library. One day, with an unexpected $50 in the budget, I seized the chance to order puzzles, which don't fit any of our budget categories. We set up a puzzle corner on two old tables, and now we suggest to bored students that they "put the United States together" or work on the world. This activity, which appeals to students of all grade levels, can be done by students alone or together. We've noticed that groups tend to work quietly. We also suggest challenges: Put the United States together in less than ten minutes, name the states bordered by an ocean, put Africa together in five minutes, and so forth. Those who complete challenges sign their names on a long banner in the corner, and we write congratulatory notes to them. Our $50 experiment has created a pressure-free learning tool for students, and 15 minutes' worth of writing "congratulations" once a week has halved our discipline problems.

— *Ginger Williams, Williston-Elko Middle & High Schools, Williston, South Carolina*

Grammar Checks Added to Word Documents

Because the English teachers use the grammar check feature in *Microsoft Word* to evaluate student writings, we needed to find a way to paste the check display in documents. You can copy the grammar check and put it in the clipboard by pushing Alt and Print Screen. Then you can paste the information in the *Word* document in the usual way. The grammar check is also useful in determining reading levels.

— *Kathy Sells, Lincoln High School, Ypsilanti, Michigan*

Guaranteed Winners

As a new librarian wanting to establish a working partnership with the faculty, I began a concentrated effort of reaching out to each English teacher. After assembling handouts, sample lesson plans, bibliographies, and booklists, I sent invitations written in the style of the common mass market mailings we all get at home, encouraging each teacher to visit the library. When the teachers arrived, I gave them pages of ideas and bonus gifts of paperback books. We all enjoyed this "open house," and the invitation served as a lighthearted beginning to serious librarian-teacher curriculum planning. The letter read:

INFORMATION ENTERPRISES
Robinson High School
Fairfax, Virginia 22032
Joe or Jane Teacher
English Department
Robinson High School
Fairfax, Virginia 22032

Dear Mr. Teacher:

Congratulations! Your name has been drawn from those of hundreds of educators to receive at least one of the following valuable gifts:

▽ a team-teaching partner
▽ free cooperative lesson planning
▽ ideas for implementing curriculum objectives
▽ a resource person for information skills
▽ assistance with AV equipment and software
▽ bibliographies on any subject
▽ booktalks
▽ assistance with students' research

You are definitely a winner. You can claim your prize at any time in the library office. However, in order to receive a *bonus gift* especially designed for English teachers, you must come to the library office during your planning period on December 15, when prizes will be discussed and nourishment provided.

In order to qualify for this offer, you must be a certified English teacher over 21 years of age. Your spouse, if you are married, must not accompany you.

Your chances of winning are 1:1. Prizes left unclaimed after three days will be given to the needy.

Sincerely, Librarian

— *Peggy Hook, Robinson High School, Fairfax, Virginia*

Guide Abstracts

To provide staff with a quick overview of educational programs on television, I pick up the *TV Guide* on Tuesday mornings and note all programs that may be useful to the curriculum. For each program, I note the title, length, channel, time, date, and a brief annotation. This list is printed and distributed to the teachers by Tuesday afternoon, giving them a minimum of three days before a program will air to discuss it with the students or assign watching it as homework.

— *Randall English, Brandon High School, Ortonville, Michigan*

Guide to Teachers' Wants

As reports, term papers, and other projects are assigned, I ask each teacher to send me a copy of the written instructions with the due date. I put these instructions in a notebook, which is divided by the teachers' names. When students come to the library for research, a quick glance in the notebook tells me exactly what the students' need.

— *Pamela I. Stein, The Bodine School, Bartlett, Tennessee*

Hard Disk Capacity in Windows

Running out of disk space at the wrong time can be inconvenient or disastrous. To avoid such computer casualties, remember to check your available disk space prior to tackling a long and involved document, especially if you are without a disk. If you are using a PC, double click the mouse on the My Computer icon and then right click on the Drive C: icon. A window will appear with the term Properties listed at the bottom. Click once on Properties. The window that appears will have a colorful pie chart. The chart indicates how much hard disk capacity your computer has, how much space you have already used, and how much disk space is available.

— *Bonnie Hunt, Marietta, Georgia*

Editor's Note: If you are using a Macintosh, simply go to the apple menu icon, click and hold the mouse as you pull down to "About this Macintosh" and release. A bar graph will appear in the window showing which programs are active, how much hard drive space is in use, and how much is available. smc

High School Scheduling

Our high school library operates on flexible scheduling, so motivating teachers to spend some of their instructional time in the library can be a problem. To stimulate participation, I set up a special schedule for English classes. Ninth graders and their teachers are invited to come once a month while tenth and eleventh graders are scheduled at least twice a year. Skills to be taught are listed on the invitation to teachers. As an added inducement, we offer this time as an extra planning period for the teacher. Also, when classes arrive in the library, students get to draw from a grab bag of small prizes. We provide word searches for students who get done with the lesson early and always allow 15 minutes for browsing.

— *Barbara Terry McDougald, Scotland High School, Laurinburg, North Carolina*

Hot Books

I wanted to keep students informed about the best sellers every week, so I made a sign with the lettering "These Books are Hot, Hot, Hot!" Leaving the middle blank, I added red chili peppers around the border (you could also use a thermometer). The poster is laminated so I can change the best sellers list in the middle without ruining the sign.

— *Kathryn Haddeland, Portales (New Mexico) Senior High School*

Instant Math in the Library

To make paying fines interesting and sometimes fun, we give students a chance to reduce their fines by calculating half of the sum in their heads. If students can do this without help, they pay the reduced fine. Many students can do the calculations easily, and others find it a difficult task. Some are surprised that math can be used in the library. The student aides are getting better at doing the calculations and find it fun.

— *Fran Feigert, Northwest High School, Justin, Texas*

Just One of the Kids

As she was making plans for a class research project, a health teacher realized she needed to refresh her own electronic search skills. Three weeks later she voluntarily attended a science research skills lesson I was teaching for sixth graders. She joined with the kids in taking notes and asking questions. And, like the kids, she left the media center excited!

— *Mary Alice Anderson, Media Specialist, Winona (Minnesota) Middle School*

Keeping Track of Tasks

To jog your memory and to help you delegate beginning-of-the-year and end-of-the-year tasks, create task cards. The cards should designate who will perform the job (student helpers, paraprofessionals, yourself) and give a description of how to do delegated jobs. I use different color cards for different areas of the library or different tasks: circulation, audiovisuals, computers, administration, facil-

ities, books, and so on. Remember to keep the cards marked "Done'-good for an emotional rush as tasks are completed.

— *Joan Enders, Monticello Middle School, Longview, Washington*

Learning Bibliographical Format

Rather than trying to remember bibliographical format taught in a formal lesson once per year, our middle school students practice at every library visit. When students come to the library with a class, they are required to write a bibliographical entry on an index card for each book they wish to check out. Cards are checked for accuracy before books can be stamped. Cards are kept on file under each student's name. At the end of the semester, we give each student his or her cards, and students compile a bibliography of everything they have read.

— *Betty Hamilton, Brownfield (Texas) Middle School*

Learning New Software

Once I have tried a new computer program to make sure it works, I ask a few students to "test drive" it for me before it is introduced to the whole school. The students selected feel important, and this is a good way to spread the word since they invariably tell their friends about the new program. I also list the new products in the librarian newsletter with the offer to present a workshop for teachers who wish to learn how to use the software. In addition, the county administration grants continuing education credit to teachers who work with a program for ten hours over a period of several weeks.

— *Melba Chandler, Crest Senior High School, Shelby, North Carolina*

Library Smiles

At the book-return table, we keep a jar filled with wrapped candy. Students who return books on time help themselves to a treat. Also, I write the name and homeroom of the prompt book returnee on a small slip of paper. Each month we have a drawing for a gift bag containing a paperback book, some chocolate, and other little items that have come my way. I can't say either of these devices has any influence on chronically delinquent borrowers, but they add to the friendly atmosphere of the library and bring smiles to student faces.

— *Sister Marjorie Stumpf, St. Savior High School, Brooklyn, New York*

Library Tourists

AAA Tour Books are excellent resources for students doing state reports since the books have information on cities and tourist attractions. The information on motels will help students who are assigned to plan a trip and figure its cost. Students and staff can donate the books after vacation time or you can call AAA for copies.

— *Anitra Gordon, Lincoln High School, Ypsilanti, Michigan*

Multicultural Activities

"Celebrating Traditions Around the World" was an all-school multicultural program promoted by the faculty, staff, and students. The music department involved students in the orchestra, band, and chorus. The physical education department volunteered an international folk dance. Students researched and presented a three-minute presentation on different traditions and celebrations.

— *Madeleine M. Hoss, Metcalf Laboratory School, Illinois State University, Normal, Illinois*

No-Cost Author Profiles

Create an author file by tearing out the author profiles that frequently appear in publisher's catalogs. Store them in the vertical file for use by students doing speeches and book reports.

— *Shirley Fetherolf, Strongsville, Ohio*

Nostalgia through the Year

We started the school year by featuring photos of our staff members in school. (We do this every four years.) Thus I was inspired to continue the nostalgia displays from past decades. For the 40s we had ration books, table model radios, sheet music, campaign buttons, and copies of newspaper headlines found in library books. For the 50s we had a portable phonograph player and records, glass milk bottles, hula hoops, and Elvis memorabilia. When we get into the 60s, 70s, and 80s, more and more people have items to include. The display gets a lot of attention since the U.S. history course parallels the time periods featured.

— *Evelyn Hammeran, Randolf (New Jersey) High School*

Number Puzzlers

An activity I've used to attract ninth graders' interest is called "Number Puzzlers." Students try to guess the meaning of a phrase such as "7diaw" (seven days in a week) or "16oiap" (16 ounces in a pound). Try "7 wonders of the world," "103 chemical elements," or "8 sides to a stop sign."

— *Louise Woodall, Sutherland (Iowa) Community Schools*

On the Road with Databases

Using the three databases available on our network, I created a set of questions on each of the 50 states and then presented students with a "question of the week." The students put cards containing their name, their answer, and the source they used into a box, and I held a weekly drawing. The first entry drawn with the correct answer received a small prize. In the media center, I displayed a large U.S. map with a small car that traveled from state to state as the questions were answered. Students used an atlas program to determine how many miles our little car had traveled each week.

— *Kristy Patterson, Callaway Middle School, Hogansville, Georgia*

Pamphlets on Parks by Students

A geography research unit taught by the librarian and geography instructors had "National Parks" as its theme. Students selected their favorite parks, conducted research, and developed pamphlets about the parks. The pamphlets included maps, points of interest, historical background, and more. A bonus activity of this high-interest, facts-intensive unit was for students to display their finished pamphlets.

— *Donna Sands, Prairie Central High School, Fairbury, Illinois*

Party Passports

In our middle school, the children carry assignment notebooks, which we call "passports." In these notebooks, they keep track of their homework. Once every 10 weeks or so, we have passport parties for those children whose passports are complete and signed by a parent or guardian weekly. (The parties may consist of talent shows featuring the teachers, guest speakers, movies, or a day-time dance.) The children who do not keep their passports up-to-date are sent to study halls during the party. I always take one of the sixth-grade study halls and work up about 20 questions, drawn from many library reference resources. When they have answered all the questions correctly, I give them a treat from the cafeteria. The children have unlimited opportunities to correct their incorrect answers, but only during their "study hall" in lieu of a party. Thus I have the opportunity to give the less-scholastically-inclined students great reference lessons.

— *Anne Ozog, Waterloo (New York) Middle School*

Posters & Chemists

Chemistry and physics teachers joined in the district's effort to emphasize multicultural education this year by assigning research on a scientist from the student's ethnic background or a woman scientist. A two-page report and a poster were required. Identifying resources for the assignment took some searching on the part of the library staff, but the results were worth the effort. Some outstanding posters were created and displayed in the library. While making a poster seems like an old-fashioned assignment, it was well received by the high school students. The teachers liked the assignment enough to plan to repeat it the following year.

— *Evelyn Hammaren, Randolph (New Jersey) High School*

Putting Fun Back into Science

To make science come alive for middle school students, I try to make connections to their world. We ask a supermarket for paper grocery bags that we return decorated with pictures and a slogan, such as "Save the

Whales." After researching two or three animals in the library, the students write and design a newsletter, which they mail home to parents. (While students are on the computer, we introduce them to some Internet sites on animals. One of their favorites is Cockroach World at <www.nj.comi~ucky/index.html>.

And a final idea is to ask students to place a soybean under their tongue for a class period. Warn them not to swallow or suck on the bean. By the end of the class period, the bean will begin to germinate, showing that the soybean has a short gestation period.

— *Danny Collins, Cedar Hill Middle School, Carrollton, Georgia*

Reading Lists for All

At the beginning of the year we make copies of all reading lists distributed by teachers. The lists are placed in report covers, labeled with the teacher's name, and displayed in a wall-mounted magazine rack. Students have easy access to the list they need. We also send copies of the lists to the public library.

— *LaMae Y. Strange, Georgetown (South Carolina) High School*

Reading Passports

The global studies teachers wanted to broaden ninth graders' reading beyond textbook assignments on countries of the world. We purchased new books about the countries being studied and added these to older titles in a bibliography of fiction and nonfiction titles. Among the nonfiction were biographies and personal narratives. Among the novels were those set in a studied country, those with a character from the country, and historical fiction. As students read books about a country, they created a page to enter in their "passport." The page contained a picture of the country's flag, current statistics, and a synopsis of the book read. Teachers or librarians could design a rubber stamp to add further authenticity to the passport.

— *Patricia Hanny, Kenmore West Senior High School, Buffalo, New York*

Recycling SIRS Index Replacements

When you receive new pages and a revised index for the SIRS binders, give the old indexes to teachers who teach the topics covered. I give them both the specific index and the cross-reference index along with a reminder that we have this resource in the library. Of course, you could add notes about other resources on the topic. Teachers can often use reminders about the wonderful materials we have. This is one more way to remember to remind them.

— *Anitra Gordon, Lincoln High School, Ypsilanti, Michigan*

Research + Hobbies = Good PR

To encourage reading and research skills, I introduced a hobby show as a collaborative effort with the English department. The freshmen students research their hobbies, and since they enjoy the topic, learning doesn't seem a chore. On a certain day, students put their hobbies on display in the library. The rest of the school is encouraged to visit and comment on the displays. The faculty and I were really impressed by the creativity of some of the students. For increased PR for the library, schedule the show during an activity that brings parents into the school. I used my show in conjunction with parent-teacher conferences. It was a big success and made the library *visible* to parents, teachers, administration and students.

— *Madeleine M Hoss, University High School, Normal, Illinois*

Research Projects Linked to The Big Six

All research projects are linked to The Big Six, a research process developed by Eisenberg & Berkowitz of Syracuse University. Media center use has increased; kids know their way around the media center; the demand for books is up; and all research projects are sensational!

— *Janis V. Isenberg, Middlebrook Elementary School, Trumbull, Connecticut*

Editor's Note: Learn more about Michael Eisenberg and Robert Berkowitz's strategies by visiting <www.Big6.com/>. smc

Researching *Animal Farm*

Before our ninth-grade English class began reading George Orwell's *Animal Farm*, each student selected a historic revolution to research in the library. While the American, French, and Russian revolutions seemed to be obvious choices, students were encouraged to choose more obscure or more modern insurrections. Examples include Corazon Aquino's "people power" revolution, Tiananmen Square, the overthrow of Romania's Ceausescu, the 1986 Haitian coup d'etat or the 1979 Islamic Revolution in Iran, among others. Using magazines and other sources, students answered factual questions about their chosen topic. Questions included: When and where did the revolution occur? Who lead the revolution? What was the cause of the revolution? What kind of reform was desired? What slogans did the rebels use? Was the revolution a success? This exercise gave students a context for reading *Animal Farm*, provided them with a basis for comparison, initiated spirited discussion of the book in class, and produced some original essay topics. Perhaps the best result was that the students were enthusiastic about the library and reading.

— *Ken Vesey, St. John's International School, Waterloo, Belgium*

Reserved Weeks for Research Projects

Because we had conflicts when teachers assigned research papers, we set up a reservation system. During inservice days before the school year begins, English teachers can reserve a week for bringing classes to the media center for research projects. There is some flexibility in the scheduling to allow for unexpected changes, but the teachers are cooperative and respect the reservations made by others. The system also reduces the anxiety students experience when there are similar research projects going on at the same time. Students and teachers get that special attention they need since the library staff can focus on their projects.

— *LaMae Y. Strange, Georgetown (South Carolina) High School*

Science Trivia Contest

As a change of pace for our eighth-grade science classes, we typed science trivia questions onto index cards and laminated the cards. We divided the classes into teams of two students each and gave each team ten questions to answer. The team that finished first (with the most correct answers) won a prize. The winning teams from each class competed against each other the next day, and each team had to answer the same questions. We awarded the *Guinness Book of World Record*s as the grand prize.

— *Phyllis Mosciski, Pinconning (Michigan) Area High School*

Science Updates

Science is one area of the curriculum that requires the latest information. Last year the biology and environmental science classes came to the library to read periodicals with the most up-to-date information chosen from a bibliography of recent articles. TOM helps us keep those bibliographies current.

— *Patricia Hare, Northwest High School, Cincinnati, Ohio*

Seating Charts with Names and Faces

Using a digital camera and the software *ClarisWorks Drawing*, teachers can create seating charts with their students' names and faces. These charts will be especially useful for substitute teachers. When seat assignments change, it is easy to edit the chart on the computer. -Laura Bratschi, Garrison Mill Elementary School, Marietta, Georgia Seventh Graders Write Science Picture Books Our seventh graders honed their writing and reading skills when they became authors of books for younger students. Students from a science class and a compensatory reading group wrote, edited, and illustrated stories that might be used to explain the life sciences to younger students. Popular titles included "Keeping Healthy with Babs Bunny," "The Quest Through the Digestive System Featuring Food the Knight," "Visiting the Blood Family," "Clementine Carbohydrate," "The Digestive Factory," and "The Flintstones and Too Much Junk Food." When the stories were printed, bound, and laminated, students tried them out on children at an elementary school.

— *Andrea Troisi, LaSalle Middle School, Niagara Falls, New York*

Sharing Resources

Scenario: Jim Social Studies assigns his three sections of modern history a research project on the period between the two world wars. He has tried to work it out so that no more than two students are researching the same question. The classes are scheduled into the library during the 1st, 2nd, and 5th periods.

Problem: How to assure that all students have equal access to our limited resources.

Solution: As each class arrives, I explain that materials will not be checked out during this period, but that their selections will be reserved until the end of the day. The student signs a reserve slip for each book wanted and brings all to the desk. I clip the reserve slip to the book card and put it in the tray. I put a slip of colored paper into the book pocket and place the book on a cart. If there is time, the books on the cart will be reshelved. If not, the next class will be told to check the cart as well as the shelves. The procedure is repeated for each class. At the end of the day, books requested by more than one student are divided among them and put on a circulation of one week instead of two, allowing all students access to the books.

Evaluation: It isn't foolproof and requires cooperation, but it has worked for us. Fewer students leave with a large stack of books, but fewer leave frustrated and empty-handed.

— *Sister Annunciata, Sacred Heart High School, Los Angeles, California*

Social Studies PR

Our sixth-grade students researched countries as part of our yearlong theme, "Celebrating Our Cultural Diversity." As an added touch, the students learned to enter the final reports on the computer and to use computer graphics to design a cover. The results were so impressive that the finished products were displayed at our public library.

— *Elizabeth Garbarino, Riverhead (New York) Middle School*

Speechmaking in Library Science Classes

Students never get enough research practice or enough public speaking practice. As a remedy for this, the ninth-grade library science class was required to wrap up with a researched speech incorporating all forms of library resources. Good research and speech techniques, from note taking to the dreaded bibliography, were emphasized. I created a simplified version of bibliography style from Turabian's *A Manual for Writers of Term Papers, Theses, and Dissertations* and the Modern Language Association on one sheet of paper, with general rules on one side and a labeled sample on the reverse side. Each year since that assignment, when students need to create a bibliography in other classes, they return to the library for a copy of that style guide. I now keep a supply ready and available to all.

— *Margaret Heydrick, Rocky Grove High School, Franklin, Pennsylvania*

Student Speeches by Videotape

We videotaped student council officer's speeches to the student body and played them over the school's TV system. The alternative was to deliver the speeches in person in an auditorium without air conditioning in late August. Some students said they felt much less nervous giving their talks on videotape. We also saved valuable school time that would have been lost in moving the student body to and from the auditorium.

— *Deborah Young Maehs, Kingfisher (Oklahoma) Middle School*

USA Today Debates

The debate page from *USA Today* is a great resource for speeches and papers, but after I had collected about 200 of these pages, I found it difficult to find specific information. Using the Macintosh LC and *Filemaker* software, I made a database with the number, date, debate title, and keywords. Now a student can use the computer to search for a topic. The entries appear on the screen, directing the student to the correct file. I also plan to add the vertical file folders to the database.

— *Deanna Kennedy, Myersdale (Pennsylvania) Junior-Senior High School*

Visual Organizers for Notes

Try using the Microsoft *Publisher* program to create a blank newsletter for class note taking. I fill in the headlines only and then my students have an easy time finding each topic as it is covered in class. The students will have each topic sorted in their notes and find reviewing easier and more productive. Add clip art for visual learners.

— *Marcie Clark, Sprayberry High School, Marietta, Georgia*

Wake Up to Black History

To promote African-American History (Black History) Month, we devised a contest that got all first period classes involved. Teachers were alerted ahead of time about the contest and its basic rules: teachers couldn't help; the answers had to be written on a piece of paper; and each class could send only one person with the answer. Our school announcements are read at the beginning of the first hour. At the end of the regular announcements, a mystery biography lasting about 10-15 seconds was read. Students in each class would quickly try to guess the name of the person and then dispatch its 'room runner' who raced to be the first to deliver the correct answer. As soon as a correct answer arrived, it would be announced along with the class that had won. Each person in the winning room would receive a yummy treat that same period. Besides teaching about famous black Americans, the game has had at least one additional benefit: since we didn't do it every day, teachers reported that students were paying more attention to the announcements. We also learned to make our clues harder than originally planned because students working together surprised us with their knowledge.

— *Carol Burbridge, Jardine Middle School, Topeka, Kansas*

What Do You Know?

I have been distributing lists of terms, names, and phrases from the book *What Do You Know?* by Jaime O'Neill (Bantam). This weekly list, based on a common theme such as geography, can be used by teachers for reference ideas, discussion questions, assignments, or just for fun. As a PR tool, I send copies to the central office for administrators and secretaries to test their common knowledge. Here is an example of one list: Are the following places islands, rivers, mountains, lakes or none of the above? Madagascar, Mindanao, Thames, Sardinia, Harlem, Titicaca, Mauna Loa, Euphrates, Via Veneto, Orinoco, Ararat, Tiber, Nicosia, Baikal. If you want to show off, in what country are they located?

— *Randy English, Brandon High School, Ortonville, Michigan*

Women's History Contest

During National Women's History Month, we run a contest for students in our high school. Twice a week we ask a question about a famous woman in history. Winners receive a candy bar and a Susan B. Anthony dollar. This is a fun activity that also gets students into the library to use reference books to research the answers. We also run a similar contest for Black History Month. Local merchants donate coupons and discount cards as prizes.

— *Judy Gallagher, Mineral Point (Wisconsin) High School*

Women's History Month Biographies

For Women's History Month in March, our library offered special booktalks that got faculty and students actively involved. In preparation, I taped short "Who am I?" profiles of famous women whose biographies were on display in the library. As each tape was played, a panel of visiting teachers held up several appropriate clues suggesting the identity of the subject. For example, for Georgia O'Keefe, we presented hats, a quill pen, and a deer skull. Students guessed the name of the person after listening to the tape and viewing our antics. A second tape about famous women from our school added to the fun.

— *Alena Napohitaro, Bellport (New York) Middle School*

Working Cooperatively

Librarians and teachers are natural partners when it comes to teaching research. I split the class with the classroom teacher, who works with students to explain the assignment procedures: narrow topic, outline ideas, and show examples. In the meantime, I teach search skills, including Boolean, truncation, keyword search difficulties (variant spellings, synonyms, and plurals), and show how the appropriate programs operate. Then we switch groups. After the initial two or three class periods, intermediate or middle school students will be ready to do their research.

— *Lois McNicol, Garney Valley High School, Glen Mills, Pennsylvania*

Managing the Library

> ## The school library is no longer a luxury, but is rapidly becoming an essential element in the equipment of every school.
>
> Public Libraries, *September 1897*

The library is a place where print resources merge with resources available electronically. Librarians have long been charged with insuring that users of the library are linked to as much information as is available and feasible. They have attempted to bolster budgets for print and nonprint resources through normal sources and through innovative programs to bring funds and donations into the library. Librarians know that unless access to all types of information resources is available in the libraries, many people will not be able to gain access on their own. In a school setting it is the staff and students who are the users. Every student, regardless of where she or he lives, no matter the economic status of the child's household, must be given access to the world of knowledge. Our school libraries are making great strides in providing that access in a location conducive to the child's quest for learning. Making that information available to students is greatly enhanced through the organization and stewardship of the library media specialists who manage libraries. These are a few of the ways they do manage the centers—to fill their centers with resources and to make those resources available to all students who visit their centers.

"Garden Party" for Teachers

When faced with the overwhelming task of weeding our 13,000 title print collection prior to automating, I invited the teachers to come to the library for a "Garden Party" the day after school closed for the summer. Armed with my guidelines, the teachers pulled books from their own specific subject areas, and I provided lunch with school funds. Not only did we weed out more than 2,000 books, but also the teachers became more familiar with the rest of our collection.

— *Carol N. Kelly, St. Paul's School for Girls, Brooklandville, Maryland*

"How It Works" Speeches

Showing how things work or how things are manufactured is a popular type of demonstration speech in our school. Students' inability to locate the needed information led us to enter HOW IT WORKS as a homegrown subject in the catalog. In addition to information about processes, books of formulas go under this topic. We have also added recent books that give substitutes for the word "doohickey."

— *Edna Boardman, Minot (North Dakota) High School, Magic City Campus*

"Please Bother Me"

Although I use my office for confidential matters, I have found that placing a work station—complete with computer, telephone, and typewriter—in the reading area makes me more visible to students, more available for help, and able to assist in student supervision. A sign on the desk says: "If you need help, please bother me."

— *Roger B. Tanquist, Fairmont (Minnesota) High School*

...and from Wrapping Paper

When I open reams of copier paper, I'm careful to do as little damage as possible to the heavy wrapping paper. At the beginning of the year, there are always some students desperately looking for textbook covers. Our school requires covers for textbooks. For a slight service charge, they can "buy" the wrapping sheets. The charge goes into the library supplies fund.

— *Sister Marjorie Stumpf, St. Savior High School, Brooklyn, New York*

A Big Calendar Is a Key Management Tool

My work is split between the high school and grade school libraries, so organization is my key to survival. I use a huge, time-saving calendar, divided into three-month sections, that tells me at a glance which skills are to be taught, who needs what equipment, which classes are scheduled, and more. The teachers also find the calendar convenient, for they can sign up for library time and equipment without wondering about schedule conflicts, especially since I am unavailable part of each day.

— *Marsha Sisson, Warrenton High School*

Another Use for Catalog Cards

I keep deleted or extra catalog cards in a box by the circulation computer for students to jot down the location of books on the shelves. A "stick-on" pen is attached to the computer.

— *Donna Ayer, South Spencer High School, Rockport, Indiana*

Answers at a Glance

For students to come to the library during a study hall, they must get a pass from the librarians in the morning. Some days, there was a long line of students waiting to find out if passes were available for their study period. To alleviate this congestion, I created a board to display periods for which passes were available that day. The periods of the day were printed in a large font, laminated, and backed with a piece of Velcro®. The period numbers are attached to the board so that students can easily see if passes are available for their study hall before they get in line.

— *Allison Trent Bernstein, Blake Middle School, Medfield, Massachusetts*

Author Cards for Orders

As I read through catalogs and review journals, I fill out a 3 x 5 card as if it were an author card, putting the price in the lower left corner and my reasons to consider the book. I keep the cards, alphabetized by the authors' names, in a box until ordering time. Books that appear on more than one card are considered first along with those by significant authors on subjects. I weed the obvious, keep the best, and check my favorites against our card catalog. When I'm done, I can easily type the final list for a "do not exceed" order to the jobber. I use the same technique for CD-ROMs, but I also include the address of the producer, the price, and machine requirements.

— *Anne Ozog, Waterloo (New York) Middle School*

Editor's Note: The same system will work using a database on your computer. Add a field for noting the source of the review. The entries can easily be sorted by author, title, or any field you have included in the database. Once the list has been pared down to those which you wish to purchase, a printed list to attach to your requisition/purchase order can be generated with a flick of the print command keys. smc

Automatic Call Slips

For our printers attached to CD-ROM products, such as Magazine Article Sum manes and Resource One, we use two-part carbonless paper. Students keep one part for bibliographic use and turn in the other as a call slip so library staff can pull their periodicals

— *Marcia Beckwith, Centennial High School, Meridian, Idaho*

AV Organization in a Zip

Try using gallon-size, self-sealing plastic bags to hold manuals, remote controls and other items that go with TVs, VCRs and other AV equipment. The bags can be labeled with a sticker; if holes are punched along one side, they can be kept in a binder.

— *Patricia Burns, Crary Middle School, Waterford, Michigan*

Awards from the Computer

Last year was our first with library automation (Follett). When award time came, I remembered that the system had been keeping track of how many books and magazines each student had checked out during the year. The computer revealed that 135 students (out of a possible 650) had checked out more than 30 items. I designed a special certificate so each of these students would receive recognition as well as their grand total of checkouts for the year. The student with the biggest record—122 items—also received a gift certificate to a bookstore. After the awards ceremony, student could be heard comparing notes on how many books they had checked out.

— *Connie Quirk, Brookings (South Dakota) High School*

Barcode Everything

Barcode and check out everything that can be taken out the door. When the item comes up on the overdues, you'll know where to find it. Any flat surface can be barcoded: CD-ROM caddies, calculators, rulers, three-hole punches. Attach shop tags with barcodes to equipment and make a book card with the same barcode (to be used in tracking the equipment). If equipment is sent out for repair, check it out for four weeks to a patron named REPAIR. Write the name of the service company on the card kept for tracking. If the item comes up overdue, it's time to call and inquire about the repair delay. If an item cannot be barcoded, for example, scissors, protractor, compass, magnifying glass, check it out as a temporary item. Use a clear catalog card protector or recipe card saver over a barcoded book card. Identify the item on a 2 x 4 inch "form" under the protector, leaving the barcode showing above it. Barcoded cards in protectors can be kept ready for use at the circulation desk, and patrons can fill out special forms before checking out items such as vertical files. Temporary barcode cards /protectors/forms in use can be filed in the charge tray like book cards; equipment cards may also be stored in the old charge tray for quick tracking of equipment

Janet Hofstetter, California (Missouri) High School

Barcodes for Current Issues of Magazines

Because current popular magazines, such as *People, Ebony,* and *Seventeen,* often disappear from the periodical rack, we keep them at the circulation desk and check them out with a barcode card. We don't barcode the magazine itself; the card stands for current issue

— *Lu Richardson, Barnwell (South Carolina) High School*

Barcoding CDs

At our school, we catalog and barcode each compact disc that circulates. The barcode is attached to the CD's case. We use a permanent ink marking pen to write the barcode number on the top of the disc so we can identify the copy if a disc is separated from its case.

— *Sharron L. McElmeel*

Being Prepared for Budget Time

Throughout the year we type purchase requisitions for "wanted" items, omitting the date and total costs until it is time to submit the requisitions. When funds are available, we don't have to rush to prepare requisitions at the last minute.

— *Jaunita L Brown, Franklin County High School, Carnesville, Georgia*

Book Fair Adjuncts

If you take time to recycle throwaway items, you can increase your book fair profits. Here are a few ideas that have been popular at our school:

▶ Postage stamps. I keep an envelope by the desk in which to deposit stamps from all the mail. For the fair, I sort them as seems appropriate (wildlife, famous people) and package them in clear plastic envelopes. Prices vary from 15 to 25 cents.

▶ Stickers. All those bonus stickers from Green Peace, Sierra Club, and Christmas Seals are priced as large single stickers or in blocks for five cents each. These go fast.

▶ Freebies. All the pencils, rulers, erasers and whatnots that vendors send as promotional material are offered at 10 cents each.

▶ Posters. We save those that come from advertisers as well as magazine inserts and sell them for 10 cents each.

▶ Magazines. Discarded magazines are popular, especially *Beckett Baseball Card Monthly, Mad* and *Sports Illustrated.* Be sure to use your discard stamp where it won't deface the cover illustration. We sell magazines at 25 cents each, except for special issues, for which we take bids.

Not only are these materials attractive and affordable to students, but our library earns about $50 per fair from these 'free' materials. The money goes into a fund to bring in visiting authors and illustrators.

— *Phyllis Ennes, Anacortes (Washington) Middle School*

Book Stretchers

We recently moved the library collection to a new building. The school maintenance department built 12 paperback display racks, which were the same length as our bookshelves, 31 inches. Handles were placed on the ends of the racks. When moving day arrived, the physical education classes worked in teams of two to fill the racks, called "book stretchers" by the students, with hard cover books for the move to the new library. When a book stretcher arrived at the new library, its contents were unloaded by shelf. Library staff members directed the stretchers to their assigned places and supervised the loading and unloading. The library was closed one day. And we have 12 new paperback display racks.

— *Betty J. Stout, Alamo Campus, Harlingen (Texas) High School*

Bulletin Board on Windows

With Windows software, we can use computer monitors as an electronic bulletin board. One teacher uses his classroom computer screen to alert students to the daily assignment, such as "Test Today" or "Library Day—Bring Your Books." The procedure uses the screen saver feature of Windows. When the screen saver is activated, the message appears on the screen.

— *Marcia Herman, Manhattan (Kansas) Middle School*

Bypassing the Budget for Best Sellers

The library budget is tied to lots of red tape—purchase orders, year-end cutoffs, and so forth. To cut down on the time it takes to purchase new books, I joined the Doubleday Book Clubs, now known as Doubleday Direct, 401 Franklin Avenue, Garden City, NJ 115301, which sells newly published books by mail order. The catalog descriptions alert buyers to the presence of sexually explicit language in novels, helping me eliminate those not suitable for the library without having to wait to read reviews. I pay for these books through the library's activity account and bypass some of the red tape of using budget funds. Money in the activity account is earned from book fairs and fees for lost or damaged books.

— *Sonjia Gilbert, South Adams Junior/Senior High School, Berne, Indiana*

Cable in the Classroom

Our school is an active user of Cable in the Classroom programming, and the media center is the collection site for the programs we tape. I send a memo to remind the teacher who requested the program. To inform other teachers who might be interested in the program but did not request it initially, we post titles on a prominent wall. These titles are changed monthly; at which time I also put up the new calendar from Cable in the Classroom Magazine. Teachers make their requests for programs to be taped from a monthly list sent to each department.

— *Shelley Glantz, Arlington (Massachusetts) High School*

Cataloging Magazines

I catalog issues of *Cobblestone, Calliope, Faces,* and *Odyssey* magazines into my Winnebago circulation/catalog system so students and teachers can quickly search the subject headings of these valuable publications.

— *Wayne Rush, Grover Cleveland Middle School, Caldwell, New Jersey*

Catching Up on an Incomplete Shelf List

When we computerized our collection from the existing shelf list, I had no idea that the "inherited" list was not complete. Soon books began to arrive for checkout with no computer record. Since the program allowed a temporary entry, we flagged these books by placing a bright color dot next to the barcode, which alerted us to computerize the record when the book was returned. We "found" about 1,000 books in the first year.

— *Faye Griffith, Venice High School, Los Angeles, California*

CD ROM Security

Because our library had a few problems with the security of our CD-ROM products, we were on the lookout for a device that would prevent the removal of our CDs from the CD-ROM players. After much fruitless searching, we designed a bottomless, backless box that fits over the CPU. Made of wood, the boxes are big enough (24 1/2" x 16" x 8 1/2") to allow for air circulation and sturdy enough for the monitor to sit on. Since we put these boxes to use, we have not had any further problems with the removal of our CD or the inadvertent breaking of our CD players.

— *Susan Kallok, Harvard-Westlake School, Los Angeles, California*

Checkout for Borrowed Supplies

Because students were not always returning borrowed items, such as correction fluid, rulers, pens, and calculators, I printed barcodes for each item on a laminated sheet. Now I lend the items out to students for a class period at a time. I have made a similar sheet of barcodes for popular magazines, such as *Teen, Seventeen, Sports illustrated,* and *Car and Driver.*

— *Laura Moe, Zanesville (Ohio) High School*

Circulating Laptops

Our high school library recently purchased laptop computers for students to take home. We also purchased backpacks suitable to house the computer and printer. I decorated each of the backpacks with a school varsity letter and a logo stating "I Love the Library." It's great publicity!

— *Patricia Kolencik, North Clarion High School, Tionesta, Pennsylvania*

Circulating Magazines

We circulate our magazines and in the past have found that many were not returned despite a $5 per magazine charge for lost items. Our return rate has gone up considerably since we started circulating periodicals in plastic bags. The students love using the bags to keep their library materials together and presence of the bags seems to serve as a reminder to return the magazines.

— *Rosalyn Spergel, Lenape Valley Regional High School, Stanhope, New Jersey*

Class Ring Collateral

Have trouble getting scissors, staplers, tape, and other supplies returned when students borrow them? Have the students leave their class rings on deposit until they return the items. Works like a charm!

— *Ann Koebbeler, La Junta (Colorado) High School*

Color Coding Books

In a school that houses grades 4-12, it's difficult for students to easily identify books on the shelves at their reading or interest levels. For that reason, we have added letters to the call numbers. Books written for grades 4-8 are marked with a red J. Books for grades 9-12 have the letters XA written in blue.

— *Diane Peacock, Long County High School, Ludowici, Georgia*

Come Heck or High Water. . .

I keep two boxes of paperback books on hand in case the library is unexpectedly closed due to construction, roof leaks, or anything else interrupting normal operation. The paperbacks are placed on a cart near the library entrance, and students and teachers can simply take one if they need something to read.

— *Travis Cox, Librarian, Bethel High School, Hampton, Virginia*

Communicating with Staff

Communication among the four staff members in our library was greatly enhanced by the simple addition of a clipboard with lined paper. We jot daily notes and reminders to each other, eliminating the need to try to remember to tell everyone everything. Now we just need to remember to read it!

— *Sally J. Martin, Westlake High School, Austin, Texas*

Company-Sponsored Subscriptions

After a bank agreed to purchase some of the magazines on our subscription list, I began looking for other groups that were supporters. I used the printed football program to identify some of the supporters and solicited sponsorship for magazines to be placed in our LMC. The result: One-third of the current magazine and holdings are sponsored by businesses in the community. I send each company a thank-you letter and photographs of students reading the magazines and newspapers.

— *Karen George, Newark (Ohio) High School*

Computerized Debts

For keeping track of student debts, we have assigned barcodes for "copier charges," "damaged books," "IOUs," and so forth. We enter them in the fines (Follett Circ + F7) and the amount owed.

— *Carol Conti, Darien (Connecticut) High School*

Coping with Cables

After spending all our money on two catalog stations and network hardware, we had no funds left for a suitable table with an electrical outlet. We made do by shoving one of our large round tables up against a concrete pillar, having a new outlet installed, and pulling the network wiring down the same pillar. The resulting mass of cables spilling over the table was unsightly, not to mention tempting for students. We solved the problem by spending $3 more for a 12 x 18 inch plastic carryall basket. The fragile network box and the surge protector fit in the bottom, the cables on top. All the cables are pulled through the plastic slats on the sides of the basket. True, we now have an ugly plastic basket on our computer table, but it's tidy. The best part is that, while our students still play around with every pull-down menu on the computers, they don't bother the cables.

— *Linda Whitmore, Cedar Ridge Middle School, Sandy, Oregon*

Cordless Freedom

Until recently, we relied on lung power to relay information to those servicing our workstations. One staff member would hold the office phone and relay the advice offered by the customer support rep at the other end. It was a frustrating and noisy situation. Our problem was solved when we bought a cordless phone. It has given us incredible freedom to move around and fix things with technical support people. We also carry the phone with us when we check the shelves for book requests phoned in by teachers, administrators, and other libraries.

— *Joyce Valenza, Wissahickon High School, Ambler, Pennsylvania*

Cross Referencing on the Computer

To supply SEE references for our public access catalog (Follett Search Plus), we enter a blank title with the cross-reference as the subject heading. For example, in the 650 field, we enter: Civil War–See–UNITED STATES–HISTORY–CIVIL WAR, 1861-1865. Then we save it with a phantom barcode number (800001) and check it out to a phantom patron (800). That way it will show no copies available if the student hits ENTER.

— *Victoria Mark Anthony, Darien (Connecticut) High School*

Date Labels for Magazines

Because the date can appear anywhere on magazine covers, we print dates on small labels and affix them to the magazines. We also place colored dots—a different color for each year—on the spines of the magazines. We can see at a glance if all the issues for a year are in the right container.

— *Mary Ann Kull, East Aurora (New York) High School*

Dessert for the Prompt

Every time a student returns library books on time, he or she may cast a ballot for a favorite dessert. On the last day of every month, we have a drawing and I make the winner's favorite dessert. I love to bake and I hate overdue books.

— *Anne Betts, Philipsburg-Osceola Area Junior High School, Philipsburg, Pennsylvania*

Disappearing Books & Magazines

Any books and magazines that frequently "disappear," such as Stephen King's novels or Teen magazine, are kept behind the circulation desk. Students can check them out, but they must ask me for them. This has cut down on both theft and defacing of materials.

— *Laura Moe, Zanesville (Ohio) High School*

Discard and Declutter

Unclutter the library and your life. Don't save anything just because you think it might be valuable someday. Check now with a public library, an antique dealer, or rare book collector to see if the 1931 encyclopedia has any value. If it doesn't, get rid of it. Resist the temptation to put things where they don't belong "just for now." Shelve it, file it, discard it—but make a decision. Also consider whether things really belong in the library. Maybe it would be better to store the three-hole punch or laminating machine in the school office. If you need it, you can always borrow it back. To avoid a buildup of junk mail, sort your mail in the school office. If you aren't interested in the products advertised, throw the advertisements in that office's trash containers. Keep a box near the door of the library for discarded books, catalogs, pamphlets, and magazines. Urge students and teachers to take items from this pile for classroom libraries, artwork, and reports. Ruthlessly go through your files, keeping in mind that professional organizers estimate no one looks a second time at 80% of the paperwork saved.

— *Andrea Troisi, LaSalle Middle School, Niagara Falls, New York*

Taking Turns for the CD-ROM

Students love to use the CD-ROM data base in our library so much that they line up to wait their turn rather than doing something else and then coming back. To eliminate lines and confusion, I devised a numbering system similar to the ones used at bakeries and delis. Students are assured a place at the computer without standing in line.

— *Charlie Makela, Prince George (Virginia) High School*

Do-It-Yourself Book Reservations

In an effort to encourage students using the Alexandria circulation system (Companion) to place their own "holds" on books, we gave coupons to students when they picked up these books. The coupons were good for extra computer time, first checkout of new magazines, and a free book or poster. More and more kids are placing "holds."

— *Connie G. Pappas, J. D. Zellerbach Middle School, Camas, Washington*

Don't Leave Study Hall Without It

At our high school of 1,500 students, we issue each student a library pass card every 10 weeks. This card gets punched when they come to the library from study hall, and each student is allowed up to three card punches per week. Once a card has been punched three times, the student must obtain a writ-

ten pass from a librarian in order to leave study hall. In order to recognize students who use the library in a productive manner, we have instituted a Gold Card program. Gold Cards are issued to students nominated by a library staff member and unanimously approved by the staff. Good for the entire year, this card provides unlimited access to the library with no need to ask for a pass. We have had positive results with this program, which we feel helps the self-esteem of students and encourages responsible behavior in the library.

— *Gail Szeliga & Kathryn Brown, Union Endicott Central High School, Endicott, New York*

Donations of Microfiche from the Hospital

Since many hospitals have converted their medical records to computer formats, they may have microfiche machines gathering dust in storage. Our local hospital recently donated 15 microfiche readers to our school library. We expressed our appreciation by notifying the newspapers of the hospital's generosity.

— *Laurence Jaffe, Lionville Junior High School, Downington, Pennsylvania*

Editor's Note: You may not need microfiche readers, but businesses often have equipment that they might consider donating. Think in terms of copy machines, LCD projectors, or computers (be sure to set minimum standards). A few years ago we were given a Macintosh Plus computer with a printer. It was seriously lacking in memory for Internet or catalog duties, no color, small screen. However, recognizing a use for it, we set up the computer in our LMC office for the sole purpose of generating call labels for spines.

The printer is always loaded with label stock. With this computer even our student volunteers can quickly generate a fresh new spine label for a worn or torn label. Over a period of a year or two we were able to replace the spine labels on all books with a large font spine label and now use the large font for all incoming books. Not only does our collection look fresh but also the large font makes finding a book much easier to read. All of this is due to donated equipment that would have served few other purposes. smc

Donations-Ask and Ye Shall Receive

After a trial of Pro Quest, none of our teachers and students wanted to go back to the Readers' Guide. The only disadvantage was that we needed microfiche readers and a reader-printer, and it is just about impossible to request these items in this day of computers, CD-ROMs, and laser discs. Not to be deterred, I wrote a letter to local corporations explaining the situation and asking if any could donate old microfiche readers or reader-printers. As a result of this one effort, I ended up with 22 readers (all in excellent condition) and a microfiche/microfilm reader printer.

— *Barbara Schoenthaler, Haysville (Kansas) Campus High School*

Donations for Fines

Have students clear their library fines with the donation of a can of food for the food bank, animal food for the animal shelter, or paperbacks for a children's shelter. We send several cases of food to the food banks every year.

— *Elizabeth Guntharp, John Marshall High School, San Antonio, Texas*

Drive That Winnebago!

I use an external hard drive as a backup for my Winnebago software system for the Macintosh. At the end of each day I just drag my system folder to my external hard drive icon to copy. It copies everything in just a few minutes. When I need to catch up on such time-consuming projects as adding new patrons or cataloging in new materials, I disconnect the external hard drive, take it home, and hook it up to my own Macintosh. Then I open up my Winnebago circulation/catalog program and get to work. When I return to school, I copy my Winnebago system folder to the drive in my main computer.

— *Wayne Rush, Grover Cleveland Middle School, Caldwell, New Jersey*

Dummies for the Collection

Some items in our collection are too large to fit on the shelves and consequently are stored in a back room. So students will not overlook these items, we put a "dummy" on the shelf. The dummies are empty golf ball boxes, covered with a self-adhesive paper, and labeled. Plain cardboard boxes are expensive so we appreciate the help of a golf shop that gives us the boxes that held a dozen balls. We are saving money and recycling too.

— *Linda Kruchten, Churchville-Chili Senior High School, Churchville, New York*

Easy Barcoding

While the fifth and sixth grades from an elementary school were housed in the middle school during a remodeling project, their library materials came with them. The problem was how to check out books since both school libraries were automated. I found that I could place the middle school barcode label over the elementary barcode since both were covered with protective labels. The elementary barcode was not damaged when the middle school label was removed.

— *Margaret Eversole, Pendleton Heights Middle School, Pendleton, Indiana*

Easy-to-Find Procedures

If you subscribe to database services such as Wilson or Dialog, make cards for common procedures and for online emergency procedures. Make a separate card for each popular file on a database, giving appropriate commands and formats from the service's manual (such as from Dialog's blue sheets). Post basic procedures for database services on a bulletin board visible from the computer used for accessing the service.

— *Janet Hofstetter, California (Missouri) High School*

Easy-to-Remember Temporary Barcodes

When I have to set up user ID for a guest, a parent, or a teacher from another school, I use his or her telephone number as the barcode. It is easy for the users to remember and works well for me. If the books are overdue, the phone number is printed on the notice.

— *Jaime Meadows, Pau-Wa-Lu Middle School, Gardnerville, Nevada*

Encyclopedias of a Certain Stripe

When students ask which of our more than 20 sets of encyclopedias may be checked out over night, we can say "any that's striped," because each such set has a different colored book tape striped diagonally on the spines. The color and angle of the stripe facilitates

reshelving since anyone can immediately see the set and sequence order in which each volume belongs.

— *Lily Loughlin, Stanford Middle School, Long Beach, California*

Faxing Lost Pages

When someone has cut pages or items out of a reference book, I call another librarian to find the pages and fax a copy to us. We get the material immediately instead of waiting for a photocopy to arrive in the mail.

— *Ann Martha, Frankford High School, Philadelphia, Pennsylvania*

Fine Art for the Collection

With book fines we buy a print of a work by a famous artist. We frame the print and put it in our collection.

— *Vicki Bell, Eupora (Mississippi) High School*

Fines—"Can" Those Fines

Each spring, our media center gets to work gathering the many overdue books held by students. We've found these techniques useful: 1) Students who bring in canned goods for local food drives along with their overdue books are exempt from fines. 2) We offer a short grace period as a "spring break" from fines. 3) We provide coupons worth 50 cents off fines (limit one per customer).

— *Sandy Barron, Tomball (Texas) High School*

Fines—Fine with These Students

Twice a year I use the money collected from library fines to buy a Christmas poinsettia and Valentine candy to raffle. Students write their names on a slip of paper, and I randomly draw a winner. Only students with no overdue books or fines are eligible. The drawing inspires those with overdues and fines to pay up so they'd be eligible, and the fine money more than covers the cost of the giveaways!

— *Jenny Lugibihl, Eisenhower Middle School, Oregon, Ohio*

First Aid for Projectors

When called to replace a projector lamp in a classroom, I am often not told what kind of bulb is needed. For such emergencies, I grab my handy "first aid" kit filled with one of each commonly used lamp plus screwdrivers.

— *Carol Burbridge, Jardine Middle School, Topeka, Kansas*

Food for Fines

Several times during the school year, clubs and classes conduct drives for food pantries. Students are allowed to "pay" library fines with a can of food. This helps clear library obligations and adds to the success of the drive.

— *Velda McMorris, Antioch Middle School, Gladstone, Missouri*

Free Reading for Outdoors Enthusiasts

Students and teachers who like the outdoors, trucks, recreational vehicles, and boats enjoy the articles in the free magazine *Chevy Outdoors*. This 84-page quarterly has articles on fishing, boating, and vacation spots. The articles do not promote Chevrolet products. There are advertisements, but no more than in many other magazines. For a subscription, write to *Chevy Outdoors*, P.O. Box 40299, Redford, MI 48240-0299.

— *Anitra Gordon, Lincoln High School, Ypsilanti, Michigan*

Free Resource for Librarians

The Librarian's Yellow Pages is an all-advertising directory organized in an easy-to-use yellow pages format. This resource lists all the sources you can imagine for acquiring library "stuff." To receive a free copy, request one at their Web site at <www.LibrariansYellow Pages.com/>.

The Librarian's Yellow Pages is also available online with search capabilities by keyword or company name. This online database is updated monthly.

— *Jacque Burkhalter, Fidalgo Elementary School, Anacortes, Washington*

Friendliest Orientation Possible

I have found a way to keep my orientation slide program up-to-date while enhancing its appeal to students. When the seventh-grade English students visit the library each September, I take pictures of them selecting books. I use this opportunity to ask them to pose next to new equipment and displays, too. As soon as I get the slides developed, I hold orientation sessions with each seventh grade social studies class. The students are surprised and excited to find that they are the "stars" of the show, and our large school seems just a little smaller to our new arrivals.

— *Cynthia K. Dobrez, Grand Haven (Michigan) Junior High School*

From Paper to Electronic Catalogs with Help

When you are switching from a paper card catalog to an electronic catalog (and doing the job yourself), enlist the help of the teachers and students. Ask the students to pull shelf cards, assign barcode numbers, and box books in the same subject areas. The teachers and students can enter the records at network computers. A contest with progress noted on bar graphs will maintain interest in the project.

— *Eleanor S. Bayles, Grenville Christian College, Brockville, Ontario, Canada*

From Paper to Electronic Catalogs with Help

When you are switching from a paper card catalog to an electronic catalog (and doing the job yourself), enlist the help of the teachers and students. Ask the students to pull shelf cards, assign barcode numbers, and box up books in the same subject areas. The teachers and students can enter the records at network computers. A contest with progress notes on bar graphs will maintain interest in the project.

— *Eleanor S. Bayles, Grenville Christian College, Brockville, Ontario, Canada*

Funding Special Projects

If you need money for a special project, consider asking local businesses for donations. After getting approval from the principal, ask the district business manager for a list of companies the school does business with. Our maintenance manager let me photocopy his collection of business cards from vendors, and then he starred "hot prospects." In the letter to companies, mention that the school is one of their customers, and that you got their names from the business manager. The letter should include a brief description of the project. You may want to provide suggested levels for contributors: $250 for benefactors, $150 for sponsors, and so on. Of course, you'll thank each contributing business both privately and publicly.

— *Anitra Gordon, Lincoln High School, Ypsilanti, Michigan*

Handy Barcodes

In our school, each student's library barcode is printed on their ID card. Because students often do not have the card with them when they want to check out materials, I print lists of barcodes by grade level and keep the lists in clear plastic covers. We can scan the codes from these sheets. Students and librarians like the system.

— *Sister Alma Marie Walls, Our Lady of Lourdes High School, Miami, Florida*

Hassle-Free Processing

To expedite the processing of books for our school library, I made a slip listing each of the steps that a book follows from the time it is received until it is ready for the shelf. Now staff or volunteers can tell by glancing at the attached slip what needs to be done to a book. Knowing the status of any new book helps me know if I can delegate a task to my student workers or if the book is at a step that requires my attention.

— *Brenda Moriarity, Ketron Middle School, Kingsport, Tennessee*

Help As Close As Your Telephone

Keep a file of toll free telephone numbers and use them when the vendors can be helpful to you. For instance, some book jobbers will look up ISBN numbers while you are on the phone. A technical support person for a major computer company walked me through every step of installing a card for an external CD-ROM player.

— *Shirley Fetherolf, McMinnville, Tennessee*

Hug-a-Book Program

We instigated a "Hug-a-Book" program, for which our Parent-Teacher-Student Organization donated seed money. We buy books we want, keeping them on a certain shelf for anyone to "repurchase" as a gift or memorial tribute. We place a bookplate in the front of the book to acknowledge the giver and the gift.

— *Laura Edwards, Coppell (Texas) High School*

Identifying CD-ROMs

Writing the school name and barcode number on the rim of CD-ROMs with a felt marker has made it much easier to keep track of them. If a disc comes back to the library without its packaging, I can easily find where it should go.

— *Marilyn Platz, Lake Windward Elementary, Alpharetta, Georgia*

Identifying Discards As You Go

During the school year, I come across books that are outdated or need to be replaced. But at the end of the year, I cannot remember what they were. My solution: I entered the subject headings "Discards (Outdated) June (year)" and 'Discards (Worn or Damaged) June (year)" in the automated circulation system. During the year, it takes only minutes to pull up a book title and click in the "discard" subject heading. At the end of the year, I print a list of all books with the "discard" heading. The same system works for audiovisuals.

— *Jaunita L. Brown, Franklin County High School, Carnesville, Georgia*

If It's Monday, Your Books Are Due!

Five years ago when there was a cutback in teacher aides, we redistributed our workload over the week. Instead of a daily due date, all books became due on Mondays. We designated Tuesday and Wednesday as the days for shelving returned books. Overdue notices went out on Thursday; cleaning and plant watering were Friday's chores. After the circulation system was automated, we retained the routine by popular request. We remind students to return books with once-a-week public address announcements, and teachers appreciate not receiving a daily overdue list.

— *Faye Griffith, Mulholland Middle School, Van Nuys, California*

In Search of Used Books

If you go to spring yard or garage sales, be alert for copies of popular paperbacks in good condition. I found a new Stephen King novel for 25 cents. I sent it with others to be rebound during the summer, and now my library has a reinforced hardback book for a small investment. Sales at public libraries are also a source of good used paperbacks, often for as little as 10 cents. One librarian I know acquires bargain used books by taking purchase orders to bookstores in college towns.

— *Shirley Fetherolf, Lakewood (Ohio) High School*

Installing Patron Station

If you are just now automating or have automated the library's catalog and still have reluctant users clinging to the old card catalog, you might be interested in how I solved the problem. I installed one patron station on a separate switch, loading a backup copy of data, and setting it to automatically boot up to the search function when the computer is turned on. An easy-to-follow set of directions for search, browse, and print functions accompanies the station, which is used after hours. Every few weeks I update the backup data so that it reflects the library's most current holdings. A clipboard for staff to request materials is kept at the station, and my aide and I check this each morning, tracking down items as needed. For sure-fire impact, you could install this station in the same location as that occupied by your old card catalog. What a surprise for those technophobics on your staff!

— *Jacque Burkhalter, Fidalgo Elementary School, Anacortes, Washington*

Instant Bibliographic Information for Audiovisuals

I've found it helpful to photocopy the reviews of nonprint items when we order them. It simplifies my cataloging chores, and we've found that teachers and students appreciate the information, which we attach to the cassettes and cases.

— *Lizbeth Messing, Traverse City (Michigan) Senior High School*

It's in the Bag

The most effective way I have found to circulate periodicals is by using gallon-size self-sealing freezer bags to hold the materials. I tape the barcode on the side of the bag along with our school's identification. The plastic bags far outlast any paper envelopes or folders that have been used in the past. A budget tip is to have the home economics department order the bags for you.

— *Patricia Kolencik, North Clarion High School, Tionesta, Pennsylvania*

Jobbers Save Time

As a solo librarian, time is really precious. To save time, I use a jobber to order all of my periodicals. The school gets a great discount, and all I need do is check the renewal list and sign the purchase order.

— *Arlene Kachka, Luther High School, North Chicago, Illinois*

Just Desserts

Recovering long-overdue items at the end of the school year is always a challenge. And putting teeth into policies that suggest seniors won't graduate until all their obligations are cleared isn't likely. So, instead of the negative approach, we sponsor an annual "Donut Derby" that rewards homerooms with clean library records. In mid-May we send out frequent notices to remind students to return books and pay overdue fines. These are delivered during homeroom. As the last week of school approaches, lists of students, arranged by homeroom number, are circulated. Announcements inform students of the final deadline, the "finish." Peers and teachers assert the appropriate pressure to make most students accountable. When the due date deadline arrives, a tally of the homerooms that "finished" the derby is calculated and dozens of donuts are delivered on the last day that all homerooms convene. These "just desserts" seem to motivate students at our school, and the library gets good PR as well.

— *Betty Jo Marling, Mater Dei High School, Breese, Illinois*

Just the Fax, Ma'am

Within our region, we fax many periodical requests to neighboring schools. Instead of discarding the copy of the requested article, I put a subject heading on it and add it to the vertical file for student use. -Patricia

— *Kolencik, North Clarion High School, Tionesta, Pennsylvania*

Keep Track of Disks

Computer backup disks are easy to lose, so I use color as a visual cue—the wilder the better—to keep track of them. Neon-colored disks don't stay lost for long!

— *Sister Mary Veronica, Xavier High School, New York, New York*

Keeping an Eye on Equipment

A perplexing problem for us was reclaiming calculators at the end of the school year. Teachers who were issued calculators always shared them with other teachers at standardized testing time. And then the test-givers collected the calculators so no one knew where to look for the calculators he or she had loaned. It seemed that no one ever kept track of the equipment. We developed a form that the teacher receiving the calculators must give to the teacher giving out the calculators. The form simply requires the teacher's name and the number of calculators received. When that teacher returns the calculators, the teacher who loaned the calculators signs the form. We used this form last year with great results. There were no lost calculators due to borrowing.

— *Lea Ann Kelley, Adamson Middle School, Rex, Georgia*

Keeping Jackets New

After spine labels, barcodes, and so forth are attached to a new book jacket, I run it through the laminating machine. Along with preserving the jacket, labels don't fall off.

— *Ginny Weber, Lowell (Michigan) High School*

Keeping Tabs on Recorded Videocassettes

We tape many videocassettes for teachers. Most of these have varying taping rights with expiration dates, ranging from fair use to unlimited. Teachers need to be able to access these "temporary" videotapes for particular topics. We now use our automation program, Surpass, to enter an abbreviated MARC record so the teachers can locate the videotapes and we can print a monthly list of tapes to be erased. We put this information in the MARC field (or subfield) tag:

> Title of video
> Edition: Taping date
> Publisher: Provider (or site) we taped from
> Date: Erase date
> Physical Description: Length of the tape in minutes
> Notes: several sentences using keywords like "factoring algebra expressions"
> Call Number: VT followed by Dewey number
> Category: TVT for Temporary Videotape

The teacher can easily access the videotape by keyword search and locate it in the media center by the call number. We can print a list using the category TVT, and MARC subfield tag 260c from greater than or equal to November 1, 2000 to less than or equal to November 30, 2000. Our printed list would contain all videotapes to be erased in November 2000.

— *Ella Stone, Lakeview-Fort Oglethorpe High School, Fort Oglethorpe, Georgia*

Keeping the Collection Intact

Theft problems? No aides? Picture your library as a convenience store: have one exit by the check-out desk, good signs, and everything arranged for self-service. I moved all the periodical back issues out of a tiny dark room onto the main floor of the library and converted the room into a videotape viewing area with a wall-mounted TV/VCR. Back magazines are used more for browsing now, and faculty and students have a place to preview videos.

— *Shirley Fetherolf, Strongsville, Ohio*

Keeping Track of Projectors and Such

In our audiovisual room, where teachers go to check out equipment, we have hung a large laminated map of the school with all the room numbers marked on it. Strips of Velcro are attached to each room, and each piece of equipment has circular key tags, marked with the equipment name and number and attached with Velcro®. We have found the best place to attach the tags is near the electric cord at the back. When teachers borrow a piece of equipment, they peel off the key tag and put it on the map to show where the equipment will be.

— *Judy Taylor, Ryerston Middle School, Hamilton, Ontario, Canada*

Keeping Track of Remotes

I use pieces of Velcro® to tape the remote controls to television sets and VCRs that are loaned to classrooms. When the equipment is returned to the library, I can easily see if the control is still attached. If it is forgotten, a gentle reminder gets it back.

— *Nancy Hughes, Matthew Henson Middle School, Indian Head, Maryland*

Keeping Track of Remotes (2)—Controlling Remotes

This suggestion is for thos—like me—who couldn't get the "attaching remotes with Velcro" idea (described in a previous tip) to

work. As an alternative, I put each remote control in a brightly colored drawstring bag. This makes the remotes more noticeable, and teachers remember to return the remote along with the television set or VCR.

— *Bev Oliver, Indian Hill High School, Cincinnati, Ohio*

Keeping Track of Remotes (3)—Preventing Remote Remotes

The TV/VCR was often returned to the library without the remote control. The problem was eliminated when I stuck one side of a strip of Velcro® to the back of the remote control and the other side to the VCR. This seems to serve as a reminder to the user to attach the remote to the VCR. The Velcro also keeps the remote from sliding around during movement from room to room.

— *Virginia Marcantel, Iowa (Louisiana) High School*

Keeping Track of Remotes (4)—Get a Grip on Remote Controls

Remote controls for TVs and VCRs at our school were often not turned in with the equipment, usually turning up days later in a desk drawer. To solve the problem, I bought a yard of Velcro® and put a two-inch piece on each remote and a matching piece on each TV and VCR. It worked like magic! We have not once had to search for the remote controls.

— *Joan Hyland, St. Croix Central Schools, Hammond, Wisconsin*

Keeping Track of SIRS

I recently replaced an old SIRS set that had many missing articles. To protect the new set, we decided to keep the volumes at the check-out desk and not allow the material to leave the library. Students may read the individual articles in the library or may photocopy them. Students must sign a special check-out book even if they only plan to photocopy an article. Articles are returned to aides, who cross the student's name off the check-out book and refile the article. Since we earn money when students use our photocopier, we give students 20 cents to help pay for copying SIRS articles.

— *Anitra Gordon, Lincoln High School, Ypsilanti, Michigan*

Keeping Videotape Items Up-to-Date

Allow teachers to help you keep the videotape collection current. Devise a simple checklist so teachers can alert you as to its relevancy to the curriculum. With each videotape checked out to a teacher, attach this form:

Was the video current?	Yes ☐	No ☐
Was it useful?	Yes ☐	No ☐
Would you recommend it?	Yes ☐	No ☐

Wh the videotape is returned, the sheet is expected to be with it. If a videotape is not current, consider discarding it.

— *Barbara Abernathy, Bremen, Georgia*

Labeled Lamps

When you store new boxes of projector lamps, write the name of the equipment on the boxes. Next time you reach for a lamp in the supply cupboard, you won't have to search your memory to recall which lamp fits which projector.

— *Judie Weiss, Waples Mill School, Oakton, Virginia*

Labeling Paperback Series

To assist the large number of students who like to read paperback fantasy or science fiction books in a series, we color code each book according to genre and then add a bright orange oblong sticker indicating that the book is part of a series. These books are filed alphabetically by author and are placed in a separate paperback rack reserved for series books. This system has increased circulation of series titles and has made it easier for students to find the book they want.

— *Elizabeth Beairsto, Springfield (Oregon) High School*

Lamp Labels

We have five different brands of overhead projectors at our high school. Each brand takes a different lamp. To ensure each projector gets the correct replacement lamp, we put a label on the projector with the number of the projector and the type of lamp it takes. When a teacher sends a student to the media department because a lamp has burned out, the student asks for the correct type. This has worked so well that we have labeled all of our projection equipment.

— *Jean Edwards, Piano (Texas) Senior High School*

Learn from Your Colleagues' Errors

You can make barcodes quickly and easily with your printer. In the days when most of us used dot matrix printers, we had to worry about changing the print ribbon often. If we did not, we ended up labeling many books with barcodes too pale to be read by our scanner. Now with many of us using laser-like printers, i.e., DeskWriters, we must be careful that our print function specifies the best quality. Our advice: If in doubt, try it out.

— *Mary Hauge, Head Librarian, West Aurora (Illinois) High School*

Library Lotto

When our circulation system stops for its periodic backups, there are short delays for students who are ready to check out books. It can be a headache, especially when a class is lined up for checkout. To fill that wait whenever it occurs, we play "Library Lotto." The student standing in line when the backup begins is declared the lotto winner. We make a big fuss, jot down the student's name for the next morning's announcements, and award a small prize. The students, who already believe the computer has a brain and a soul, think it singled them out.

— *Peg Angel, Shawnee Middle School, Fort Wayne, Indiana*

Library Pride

We give a "library pride" slip to students when we see them doing something to make the library a nicer place to be. The student who gives up his or her computer game at lunch so another student can do research, who straightens the encyclopedia shelves, or who is quietly reading would be given a slip. Name and homeroom are written on the slip, which is entered in a weekly drawing for a prize. The winners are also presented on the school video announcements. We enjoy giving equal time to rewarding the plentiful good behavior instead of always focusing on reprimanding students.

— *Cindy Dobrez & Lynn Rutan, West Ottawa Middle School, Holland, Michigan*

Library Reward Day

One day each month at the middle school is designated as Library Reward Day. The library is open only to those homeroom classes with the best records for returning materials on time during the preceding month. As I prepare overdue notices, I keep a running tally of the number for each homeroom. The 8 classes (out of 32) with the best record for the month (fewest students with outstanding debts) are selected to be rewarded. For several days, these homerooms are recognized on the bulletin board and in the morning announcements. When the winning homerooms come to the library, students are allowed to play games, watch videotapes, talk, look at magazines and newspapers, "play" at the computer, or do whatever they would like to do in the library when not required to work on an assignment. While the reward day does close down the library for more serious uses, it does a great deal to encourage individual students to care about clearing up library debts. Teachers help by encouraging students to avoid overdues. Library Reward Day is a form of positive reinforcement that really works at our school.

— *James B. Gross, Taylor County Middle School, Perry, Florida*

Library Wish List

Keep a list of "wishes" (books, equipment, and other materials your budget will not cover) and their approximate prices in a handy place. Graduating classes, booster clubs, PTAs, and other groups often have a sum of money left over at the end of the year and will need to find good ways to use it up. Be ready!

— *Julia Gilreath, Beatrice (Nebraska) High School*

Library-Specific Bookmarks

Middle school students like bookmarks and they especially like the ones that are specific to our library. I have grouped some of their favorite kinds of books under 15 different headings, for example, "Trying & Crying

Times," "Animal Stories," and "War Stories," and printed bookmarks for each. Our print shop adds a small illustration and prints the bookmarks on brightly colored paper.

— *Pat Atkinson, LaGrande (Oregon) Middle School*

Up Front with What's on Hand

Our magazine holding is available as a computerized list that can be easily updated. I tape a hard copy of the current listing and keep it near the magazine index so students can immediately see which magazines are on hand.

— *Suzette Turner, Rockport-Fulton High School, Rockport, Texas*

Lost Paperbacks

When students lose a paperback from our library, they are given the choice of either paying $3.50 or bringing in two paperbacks to replace the one they have lost. The paperbacks must be in good condition and appropriate for the high school. Students understand that two-for-one is the going rate in most used bookstores.

— *Joy M. Harrison, Buffalo (Missouri) High School*

Low-Tech Security System

If you don't have an electronic security system, here are some simple strategies to prevent reference books from slipping out the door:

1. Do not allow students to wear coats or bring book bags, backpacks, or gym bags into the library.
2. Stamp library books, especially encyclopedias, on all three edges with the library stamp. An adult standing at the exit will be able to spot a library book in a stack of textbooks.

3. Give students a colorful bookmark as they check out books and ask them to have it sticking out as they leave so the person at the door can tell which books have been checked out.
4. Three or four minutes before students are scheduled to leave, ask them to return reference books to their proper places. Staff members can then check to see all encyclopedias are on the shelf.

We have excellent cooperation from students when we explain the reasons for these procedures.

— *Lucinda Deatsman, Mansfield (Ohio) Senior High School, Cline Avenue Campus*

Lunch Time Passes

In our middle school, students may come to the media center anytime during the morning periods to put their names on a list for a lunch time pass to the media center. Parent volunteers check the passes and the list as students come to the media center. The students must also report the work they expect to do in the media center. This has worked well as a screening process and keeps students who use the media center passes on task.

— *Nancy Bahr, East Middle School, Plymouth, Michigan*

Magazine Binding on a Budget

We were having a problem keeping loose issues of magazines in order and couldn't afford professional binding. A student assistant came up with the solution. We "hinge" a month of weekly or a quarter of monthly magazines together with adhesive tape and bind them together with duct tape (less expensive than conventional book tape). The name of the magazine and dates are written on the binding. A notation for any missing issues can also be added.

— *Gail Irwin, Leetonia (Ohio) High School*

Magazine Collateral

We cut the theft rate for current issues of popular magazines from 70% to 5% by requiring "collateral" from student borrowers. Collateral can be anything of value—watches, rings, car keys. We keep the items in a locked box behind the circulation desk until the magazine is returned.

— *Gina Warren, Lacombe (Alberta, Canada) Composite High School*

Magazine Management

We tape the spines of magazines with paper tape using a different color for each year. Besides the advantage of easily spotting misfiled magazines, the tape reinforces the covers. To help keep the magazines filed in proper order in a given year, draw a diagonal line across all the spines in a stack; a broken pattern means an out-of-sequence magazine. (White correction fluid shows up on dark paper tape.) Another trick is to put the dates of all magazines on a white label in the upper left-hand corner of the cover. This saves searching all over the cover for dates that sometimes hide behind mailing labels.

— *Mary Hauge, Head Librarian, West Aurora (Illinois) High School*

Magazines on the Mac

To keep track of our magazine subscriptions, we prepared a database using *Microsoft Works* for the Macintosh computer. We set a field for each month of paid subscriptions and added a record for each magazine to which our library subscribes: We can check the database at any time to determine the status of the magazine receipts, and it is easy to check in magazines on a daily basis.

— *Hannah B. Hollifield, Central Davidson Senior High School, Lexington, North Carolina*

Mail Management

To organize the stacks of mail for the library, we instituted a daily system. Magazines are processed immediately with a quick scan of the contents to look for topics in demand. Student assistants open the junk mail, giving it a cursory glance and tossing whatever is unimportant. Catalogs are piled into a box labeled "considerations," and invoices are pulled out for immediate action. This organized way of handling the mail as it arrives keeps my desk and office from looking like an explosion at a paper factory when the superintendent drops by for an unexpected visit.

Shirley Fetherolf, Lakewood (Ohio) High School

Make Researchers Fast on Their Feet

Place your library's computers on standing workstations to encourage serious research and discourage talking and loitering. Students who can't sit down tend to get their work done more efficiently.

— *Carol Elrod, Spalding University, Louisville, Kentucky*

Make Your Own Paperback Labels

Need labels for the spines of your paperbacks? If you've been deterred by the cost of commercial labels that have too many Ys and not enough Ks for Stephen King's works, make your own labels using a computer and a laser printer. Make a page of letters in the amounts you need. The letters should be 72 points high and in bold print so they can be seen at a distance. Be sure to leave enough space between the letters so they can be easily separated. Have the sheet run off by a copy company that makes label pages—gummed sheets with perforations. Order enough copies to last a semester. When you reorder, you can redesign the sheet if you find you run out of certain letters. Be sure to keep a copy of the master sheet on file.

— *Anitra Gordon, Lincoln High School, Ypsilanti, Michigan*

Manage Your Mail

A simple system of file folders can help you manage floods of incoming mail and keep your desk tidy, too! Label five folders by days of the workweek; label the sixth one "next week." As mail arrives, put it into the appropriate folder and tag urgent items. When you've finished, put five of the files aside so you can concentrate on the current day's folder at an uncluttered desk.

— *Sandy Nelson, Lee County Schools, Fort Myers, Florida*

Management Tips

Here are some practical tips for managing the media program efficiently so you have time to work with technology and some tips for managing technology.

▶ Don't do unnecessary work. Automation has eliminated many labor-intensive tasks (typing and updating bibliographies or overdue lists). When deciding which tasks to eliminate, ask yourself: Does it make a difference to the learner? Can someone else do it?

▶ Write down ideas before you forget them. Better yet, keep your ideas and "to-do" lists on your computer.

▶ Computerize anything that can be! Use spreadsheets and databases to keep track of things like equipment and supply bids and quotes, budgets, program statistics, warranty and repair information, software costs, and orders. Update these files often so record keeping does not become an overwhelming task.

▶ Develop templates for letters and reports.

▶ Ask vendors to provide written price information when you are ordering quantities of supplies. This saves you the time of looking through catalogs or making phone calls.

▶ Develop good relationships with vendors so you can rely on them for help and information.

▶ Use your automation system to keep track of anything and everything that circulates. When possible, customize records to enable students to locate resources independently.

▶ Try to limit book purchases to vendors who supply electronic cataloging records. When electronic records cannot be purchased, copy cataloging from another electronic catalog such as the one at the public library or local university.

▶ Record purchase order, warranty, price, and serial number information for all capital items in your automation system. This information is invaluable in case of theft or repair under warranty.

▶ To the extent that is possible, have the same software and utilities on all computers.

▶ Use your old card catalog for storing bulbs, batteries, cables, and other small supply items. Keep these items in alphabetical order.

- Be selective in regards to what mail you actually open and read.
- Keep file cabinets manageable by throwing something away each time you file. Cut down on what you need to file by keeping your own information in electronic format. Discard outdated technology information.
- Use telephones, faxes, and e-mail for correspondence when possible.
- Keep important paper work and manuals on a given item, including the network, in one place.
- Weed materials in all formats continually. Weeding is not a huge task if you pull materials as you come across them.
- Develop the habit of making good decisions quickly. Rapid changes in technology require that you not wait for something better to come along.
- Just do it!

— *Mary Alice Anderson, Media Specialist, Winona (Minnesota) Middle School*

Managing Circulation Cards

For an easy and efficient way to manage circulation cards in an elementary school library, buy a three-ring binder approximately three inches wide, a pack of slide protectors, and poster board in a different color for each of the grades in your school. Cut the poster board into two-inch squares to fit into each slide holder. After assigning barcodes on the automated system, place the barcode and the name of each student on a two-inch square card. Label one or two protector sheets for each teacher in your school. Arrange barcoded squares alphabetically in the slide protectors by class roll. Place the binder on the circulation desk where it is available for each class or patron who visits the media center. No more lost cards, frustrated teachers, or

re-made check-out cards. At the beginning of the next year, simply update the computer and rearrange students in their new classes. Delete the graduating class and assign those barcode numbers to the incoming group. You never have to make cards again!

— *Vicki Bland, North Fayette Elementary School, Morrow, Georgia*

Managing the Lunch Hour Crowd

In order to keep the number of students in the media center manageable during the lunch hour, I made color-coded, laminated passes for each lunch shift. We determine how many passes should be sent to the cafeteria for each shift. The administrators on duty in the cafeteria require students to sign for a pass before leaving the cafeteria. Students use that pass to sign in at the media center, where the passes are collected to be reused.

— *Janice P Saulsby, Westridge Middle School, Orlando, Florida*

Media Center Menu

Dressed in black tie and tails and carrying a silver tray piled with library "menus," I visit incoming fifth-grade classrooms at the beginning of the school year. This menu provides students and their parents with information under such headings as House Specialties, Take Home Fare and A La Carte (audiovisuals). Included within the menu is a contract, which lists library procedures. Before they can use the library; students sign and return the contract. This way, both students and parents know procedures as well as what materials are available. (Older students, in grades 6-8, receive menus from Book Woman, who carries a shopping bag full.)

— *Antonia D. White, F. A. Martin Middle School, Lafayette, Louisiana*

Milk Containers for Spacing

If you want to keep your books close to the shelf edge, but your bookshelves are too deep, start collecting half-gallon milk or juice containers. Cover the clean, empty container with any decorative paper and place it behind the books. These "bricks" will push your books closer to the edge and keep them from migrating to the back of the shelf.

— *Barbara Resnick, Queens Vocational High School, Long Island City, New York*

Mini-Library for Study Hall

If study hall supervisors have students with "nothing to do," a "mini-library" may help. Our library provides an encyclopedia set, dictionaries, an atlas, paperbacks, and course textbooks on a book cart that stays in study hall. Students do not have to go to their lockers for materials, and when study halls move from room to room, the cart can go too. Students who check out items return them at the end of the period for the next study hall's use. We do allow students to come to the library from study hall, but this "mini-library" helps when there are scheduled classes in the library.

— *Laura Werner, Oakland Junior High School, Columbia, Missouri*

New Use for the Old Card Catalog

Our card catalog works perfectly as a storage system for the assorted bulbs, batteries, cables, adapters, and other odds and ends used with electronic equipment. All items are stored alphabetically and can be found efficiently when a teacher suddenly needs a replacement bulb or when a cable isn't working.

— *Mary Alice Anderson, Media Specialist, Winona (Minnesota) Middle School*

No More Chalk

If some of your teachers are becoming disgusted with their overhead projectors and are ready to return to chalk, offer to clean the lenses on their overheads. Teachers may not know that poor projection is often due to dirt on the Fresnel lens as well as on the outside glass. Another service is to provide access to extra overhead projectors so that teachers can try a different machine if they choose.

— *Linda Beasley, Southeast Guilford High School, Greensboro, North Carolina*

No Pass Barriers

We do not require students to secure passes in order to use the library during study periods. The students simply show up before the bell, sign in after the bell rings, and stay for the period. Copies of the sign-in sheet are sent to the study halls. We believe this easy access attracts many kids who would never exercise the forethought to get a pass and others who come to the library solely for recreational reading. If there is a behavior problem, we require the student to have a subject pass for a brief time (one week for misbehavior such as noisiness and one month for anything more serious). If we have classes in the library and have to restrict attendance, we make an announcement on the public address system. This has been my policy for 21 years. It has worked well. In fact, I am horrified by the idea of putting up barriers to student use, such as passes. I find that students accustomed to using the library freely have fewer problems in finding materials.

— *Bobbie Chase, Wachusett Regional High School, Holden, Massachusetts*

Notebook of Maps

To store the many maps that I receive, I purchased a box of clear vinyl pockets and a notebook binder. The "map binder" contains the maps alphabetically and is kept at the circulation desk for easy access.

— *Linda Lenahan, Sacred Heart Academy, Louisville, Kentucky*

One Size Fits All

All students in our school district are given an ID number. We use these numbers in our circulation system. There are several advantages. If a student moves to another school in the district, the number remains the same. And, most students have memorized their school ID number.

— *Pat Hare, Northwest High School, Cincinnati, Ohio*

Organization by Cup Hooks

I have organized my office by designating fixed locations for certain objects—especially clipboards and mugs. I bought a box of cup hooks and installed them above the sink and behind the check-out counter. I use the hooks to hang "shelf markers" on our wood bookshelves.

— *Elizabeth Hanelt, Don Julio Junior High School, North Highlands, California*

Organizing Icons & CD-ROMs

Because we now have more than 50 CD-ROMs on our network, the menu was becoming unmanageable and confusing for students. To improve organization, our Windows Program Manager icons now appear under a Dewey number plus a verbal heading. For example, accessing 800-899 Literature brings up *Disc/it* and *Discovering Authors*. We also offer word processing programs and other CD-ROMs under separate icons. This has made a real difference in student access.

— *Jacqueline Seewald, Red Bank Regional High School, Little Silver, New Jersey*

Overdue Notices to the Bindery

Since books sent to a bindery are often out of the library for months at a time, I often forget which titles are at the bindery. I solved this problem by creating a check-out file for these books on the circulation system. I enter the bindery's company name as the patron and check out the books to that name. I am careful to set the date due far enough in the future to avoid generating overdue notices to the company.

— *Jim Miller, Martin Luther High School, Greendale, Wisconsin*

Overdue Popsicles

End-of-the-year overdue and lost books getting you down? Then offer any class that can get all books turned in or paid for by your deadline a popsicle party. It's surprising how such a simple incentive and a little positive peer pressure get those books in. I watch for grocery specials ahead of time so I can stock up on popsicles.

— *Cathy Bonnell, Ironwood Elementary School, Phoenix, Arizona*

Overdues Are HOT

"The library is HOT to get your overdue books back! Bring the books back between Friday, May 21 and Friday, May 28 and get a HOT BALL!" read our end-of-the-year overdue notices, which were printed out in hot colors—pink, green, yellow, orange, and purple. Red construction paper "hot balls" with the announcement "The library's HOT for your overdue books" was placed around the school. When the overdue books started to come in, we were fairly flexible, but students could not check out a book and return it for a hot ball. By the end of the week, our overdue list and our supply of hot balls were wiped out.

— *Linda Wood, South Kingstown High School, Wakefield, Rhode Island*

Packaged Answers to Project Questions

For those class projects in which all the students come to the library media center asking the same questions, I write a checklist of resources. Students can pick up the list and be more independent in their research. And, the staff doesn't begin to sound like a broken record, repeating and repeating the same answers.

— *Allison Trent Bernstein, Wayland (Massachusetts) High School*

Paperback Organization

Although we do not catalog our paperbacks for recreational reading, we do have enough to make finding an individual title difficult. We have quartered the problem by dividing our paperback collection into four portions of the alphabet by title to match the four sides of our paperback rack. Each portion, A-D for example, is given a colored label in the lower left-hand corner of the cover. Library volunteers can keep the color-coded paperbacks sorted easily, and students only have to look through the one-fourth of the alphabet in which their title would be found.

— *Deborah Locke, Westbrook (Maine) High School*

Pay Photocopier Pleases Patrons

A local company that supplies photocopy machines to drug stores and public libraries installed a machine in our school at no charge. Copies to patrons cost 10 cents each. The company provides the toner, paper, coin change machine, and technical help.

— *Margaret Tabar, Breck School, Minneapolis, Minnesota*

Periodical Reinforcement

Our magazines circulate and often lose their covers from overuse. To prevent damage, we place 1/2 inch reinforcing tape along the outside of the spine and fold it over the ends into the center of the magazine.

— *Judith Beavers, Logan Elm High School, Circleville, Ohio*

Personalized Overnight Labels

We have many carts of reserve books on overnight checkout for different teachers' classrooms. The books have one-night checkout labels to identify books that should be returned to a reserve cart. The problem was which cart should the book return to. To solve this problem, we purchase removable labels for the ink-jet printer. Using the label program on the software Print Shop (Broderbund), we can personalize labels for each reserve cart with teacher's name and a cute graphic related to the subject. We now can easily return books to the right cart. And the teachers feel special.

— *Anne Hudson, Pope High School, Marietta, Georgia*

Plastic Food Bags to the Rescue

Our high school lacks an automated security system, and an alarming number of books, SIRS articles, and vertical file materials were "walking away." Large, self-sealing, plastic bags helped us stop thefts. First, we made a rule that students leave all backpacks outside the library. All notebooks and folders were left on shelves just inside the door. Students can bring note cards, individual sheets of paper, and pens, which they store in the clear, plastic bags we furnish when they enter the library. Now, at a glance, library staff can see what students bring in and what they take out. These procedures have stopped all but the most determined students from walking off with library materials.

— *Peggy Brochers & Pat Shaw, Brazoswood High School, Clute, Texas*

Portable Air Tank

Tired of buying those expensive cans of pressurized air to clean computer hard drives and keyboards? If so, you need to invest in a portable air tank. A 12-gallon tank sells for approximately $29.95. These can be purchased at discount stores or any home improvement or auto store. Simply fill the tank and use it to blow dust from the computers. Media specialists can also use the tank to clean filmstrip projectors, overheads, and so forth. Tanks don't have to be refilled often. When they run out, just refill at a service station.

— *Lorrie Barnette, Midway Elementary School, Silver Creek, Georgia*

Poster Storage

What to do with all those posters? Beg a few liquor boxes from your local wine merchant. You can cut them down, cover them, decorate, whatever. Roll your posters and number them and their neat matching space and make a list for reference. You can place the boxes on their sides or stand them up.

— *Marjorie Lewis, Scarsdale (New York) Junior High*

Preteen and Teen Paperback Clubs

As the new junior high and high school librarian, I noticed that students were not receiving the paperback book club offers they did in the elementary grades. After securing permission from administrators and staff, I distributed orders for four different teen paperback clubs four or five times during each school year. Our school received one free item for every five ordered. This earned 267 free paperbacks for our budget-strapped library. Duplicate and extra copies are used as library contest prizes or for student library assistants. At the beginning of each year, I send a memo to all students about procedures for placing orders.

— *Marilyn Parchert, Westmer Secondary School, Joy, Illinois*

Preventing Magazine Mischief

Keeping up with periodicals used for research by high school students can be difficult. In spite of security measures, whole issues are taken or articles are cut out. Teachers have helped me solve the problem by requiring all students to turn in copies of the magazine articles used in researching their papers. This is no problem because a copier is available in the library. Since this procedure has been followed, students seldom feel the need to take articles.

— *Patricia Poe, Progreso (Texas) High School*

Prodigal Books

We have a very mobile student body, and we frequently find books from other school libraries in our return box. If the markings on the book clearly indicate who owns the book, we mail it to the home library. It occurred to us to stamp each of *our* books on the title page with our full school name and mailing address. Now we get more of our wandering books back.

— *Edna M. Boardman, Minot (North Dakota) High School, Magic City Campus*

Quick Checkout of Magazines

An easy way to check out magazines and pamphlets without cataloging and barcoding is to create removable tags. For the barcodes, I select low numbers that have not been used for cataloging books. I print these numbers in a large, bold font on a sheet of paper, leaving lots of white space around them, and laminate the sheet or cover it with contact paper. I then cut out the laminated numbers as individual tags, which are taped to the magazine at checkout. When the items come back, I remove the tag. You can leave the tape on the magazine so you don't tear the cover. Many magazines have glossy surfaces, and the tape easily peels off. I find this method easier and quicker than barcoding envelopes and putting the magazine in an envelope.

— *Anitra Gordon, Lincoln High School, Ypsilanti, Michigan*

Quick Fix for Overnight Reserves

When the biology teacher asked us to put copies of recent magazine articles on overnight reserve, I color coded the articles, the sign-out cards, and the folders in which the articles were kept. I ran out of colors and had to create some two-color designs. The system helped the library aides quickly match sign-out cards to the returned articles.

— *Lucille Bedau, Rosati-Kain High School, St. Louis, Missouri*

Recycling Return Envelopes

When junk mail arrives, we go through and pull return envelopes that we do not plan to use. When students pay late fees, we use these envelopes—one for each student. The outside has the date, student name, homeroom, and amount inside. The envelopes are sealed so the librarian can take the funds home each night for safekeeping. All envelopes are turned in at the end of the month, and the library account is credited.

— *Mary Lou Gault, Archbishop Hoban High School, Akron, Ohio*

Recycling Videotapes

If you tape daily (for example, Learning Channel programs), use 31 tapes, numbered 1-31. Use tape #4 on January 4, February 4, March 4, and so forth. Teachers will then have a month to ask for a tape before you erase the program. Since teachers usually make requests from a dated schedule, this numbering method makes it easier for everyone to find the correct tape.

— *Janet Hofstetter, California (Missouri) High School*

Reducing Hall Pass Hassles

A time/date machine has been a great time- and step-saver for me. Students can stamp their own hall passes when they enter and when they leave the library.

— *Virginia Hill, Shackelford Junior High School, Arlington, Texas*

Reference-Overnight Checkout

In our never-ending struggle to get reference material back on time, I used a desktop publishing program to make contracts the same size, shape, and color as our green reference check-out cards. I ask the student to read the contract, which states, "I understand that this reference item is due back before first period on the next school day, ___(date)___. I will pay 25 cents per period or $2.00 for each entire day that it is late." I ask the student to tell me what the contract means before I allow him or her to complete the card and the check-out process. With use of the contracts, we have had good luck getting our reference material back in time, and students cannot say they did not know when the items were due.

— *Jane A. Wilson, Emerald Junior High, Greenwood, South Carolina*

Reference Cards Simplify Cataloging

When cataloging and entering information about MARC tags, fixed-field codes, and user-defined categories, I found it cumbersome to refer to manuals and difficult to rely on my memory. To solve my dilemma, I created reference cards that I use as I catalog items on my automated system. I have cards with tag numbers for names, titles, and subjects; cards for the fixed fields with their codes; cards for loan types; and so on. The cards provide quick reference at my office workstation and can be amended as needed. I also use these cards to check information supplied by vendors. After loading the MARC records supplied, I check the record to make sure it conforms to the information on my list.

— *Pat Lemmons, North Henderson High School, Hendersonville, North Carolina*

Reference Circulation

Our greatest book losses have consistently occurred in the reference and teen life sections, both widely used by our 1,300-student population. To safeguard the books and yet make them available, we enlarged our reference section to include some popular nonfiction and fiction books. The fiction titles can be checked out for one week. The nonfiction books are checked out on a two- or three-day, weekend, holiday, or period basis. These checkouts may be renewed for the same time period. The idea is to keep a closer check on these books and to ensure that they are not monopolized by one student or group of students. This policy has cut our losses by more than half and has eliminated some of the frustration for students who find that a popular or needed book is checked out for two weeks.

— *Millicent Cade Hoskin, Central High School, Memphis, Tennessee*

Requesting Resources

We used to use such a variety of resource request forms that even the librarians got them confused. Now we have developed a new, all-purpose form printed on self-carbon paper. Now students get a copy of their requests. We encourage students to attach the form to the notes they take from the resource so they will have needed bibliographic information when it becomes time to make their reference list.

— *Annette Thibodeaux, Archbishop Chapelle High School, Metairie, Louisiana*

Requests & Problems

When you enter the school building every morning, are you swamped with troubleshooting questions, software needs, and book requests? My solution is a notebook placed near my desk in the media center. Teachers can fill out a form in the notebook, which is divided by requests and problems. I will even write the requests if someone does catch me on the run. The notebook keeps me organized and also provides a log of services provided.

— *Olivia Goodwin, Kennesaw (Georgia) Elementary School*

Reserving Space in the Library

Classroom teachers can reserve three areas in the school library: the library, the library classroom, and the technology center. To help us keep track of who's coming in and when, we divided each day on a monthly, 8" x 11" calendar into three sections. These calendar pages are kept in a three-ring binder at the circulation desk so that teachers can reserve specific areas for their classes.

— *Karen Wareham, Harvard-Westlake Middle School, Los Angeles, California*

Rewarding Teachers for No Overdues

During the last few days of the school year, I give treats (cookies or candy) to any teacher whose homeroom students have no outstanding fines or overdue books. This is a small way to show appreciation for the teachers' help in distributing overdue notices all year long. It also motivates teachers to prod students who still have library obligations at the end of the year.

— *Mary Kaschak, Roosevelt Middle School, Newark, Ohio.*

Save Time Maintaining That Computer Lab Next Door

Is time managing the computer lab next door eroding time spent on library management? Do you find staff always asking you to help

oversee the lab and does it fall on you to keep track of the disks? Students leave disks out and teachers forget about disks when in a hurry. We use a system that works well to limit the time I have to spend in the lab. First, place each disk in a plastic bag. Put large numbers on the outside of the bags for easy identification. Hang the bags in the lab using towel racks. Be sure to display a list of the software and the bag number in an obvious place so your staff can find the titles of software they want quickly. I also include a detailed guide about all the software. This includes the subject area, the grade level, and a summary of the program.

— *Robert LeCour, Columbine Elementary, Woodland Park, Colorado*

Editor's Note: Another alternative is to purchase AV storage boxes minus the inserts from a library supplier such as Demco or Highsmith. Put all the disks in one set in the box, label the box, and store on shelves in the lab. smc

Saved by the Bindery

With skyrocketing book costs, administrative concerns about keeping budgets down, and damaged or vandalized books, I often get a tight knot in the stomach. Invariably the pilfered portion of a book is the page or section a whole class needs. The book is often irreplaceable, or else my book budget has been expended and replacement funds are unavailable. I use the interlibrary loan system to obtain the same book, photocopy the missing page or pages, and send the book to the bindery for professional repair. In this way I have salvaged volumes for the price of a bindery charge. To prevent future damage to books, if a pattern is discerned, I place them on reserve.

— *Frances C. Shea, Rumson-Fair Haven Regional High School, Rumson, New Jersey*

Saving Back Issues

To keep back issues of magazines in order, tie thin, strong cord (for example, Knit-Cro-Sheen) around the magazine vertically, the way a bamboo newspaper stick holds a newspaper. Then, tape it inside the center and use the cord to secure the magazine inside a loose-leaf binder. You can also tie sections within the binder together.

— *Linda Strauss, Tottenville High School, Staten Island, New York*

Saving Paper in the Information Age

Computer printers and copiers require massive amounts of paper. To conserve paper, we provide, at no cost, paper that has been used on one side. We get stacks of used sheets from teachers and students. If someone needs to run a computer printout or a photocopy on clean sheets, he or she provides the paper.

— *Debra Fullhart, Southview High School, Sylvania, Ohio*

Saving Supplies & Time

We have devised a check-out system for school supplies, such as calculators, scissors, and glue sticks, that are often borrowed but sometimes not returned by students. The items are placed in manila envelopes or plastic baskets with a book pocket and borrower's card. We have gone to a similar setup for popular magazines. Finally, to cut down on the number of students going to the lockers for a forgotten computer disk, we keep a disk for students' emergency use. Students can save their work on that disk and then retrieve it later for their personal disk.

— *Christie Frost-Wendlowsky, Spencer-Van Etten Middle-Senior High School, Spencer, New York*

Sharing the Questions and the Answers

When the high schools, middle schools, and intermediate schools in our district were in the process of automating, the librarians held biweekly "share sessions." Our purpose was to assist each other and share what our individual teams were doing. The schools took turns hosting these meetings. We had an agenda of topics to discuss. If a question required calling a company representative, one person was designated to make the contact and follow through with the matter until it was resolved.

— *Diane Crowe & Virginia Holcombe, Nimitz High School, Houston, Texas.*

Shoe for a CD-ROM

The popularity of CD-ROMs has created a security problem in the media center. A small lab of standalone computers is loaded with multimedia software that requires CD-ROMs. Students can go into the lab to work on multimedia presentations or to use electronic encyclopedias. The theft of CD-ROMs was a serious problem until I required students to leave one shoe at the circulation desk for each disc checked out. The shoes are returned when the students return a disc. Students always remember to pick up their shoes at the end of the class period.

— *Jill Davidson, Eagle's Landing Middle School, McDonough, Georgia*

Shopping for Posters

As posters and maps come to us in magazines, advertisements, and various other sources, we laminate them, label them with a Dewey number, and barcode them for checkout. We use clothespins to attach them to a clothes hanger as you would a skirt. They are then arranged by Dewey number on a clothes rack. This allows teachers to browse the section they need, much as they would shop for clothes.

— *Carolyn Clemensen, South Paulding Middle School, Dallas, Georgia*

Short Story Index

We make full use of the feature of the Molli Automation System (Nichols) that allows unlimited subject entries. When we receive a new anthology of short stories or plays, I enter the titles and authors in the subject field. This gives us a short story and play index for this library.

— *Mary Frances Woulfe, Parker Mid High School, McAlester, Oklahoma*

Signage Eliminates Confusion—and Gives Teachers a Little Recognition

We were having a problem explaining to teachers which of the three sections of the library their classes would be assigned when they came to the library. Incoming students never knew where to sit. We purchased three sign boards, one for each section, with changeable lettering. The six class hours are listed with the teachers' last names. Our sign-up book also has matching section numbers. Before school, we can put teachers' names on the sign boards for the sections. These signs seem to make the teachers feel important to the library staff and eliminate student confusion about where to sit.

— *Nancy Bahr, Brighton (Michigan) High School*

Slippery Book Remedy

To keep books from sliding down while they are being stored on book trucks, I placed non-slip bathtub appliqués to the book truck shelves. Now the books stand up even when the trucks are moved.

— *Jana Greene, Boaz, Alabama*

Software Statistics

To gather statistics on the use of computer programs, we ask students to request a bar-coded card for each program they use. When they are finished, they return the cards to a basket at the desk. We do not take the time to physically check the cards out to the students because we "reshelve" them on the Follett Unison circulation system. From these statistics, I regularly report to administrators and school board members. When it is time to renew an expensive subscription, I can easily check the usage figures to see if we are getting our money's worth. Our students know that usage determines what we have in the library, so they don't complain about asking for the cards. We do require physical checkouts for Internet usage as well as a log of sites visited (to be returned with the card) so we can track specific students' use of the Internet.

— *Janet Hofstetter, California (Missouri) High School*

Soliciting Book Donations

With budget cuts, we have tried various ways to get free books for the library. We have been successful asking physicians for last year's copy of the *Physician's Desk Reference*. Members of Congress may donate Congressional Research Service Reports or a copy of the state manual. Call local attorneys for old copies of law books. Everyone I have ever contacted has been very obliging.

— *Patricia Kolencik, North Clarion High School, Tionesta, Pennsylvania*

Sponsor a Book Pays Off for Library & Students

At the beginning of each school year, popular novels and other books for recreational reading are featured in a special display in the media center. The purpose is to promote a Sponsor a Book program. Student government officers explain the program to classes that visit the display. Parents can view the display during open house and parent-teacher conferences. A list of recommended selections is distributed within the school community. To sponsor a book, individuals agree to purchase a book for the library collection. Their names as sponsors will appear on a bookplate, and they can read the new book before it is put on the shelves. They are also entered in a drawing for prizes. During the last three years, the effort has raised over $8,000.

— *Joey Schauenberg, Student, Moline (Illinois) Senior High School*

Spring Book Requests

Each spring I ask teachers for purchase ideas. The sheet is decorated with clip art and then divided into sections for books, magazines, and audiovisual materials. I always ask teachers to be as specific as possible and to attach any reviews, catalog pages, or order cards to their request sheet. I get more responses to this survey than any other because teachers know in the fall I will hand them the material they requested.

— *Diane C. Pozar, Wallkill (New York) High School*

Staff Helps with Weeding Process

We enlisted the help of staff members for weeding science and technology books. Armed with stickers and general guidelines, they found books with inaccuracies and outdated practices, for example, information about pesticides used by landscapers. The science teachers did this confidently, knowing we librarians would check their recommendations.

— *Louise Beattie, Davies Vocational-Technical School, Lincoln, Rhode Island*

Sticker Those Floppies

Put a label (library logo stickers are good) on floppy disks that belong to the media center. Use color coding (either stickers or different colored disks) to differentiate among different kinds of software: games, databases, and so forth.

— *Patricia Burns, Crary Middle School, Waterford, Michigan*

Storing Computer Programs

Many computer programs are packaged in "wimpy" cardboard. We put each program into narrow, plastic file boxes and label the front with the cataloging information. The program sits on the shelf without leaning.

— *Barbara Coleman, Emerson Middle School, Lakewood, Ohio*

Student Barcodes

Our students have barcodes, but no library cards. We give sixth graders their barcode number during orientation and ask them to memorize it. In case they forget, we keep folders containing each grade's numbers at the check-out desk.

— *Nan Bohannon, Sharp Middle School, Covington, Georgia*

Editor's Note: Most automation systems have the capability to pull up a patron's barcode if the last name of the patron is typed into the system. This backup feature could eliminate the need to keep a paper copy of the numbers. Memorization is reinforced if the same number can be used for other functions within the school, such as a computerized lunch account system. smc

Student Barcodes-Another Idea

Rather than having students responsible for barcoded library cards, I have filed the cards by class and inserted them in plastic sheet protectors kept in a notebook at the circulation desk.

— *Barbara Cuthbertson, St. Mark's Episcopal School, Ft. Lauderdale, Florida*

Student Barcodes—Classes by Color

Student barcodes in our circulation system are organized by homeroom and kept in a notebook on the circulation desk. When you open the notebook to any class, all class members' cards are visible. The barcodes are mounted on 1-1/2" x 3" cards that can be fed through a dot matrix computer. Cards are taped to construction paper cut to fit inside plastic sleeves, which can be scanned. Each grade has been assigned a different color, so even kindergarten students can quickly find their class. At the beginning of each school year, I just slit the tape with a sharp knife and rearrange the cards by the new classroom rolls.

— *Lisa Delgado, South Jackson Elementary School, Athens, Georgia*

Student Check-In of Books

If you're looking for ways to create time for some of the many new tasks facing you, reconsider some of your traditional tasks. For the past two years, we delegated book check-ins to the students themselves. Our students have proven they are capable. One computer is reserved for check-ins only. The students have learned to identify the appropriate numbers on the barcode label, and they enjoy keying their numbers into the computers and dropping their books into the box below.

— *Barbara Abernathy, Bremen, Georgia*

Student Log Sheet

To maintain a better management system for students entering the library during school hours, we established a log sheet for students to sign when they first come in. The log sheet includes the name of the student, class, and the times the student entered and left the library. The log is used in conjunction with passes from teachers. When students sign the log, they place their pass in the student pass slot, which is directly above the log. This system allows easy monitoring of students in the library and provides a record of library use.

— *Lydia E. Jenkins, Alice Deal Junior High School, Washington, D.C.*

Students Refer to Bibliographies

We have removed our bibliographies from the professional shelves and placed them on an index table in the middle of the library. These bibliographies are highlighted with signs and used for both library skills lessons and leisure reading selection. By teaching our students to use bibliographies, we're providing another book selection tool while easing the frustration of those who say "I can't find anything good to read."

— *Deborah Cooke, Salem Middle School, Richmond, Virginia*

Support Group for Rural Librarians

None of the rural school districts in our county has more than one high school librarian, and several districts have only one librarian for the entire district. I suspected that other librarians shared my frustration over having no one with whom to share ideas and problems. So we formed our own informal discussion group, which has grown to include five surrounding counties. Our twice-yearly meetings are held in the library of a volunteer librarian who serves a light lunch, plans topics for discussion, and conducts a tour of what's new in that facility. We have neither officers nor fees. We offer solutions to shared problems, brainstorm better ways to handle situations, and bring items for "show and tell." Usually about a dozen librarians attend. I always leave refreshed and excited about new ideas to try in my home library.

— *Joan Driver, Van (Texas) High School*

Sweet Returns

During December we keep a huge carafe of Hershey kisses in red and green foil on the desk for anyone who returns a book that month, overdue or not. The incentive helps get lockers cleaned out before vacation. Some kids have fines, but somehow the enticement of the candy motivates them to return their overdue books.

— *Evelyn Hammaren, Randolph (New Jersey) High School*

Switch Peripherals

The servers for three networks at our school are housed in a workroom off the library office. Since space is limited, we purchased a data switch for the three monitors and keyboards to use with the three servers. Now all three networks can be used by one keyboard and monitor leaving two keyboards and monitors for spares that can be used elsewhere.

— *Penny Peterson, Carl Cozier School, Bellingham, Washington*

Tabbing Journals

I love my professional journals, such as THE BOOK REPORT, but finding time to make the most of them was a problem. Now I keep a small sticky pad next to me as I quickly survey the latest issue of each journal. At the top of the page of an article I want to read, I stick a note marked with its subject. On the outside edge of a page that has special notations on unusual order sources, free materials, or anything else I want my aide to deal with, I stick a note with quick instructions such as "order" or "make copy." I pass the journal to my aide who deals with the side tabs, removes them, and puts the journal in a file box, top side up with my subject tabs showing. I keep the box on my desk for whenever I have a moment to read. I leave the top tabs on some articles that I want for future reference, and consequently, I have a ready-made file.

— *Judy Andrikopoulos, Encampment (Wisconsin) School*

Taking Work Home 'on the Drive'

I use an external hard drive as the backup for our circulation system, *Circ/Cat* (Winnebago) for the Macintosh. At the end of each day I copy the system folder on the hard drive. It copies in just a few minutes. When I need to catch up on such time-consuming projects as adding the names of new students or cataloging new materials, I disconnect the external hard drive and take it home with me, where I hook it up to my Macintosh. When I return to school, I copy the system folder to the drive in the circulation computer.

— Wayne Rush, Grover Cleveland Middle School, Caldwell, New Jersey

Three Grace Days for Overdues

To cut down on the number of overdue books, I extended the loan period from two weeks to four weeks, which better coincides with class assignments. Also, on Mondays, I send lists of students who will have overdue books by Wednesday to their English teachers. The three-day grace period built into the circulation program assures that all students will be notified in time to renew or return books without penalty. Teachers have made the list a part of their Monday morning routine. Students usually respond that day or the next.

— Connie Weber, Churubusco (Indiana) Middle/High School

Timely Videos

A previous hint in *THE BOOK REPORT* was a suggestion to put the length of videotapes on the check-out cards. Since we have a computerized circulation system, we no longer have check-out cards. The running time of the videotapes is on the catalog cards, but teachers usually bypass the card catalog and come to me to ask the time. To simplify matters, I used a permanent marker to write the running time directly on each videotape. If the time was already on the videotape in small print, I highlighted it so it could be found easily.

— Donna Walters, Ben Franklin Middle School, Valparaiso, Indiana

Top Class Awards

A well-used library sometimes has that lived-in look: chairs askew, trash on the floor, books on tables, microfiche scattered around. To help clean up our act, we instituted Top Class Awards. Announcements and posters promoted the competition. Classes are observed while they are in the library for a cooperative learning attitude, which includes noise level, on-task behavior, being helpful, sharing with others, and leaving the library neat. Top Classes receive certificates, while individual students in the class receive free overdue fines or a free period in the library during homeroom. The best class of the semester will receive a pizza party.

— Sandy Barron, Tomball (Texas) High School

Tracking Down AV Equipment

With all the other closing procedures, equipment inventory at the end of the year has always been a headache. To smooth the process, each spring I ask teachers to fill out a form listing all the equipment they have in their room at that moment. We also ask that they return anything they are not using. Much of the equipment is returned, and we can begin cleaning and repairs. We also have a chance to see where everything is and to begin to look for missing items early. By June almost everything is in order as the last few pieces of equipment float in.

— Karen Zapasnik, Deerfield Beach (Florida) High School

Tyvek® Envelopes to the Rescue (1)

The most effective way I have found to circulate magazines is to use the lightweight plastic envelopes made of DuPont's Tyvek®. I put a barcode on the envelope and check out it and its contents as temporary items. These sturdy envelopes, available in office supply stores, last a long time.

— *Kathleen Williams, Burlingame (Kansas) High School*

Tyvek® Envelopes to the Rescue (2)

We use Tyvek® envelopes to circulate items that do not have a barcode. We put a barcode for temporary items (using the numbers 10-150) on a supply of envelopes. Matching barcode numbers are put on book cards before the cards are clipped to the envelopes. When students request magazines, pamphlets, or vertical file materials, we put the item in an envelope, remove the matching card, and clip a check-out slip on the card. The name of the article and the date are written on the checkout slip, which the student signs. Whenever we have time at the circulation computer, we "wand" the barcode on the card and type the number of articles checked out to the student. The cards are filed in numerical order near the circulation desk. Students must return the materials in the barcoded envelope. The materials are easily checked in by the barcode on the envelope or on the card. The envelope and card are matched again and ready for another circulation.

— *Wanda Stimpson, Minico High School, Rupert, Idaho*

Tyvek® for Circulating Library Items

Tyvek® envelopes are the best for circulating temporary items. They outlast manila envelopes, even when the latter have been laminated. Tyvek® is that wonderful, space-age material that is impossible to tear. Put a barcode at the top of each envelope, and they can be used again to circulate interlibrary loans or anything that doesn't have its own number in your database. When we check out such an item, we scan the barcode on the envelope, enter the title as a temporary in the computer, and write the title on the envelope with a fine point permanent ink marker or ballpoint pen. (This is helpful if a patron checks out more than one temporary item and is likely to mix up the envelopes.) When the item is returned, check to be sure that what is inside matches what is written on the envelope, scan it, and draw a line through the title on the envelope. Then it is ready to be used again.

— *Eliece Edge, Alvin (Texas) Junior High School*

Use Your Automated Card Catalog for Booktalks

I inserted "Booktalk" as a local subject heading for the books on which I have written booktalks. I then replaced the summary note of the MARC record with my homemade heading. Now, when students use "Booktalk" as a subject, they get a list of 65+ titles. I also link sequels and companion books for suggested reading. We have had several classes use our "Booktalk" function for class reading assignments. "Booktalk" also gets a workout each day during lunch as students search for leisure reading. As time permits, I am adding older fiction books to the "Booktalk" function.

— *Elli Gillum, Albany (Georgia) High School*

Using Coded Subject Headings to Create Bibliographies

One of the great timesaving features of an automated catalog is its ability to create simple bibliographies with only a few keystrokes. For more complex, extended bibliographies, I create subject headings that allow complex bibliographies to be written. The following steps outline the process: Create "code" subject headings for each major bibliography. I begin all code terms with BIB, followed by three letters that are an acronym or abbreviation for the subject. For example, the code heading for American Historical Fiction becomes BIBAHF. The code for the Community Interaction and Awareness class becomes BIBCOM. It doesn't really matter what code is used as long as the term is a nonsense word. By starting all my code subject headings with BIB, I can easily search for any codes I may have forgotten. Add the code headings to existing material records using the "edit materials" program. (We use the MS-DOS version of the Winnebago CIRC/CAT). Add code subject headings to new materials as they are added to the collection. Now, when a teacher requests a bibliography, I simply search the catalog by the code term and print it using the "print bibliography" function. I also post a list of the special bibliographies next to the catalog terminals for students to use.

— *Doug Johnson, St. Peter (Minnesota) High School*

Using the Card Catalog for Storage

When our library became automated, I decided to use the old card catalog to store the students' library cards. This worked well because the students changed classes and could not always return to their homerooms to get their cards when they needed to check out a book. The old card catalogs are also useful for storing disks.

— *Cariel Thomas, Waco (Georgia) Elementary School*

VCR Workshops

Since teachers often seem confused about using VCRs, we offer a workshop titled "Everything You Wanted to Know About Your VCR But Were Afraid to Ask." I begin the session with an explanation of the common reasons the machines need repair. I show them the VCR head and explain the difference between two and four heads. I demonstrate how to clean the heads properly because this is the main problem with most machines. I also stress the need to buy quality videotapes. Several of our school machines have been broken by inexpensive tapes that teachers have brought from home. This after-school workshop has been offered several times with good response. It takes only a few minutes and saves me from explaining the same information over and over.

— *Karen Zapasnik, Deerfield Beach (Florida) High School*

Vendor Calls

I like to stay in touch with vendors, but calls were getting out of hand. For the past three years, I have had a policy of accepting sales calls only on Fridays from 7:30-11:00 A.M. Teachers now realize I will be interrupted during this time, and so they do not schedule initial research visits for their class on Friday mornings. And I don't feel guilty for time spent on the phone with vendors.

— *M. J. Tate, Union High School, Dowagiac, Michigan*

Vertical File—A Budget Enhancer

To stretch the library budget, I keep a vertical file of contemporary news items, for example, "Operation Desert Storm." When a current event item becomes obsolete, it becomes part of the historical file. Vertical files are also enhanced by attaching an index of magazine articles that we have on microfiche but that are not in the *Abridged Readers' Guide to Periodical Literature*. This increases use of microfiche magazines and adds quantity and quality to student library research.

— *Vivian Glenn, Morgan High School, McConnelsville, Ohio*

Vertical File—Gathering and Promoting Use—Automating the Vertical File

To encourage the use of the vertical file, I have entered "vertical file" as the author and the drawer number as the title. Under the subject field, I enter all files contained in the drawer. When students do a subject search in the catalog, they will be sent to the vertical file.

— *Mary Frances Woulfe, Parker Mid High School, McAlester, Oklahoma*

Vertical File—Gathering and Promoting Use—Comprehensive Cataloging

Our online card catalog is the key index to all the resources in the library, including two resources that are often overlooked—the vertical file and *CQ Researcher* (Congressional Quarterly), a weekly report that treats subjects in the news but has only periodical indexes. Since I feel so strongly about students not missing these resources, I list them in the online catalog by subject. Each vertical file subject heading is listed with a note to check the vertical file. A subject heading and

the bibliographic information list each *CQ Researcher*. We find students use these resources more now that they are in the online catalog.

— *Vonna Pitel, Cedarburg (Wisconsin) School District*

Vertical File—Gathering and Promoting Use—Requesting Material

I created a generic letter requesting free materials. I then used the *National Directory of Addresses and Telephone Numbers* to create a database of addresses from the government section. I used the mail-merge feature of our software to send my generic letter to the agencies. I enjoyed such a tremendous response and received so many positive comments that I repeated the process using the health section. Again I enjoyed the same results.

— *Jan Goetzinger, Tomah (Wisconsin) Middle School*

Vertical File Cross-References

After years of trial and error with the vertical file, I have finally found a way of increasing its use that seems to work. All vertical file folders now have catalog entries filed under subject headings. For example, under "Acid Rain" there is an entry saying "Information on this subject is located in the vertical file. Please ask for help at the circulation desk." In the past, students knew that the vertical file existed. Now they have better access to what it contains.

— *Annette Thibodeaux, John Quincy Adams Middle School, Metairie, Louisiana*

Vertical Files—Gathering and Promoting Use—Adding to the Computerized Catalog

Building to the idea of adding vertical file headings to the computerized catalog, I have added Newsbank and SIRS subject headings. Enter the subject as a "Main Entry—Personal Name"—tag #100—and as a subject-tag #600. Use the 600 "d" subfield for the notation to "also check Newsbank" (or vertical file or SIRS). In SIRS designations, be sure to indicate the volume number.

— *Thelma Seevers, Blair (Nebraska) Community High School*

Vertical Files—Management

At our high school, seven file cabinets are located in a special vertical files room. Two card trays containing subject and cross-reference cards are available on the top of one cabinet. Deposit boxes are found on the top of the other cabinets. After students use the folders, they place them in a deposit box instead of refiling them. This prevents misfiling and allows me to check the folders for repairs and to put a usage date on the front of the folder. I clip two local papers and *USA Today* year round. Students request articles on genetics for biology class, peer pressure and stress for mental health, authors for English classes, and various diseases for health class. All authors are filed alphabetically by nationality in the same drawer, and all diseases are filed alphabetically in two drawers. Students often go to the vertical files first because the information is more recent than that found in books. Even the periodical indexes are one month behind our vertical files.

— *Margaret Waltzer, Dominican High School, New Orleans, Louisiana*

Video Reminders

In many cases, additional materials, such as viewer's guides, are available for videocassettes. To indicate this, we place a colored dot (bright orange) on the check-out card. The dot also reminds us to retrieve the material from forgetful teachers when the cassette comes back.

— *Lilias Gordon, Bishop Gorman High School, Las Vegas, Nevada*

Videotape Storage & Retrieval

Our videotapes are color-coded by subject with large (one inch) press-on dots, making them easy to shelve and find. We add accession or Dewey Decimal Classification numbers to the dots and store the videotapes separate from other AV materials and software. This makes them accessible to teachers, who are asked to check out each videotape.

— *Jo McLean, Wills High School, Smyrna, Georgia*

Visibility for the Verticals

Instead of hiding vertical files in drawers, put them in colorful hanging folders under a bright mobile labeled "FIND WHAT YOU WANT HERE" and set them out in plastic crates on a table or counter. Those files filled with freebies and samples will be especially popular.

— *Sharon McWilliams, Spalding University, Louisville, Kentucky*

Weed It or Keep It?

If your library is automated, you can use your computer to obtain circulation statistics that will help you decide whether to remove a book, leave it on the shelf, or boost its circulation by promoting it. Here's how: At the end of the school year, print out circulation statistics from a specific range (i.e., 000-099, 200-299, Fiction A-H). Some library software packages can print out a list of books by copyright date. This feature provides you the capability to make weeding decisions without having to check every book on the shelves. If a record of weeded/deleted/discarded items is needed, screen print the "catalog card" from the online program, then delete the record. This saves card filing and card retrieving time.

— Sandy Nelson, Lee County Schools, Fort Myers, Florida

Within Arm's Reach

Since much of my work is done around the shelf-list area and in the periodical room where I have a computer station, I keep basic supplies in both places. In an empty shelf-list tray, I keep note paper, tape, labels, paper clips, scissors, pens, and a utility knife. In the periodical room, I use a Princeton file to hold basic supplies for working with the periodicals as well as computer supplies. Since the supplies are concealed, I can be sure they will be there when I need them.

— Jane A. Wilson, Emerald Junior High School, Greenwood, South Carolina

Working with Microsoft Works

I use the header/footer field of my *Microsoft Works* word processing program to save the telephone and fax numbers of the company to whom the letter is addressed. I check off the space marked "Don't print the header/footer on the first page," and the information does not appear on my one-page letters. The phone numbers are saved with my files and are available whenever I have a problem. If I want a version for a hard copy file, I can run a second copy with the "Print on page 1" turned on. If a hard copy is saved, the file name and date last updated can be added to the header/footer area so the matching computer file can be easily retrieved later. *The Microsoft Works Reference Manual* gives details on how to create headers and footers and how to use the special codes for filenames (&F) and dates (&D).

— Melanie J. Angle, McEachern High School, Marietta, Georgia

SECTION 5

Library Skills

> ## The illiterate of the 21st century will not be those who cannot read and write, but those who cannot learn, unlearn, and relearn.
>
> *Alvin Toffler*

Building lifelong learners is part of the mission of many schools and should be the mission of all libraries. For it is not the knowledge that is imparted that will be of greatest importance but the ability to gather new knowledge throughout one's life. It is that ability to seek and interest in obtaining new information that will have a major impact on the success of that person's life. It is estimated that during any one person's life-time that person will change careers from three to five times. With each change will come a need to learn skills to accompany that career. Any tools we, as library media specialists and technology specialists, can help students obtain will be tools that will impact their ability to become and remain a lifelong learner. Sometimes that skill is more easily learned if we can make the situation comfortable and non-threatening. So here are some suggestions for teaching library skills as well as some tips for making students comfortable and interested in becoming skilled information gatherers.

Word-of-the-Week

To help teach library vocabulary words, each week a library word is designated as "Word-of-the-Week." As classes come in for their library times, the word is introduced and the meaning discussed and illustrated. We begin with words such as author, fiction, spine, and so on. The students are then encouraged to search at home and find the word in a magazine or newspaper, in a book, on a container or any place else they care to look. During the week, students bring in the words they have found, tell what the word means, get a prize (sticker, candy, bookmark), and sign their name on the "I'm a Word Detective" chart. The students really enjoy the activity, bringing in bags full of items with library words on them!

— *Louise Kehoe, Hemlock (Michigan) Middle School*

A 'Love-ly' Valentine Contest

For a Valentine's contest, we asked students to do a keyword search on our online catalog to find out how many books in our library have the word "love" in their titles. Our students are familiar with keyword searching, but few ever limit their search to just titles, subjects, or authors. The only guidance we gave was to tell them to read the search hints on the computer screen. Students who figured it out had to show a library staff member every step of the search. The first 15 students to accomplish this received a small box of chocolates-a sweet reward for a job well done.

— *Patti Moser, Concord-Carlisle High School, Concord, Massachusetts*

Bibliography Cards for CD-ROMS

Using the citation form required by teachers, I have printed bibliography style cards for every CD-ROM program available to students. The cards are displayed on a bulletin board located near the computers. When students are using a program, they can easily refer to the bibliographic information on the style card.

— *Robyn L. Matthews, Thomas E. Harrington Middle School, Mt. Laurel, New Jersey*

Catalogs Help Teach Dewey System

Rather than discard the beautifully illustrated publishers' catalogs I receive throughout the year, I save them for my library skills classes. Most of the catalogs are organized by subject area, which makes them perfect sources of pictures for the Dewey Decimal Classification System posters that students make. These posters depict how the system refines and narrows each area of knowledge as it progresses from the first, second, and third summaries and on through specific descriptions. By finding pictures that represent each class number and its subdivisions, students can visualize the logic of the system in their own unique ways.

— *Sylvia Perrine, Emerson Junior High School, Fostoria, Ohio*

Color-Coded Handouts

When I give a number of handouts to students, I reproduce the handouts on paper of different colors so I can easily see that students are looking at the correct sheet. The colors also help in organizing handouts in my files.

— *Allison Trent Bernstein, Blake Middle School, Medfield, Massachusetts*

Current Biography & Back Issues

At the beginning of each year, our ninth graders spend a week reviewing the use of the card catalog and reference sources. As a culminating activity, they each prepare speeches using three library sources to collect information about a famous person. We found that *Current Biography* can be a valuable key to information in back issues of periodicals. We use it to determine the death dates of famous people. We then refer to the weekly magazines following close after that date or to those issued on the 10th or 25th anniversary of the subject's death. This method provides a wealth of information.

— *Marilyn Shelley, Garnett (Kansas) High School*

Custom-Made Periodical Index

To help students learn to use research tools they will encounter in college libraries, I made a periodical index. I listed all the titles the library subscribes to and the issues available, including the different forms in which the issues are available: regular issues, microfiche editions, and bound volumes. Once students learn to use the index to find out what periodicals are available in the library, they enjoy being more independent in their research.

— *Dorothy Dennis, Seminole (Texas) High School*

Dewey Decimal Ball

Learning Dewey decimal skills is more fun when students are playing Dewey Decimal Ball, a game that can be adapted to fit the sport of the season—baseball, football, or basketball. Draw a picture of the playing field or court on the board. Hold up a book and read the title. If the student (or team) identifies the Dewey number by hundreds correctly, they move a base, get a first down, or make a basket, then get another turn. Who needs boring worksheets?

— *Janice Jones, Piedmont Hills High School, San Jose, California*

Exploring Reference Books

To get students to use all types of reference books and encourage use of the card catalog and Dewey numbers, we made up reference question cards. Each 3 x 5 card has the name of a reference source and a question that can be answered in that book. Cards are numbered and kept in a box. Students choose a question card, then find the book and look up the answer. On their paper, students are instructed to write the number of the card, the Dewey number, the title of the book, and the page number of where the answer was found, as well as the correct answer. A master sheet makes checking papers easy. Students of all ages enjoy this activity, which can be used individually or as a team competition. Just make sure all books are available.

— *Helen Shaw, Clarion-Limestone Area High School, Strattanville, Pennsylvania*

Help for First-Time Researchers

Middle school students are faced with their first research paper assignment, and the English teachers insist that they follow a certain style in citing sources. I made individual style sheets for all types of sources a student might use—book, encyclopedia, newspaper, magazine, microfiche, computer software, or interview. Each sheet includes a form on which the student can record needed information, a sample of a correct citation for the source, and space for the student to write the citation for the information recorded. Copies of these sheets are boxed by type and kept accessible to students as they work in the library. Students find research easier, teachers like the system, and best of all, I don't have to answer repeated questions about citations.

— *Maureen McCarron, Carroll Middle School, Fort Wayne, Indiana*

Homecoming Contest Boosts CD-ROM Skills

Grolier's *Electronic Encyclopedia* was installed in our library at the beginning of the school year. In an effort to get students to learn to use it, we offered a contest during Homecoming Spirit Week. Our principal donated 10 free tickets to the homecoming game, and students qualified for daily ticket drawings by coming in for instruction on the use of the encyclopedia and showing a topic printout to the librarian. This helped many students become comfortable with our school's first venture into the new technology, and these initiated students in turn helped their peers with searches.

— *Patricia S. Fleming & Joe Myers, Berkeley High School, Moncks Corner, South Carolina*

Model Bibliographies

Our students were having difficulty writing bibliographies when using the computer for research. I put a model bibliography beside each workstation so they'd have a format to follow.

— *Suzette Turner, Rockport-Fulton High School, Rockport, Texas*

Online & Hard Copy Searches

Frustrated by having only one online encyclopedia for a whole roomful of kids? To make this information more accessible, I bought a print version of Grolier's *Academic American Encyclopedia* for students to use in conjunction with the CD-ROM version. They first look up their topic on the computer using the keyword search. Then they browse through the articles until they find the ones they need. At that point, they turn the computer over to a waiting classmate and locate the identical article in the print encyclopedia. This method maximizes use of the CD-ROM version of the encyclopedia for searching and browsing and eliminates the need to use it for time-consuming studying and note taking. When you have one CD-ROM and 500 students who want to use it, this is the only way!

— *Jacque Burkhalter, Fidalgo Elementary School, Anacortes, Washington*

Online Catalog Help

To help students become independent users of our online catalog, I prepared an instruction booklet for each search station. It has an outline of the procedure for searching various menu options such as Title, Subject, and Keyword. Also included are instructions and examples for using Boolean operators, truncation, wild card, and limiters.

— *Hannah Hollifield, Central Davidson Senior High School, Lexington, North Carolina*

Orientation on Video

With 35 reading classes, I got tired of presenting the same orientation lesson over and over, so our theater arts teacher offered to help me produce it as a videotape. I wrote the script, and the seventh-grade theater arts class played the role of a reading class on its first visit to the library. We plan to update the videotape and produce new programs about using the card catalog and reference books.

— *Katie Sessler, Andrew Jackson Middle School, Grand Prairie, Texas*

Orientation Video

For several years, we used a professionally produced videotape for freshman orientation in the media center. Though it was very well made, the students did not seem to relate the information presented in it to our library. This year, I decided to make my own videotape of the library. My co-star came in the form of a six-foot cardboard cutout of Darth Vader that I had purchased from a catalog. When Darth wanted to check out his favorite book, *Invaders of Earth*, he was sent to the office to get an ID card, and when he came back, of course, he had a library pass. Though I was afraid the students might think this was all too silly, they really did seem to enjoy watching the videotape. Some of the ninth-grade classes even gave it a round of applause.

— *Elaine Chambless, Kendrick High School, Columbus, Georgia*

Pencils for Answers

As a way of introducing freshmen to the library and creating interest in it, I conduct a trivia contest throughout the year. All answers can be found in the library or online. I ask a series of questions, usually two or three, on a related topic in the daily bulletin. Students with the correct answers receive a prize, such as a novelty pencil. Friday is challenge day. The questions are harder but the prize is bigger, usually a pencil sharpener. This year I was a victim of my own success. I ran out of prizes in mid-September.

— *K. Preslopsky, Wright City (Missouri) High School*

Prime Time Library Skills

Once I have introduced the Dewey decimal system to the seventh-grade classes, we play a game in which students have to apply an understanding of the system. I name a current television show, and they tell me where it would be classified if we wanted to assign Dewey numbers to the show. Examples include *L.A. Law* (300s), *Coach* (700s), and *Doogie Howser* (600s). This exercise has evoked some lively discussion—such as whether *Northern Exposure* should be classed in the 600s or 900s.

— *Cathy Evans, Memphis (Tennessee) University School*

Quick Reference for Footnotes

I put copies in plastic protectors of the pages from *Nine Steps to a Quality Research Paper* by Harry Stuurmans (Linworth, 1994) detailing style for bibliographies and footnotes. Students who need an example or a quick refresher on style can refer to these pages or make copies.

— *Anitra Gordon, Lincoln High School, Ypsilanti, Michigan*

Research Lessons to Go

Whenever a class is ready to begin a long-range research project, I try to arrange an orientation session in the classroom. Usually this takes place on the day before the class's first scheduled period in the media center. Taking a book cart of reference materials, I present an overview of the research process, review bibliographic formats on the blackboard, and discuss topics, research shortcuts, and anticipated problems. I try to involve the teacher in as much of my presentation as possible. This one-day in-class visit lets students know that the teacher and I are working as a team. Students are assured that I understand their assignment, know what the teacher wants, and am in a position to help them track down the kind of information they need. Students tend to be more focused when they begin their research, and seem less reluctant to ask for help. Even a 15- or 20-minute overview seems to make an impression.

— *Kathleen McBroom, Fordson High School, Dearborn, Michigan.*

Scavenger Hunt

Our seventh-grade library advisory decided they would like to instruct sixth-grade classes in library research. Since the sixth graders were studying Ancient Egypt, the seventh graders wrote a scavenger hunt, When, Where, Who Stole the Mummy? To solve the hunt, sixth graders used the online catalog, dictionaries, magazine index, almanacs, or electronic encyclopedias.

— *Nancy Finch, Rippowam Magnet Middle School, Stamford, Connecticut*

School-wide Jeopardy Show

For our state's Right-to-Read Week, we took the *Jeopardy!* game, which many teachers had adapted for class use, and opened it up to the entire school. We chose topics based on books and reading and gave all interested students a short pretest. The top three finalists got to be the contenders for the "big" game, which was videotaped in the library with a small "studio audience." This year we will either have an assembly or broadcast the game on our instructional TV system. We add as many realistic touches as possible, which helps students catch the spirit of the game.

— *Paula J. LaRue, Lincoln Junior High School, Van Wert, Ohio*

Self-Directed Library Orientation

Through the years, I've tried different approaches to library orientation. Two years ago I began using self-directed learning with seventh graders. With the students I reviewed cooperative learning and established work groups. In each group, one student was named to record the members' answers to these questions:

► What kind of information do you expect to learn about the library?

► What do you need to know before you can effectively use this library?

► If you were the librarian/teacher/tour guide, what would you teach?

After the small groups developed their lists, we met as a large group and shared the items on each group's list. (This gave me the opportunity to ascertain that the students were covering the important features of the library.) Students were then directed to find the answers to their specific questions, such as where are the periodicals housed and how long are books checked out? In a wrap-up session, students told me what they had found. They could also ask about resources. I expect to continue using this technique and will refine it over the years to ensure that the experience is educationally sound.

— *Sally Mortier, Peoples Academy, Morrisville, Vermont*

Split Into Small Groups

As we work with teachers on resource-based units, we divide classes into thirds and assign a group to each media specialist. Each group works exclusively with their assigned media specialist, as well as with the classroom teacher. Small groups of 12 or fewer make it easier for students to focus on their work and get the individual help they need.

— *Jean Bailey & Judy Davidson, Lithonia (Georgia) High School*

Using Books for Research

That high school students know how to use nonfiction books for research is an assumption that may not be true. As I help students assemble information for their bibliographies, I find that many of them are not familiar with the parts of a book and do not know how to use a book's index to find information. I developed two instruction sheets for students: one defines the parts of a book and the other explains how to locate and use the index. Teachers go over these information sheets with students before they launch them on their projects. I have also made some activity sheets if teachers want students to practice before they begin researching.

— *Gloria Ziolkowski, Thornton Township High School, Harvey, Illinois*

World Almanac & *Jeopardy*

When I used commercially prepared work-sheets in teaching how to use *The World Almanac*, the students pronounced them boring. To enliven this part of information skills teaching, I asked pairs of students to look through the book and find 10 facts dealing with a topic they were studying. Then they wrote a question to go with each fact. I used the questions and answers to devise a *Jeopardy*-like game board.

— *Allison Trent Bernstein, Wayland (Massachusetts) High School*

SECTION 6

Odds and Ends

> **The main impact of the computer has been the provision of unlimited jobs for clerks.**
>
> *Peter Drucker*

Much of the odds and ends in a library media center are the details that can make a library run smoothly, make the facility look attractive, and give the facility an organized look. Some of these activities could be considered public relations, such as presenting an image of organization that is part of the persona of building that level of credibility needed to have successful public relations activities. These same odds and ends can help keep patrons coming back—if the center is attractive and comfortable. The computer that has created "unlimited jobs for clerks" has also made unlimited jobs for others of us who are part of a service-oriented center. Any tip for making the center more attractive, easier to be in, more useful, and student friendly might have ended up in this section but might have, on a different day, been placed in one of the other sections. Such is the nature of "odds and ends."

"Info Packs" from the Library of Congress

"Info Packs" packets, generated by the Library of Congress's Congressional Research Service, are available through state representatives. A boon to students doing research, they usually include an issue brief, bulletins, government arguments, copies of magazine articles, and general information sheets. We have used them for reports on capital punishment, abortion, acid rain, social security, AIDS, drug legalization, and education.

— *Anitra Gordon, Lincoln High School, Ypsilanti, Michigan*

"New" Projector Carts

I had several three-tier carts available for teachers to use, but the teachers complained that the carts were too tall for overhead projectors. Buying new carts was too expensive. My solution was to ask the maintenance staff to chop off the top tier and repaint the carts. Our new shortened carts are really in demand.

— *Amy Pritzl, Tomahawk (Wisconsin) High School*

Book Covers from Highway Maps

Since textbook covers were in short supply this fall in our school, we made old highway maps from the library's collection available to students. The kids enjoyed choosing a state for their book covers, and we recycled yet another paper product.

— *Evelyn Hammaren, Randolph (New Jersey) High School*

Colorful Clips

When I am photocopying several different items at a time, sometimes it is difficult to keep the masters separate from the copies. To solve the problem, I quickly place a brightly colored paper clip on the master. If I am in a hurry or get interrupted, I can easily group the masters together so they don't get lost in the shuffle.

— *Sandy Iwai, Whittier/Naples School, Long Beach, California*

Conventional Wisdom

If you're going to a convention, workshop, or other professional activity, take along either name and address labels or one of the new self-inking address stamps. Things go easier and faster when you register for the dozens of offers and raffles available.

— *Anitra Gordon, Lincoln High School, Ypsilanti, Michigan*

Cooperative Custodian

Like socks in the washing machine, pencils and pens seem to have a way of disappearing from the library. Our custodian overheard me lamenting this problem and commented that he was sweeping up many pens and pencils as he cleaned the classrooms and hallways each night. He offered to take just a few min-utes to collect them instead of throwing them away. Now students are amazed by the number of pens and pencils we have for use in the library. Some have even recognized and reclaimed their own property, which they thought was "lost forever." Students now rely on the library when they need to borrow a pen or pencil for class use. Remarkably, these are almost always returned.

— *Patty Benedum, Cheat Lake Junior High School, Morgantown, West Virginia*

Covering Up Old Books

We cannot afford to replace all of our "old-looking" books. For the hard cover books that look their age, I pasted a printout of the title, author, and Dewey number over the spine. I secured the printout firmly with tacky plastic. I have also created new dust jackets using construction paper and a plastic jacket cover.

— *Elizabeth Hanelt, Don Julio Junior High School, North Highlands, California.*

Envelopes for Computer-made Greetings

Finding $8\frac{3}{4}$ x $5\frac{3}{4}$ envelopes for single fold greeting cards (such as those made in *CreateACard* by American Greetings) was a challenge. Most business supply stores only stock booklet envelopes, with flaps on the sides, or the pricey sets of paper and envelopes. Then we found "announcement envelopes" available from Quill in packages of 50.

— *Carol Burbridge, Jardine Middle School, Topeka, Kansas*

Friends Who Might Have Been

In our "Friend for Life" contest, we display pictures of staff members when they were in middle school. By putting money in labeled jars, students vote for the teacher they would most likely have had as a middle school friend. This has been a highly successful fund raiser for the library.

— *Nancy Hughes, Matthew Henson Middle School, Indian Head, Maryland*

Good 'n' Cheap Boxes

If you need boxes in large quantities, check with your local bulk mailing services. They can be a terrific source of sturdy boxes at a low cost, if any.

— *Patricia Burns, Crary Middle School, Waterford, Michigan*

Grime Fighter

Ronson's lighter fluid is great for removing misplaced labels, tape, chewing gum stuck between the pages of a book, and accumulated grime on book covers. It evaporates without leaving a stain on paper.

— *Sister Annunciata, Sacred Heart High School, Los Angeles, California*

Half a Dozen Uses and More for Donated Books

Let parents and the community know that you appreciate donations of books and magazines. In our school, art classes and others use the extra magazines for projects and for classroom reading. I add some of the book donations to our collection, but most of them are offered free to students. I count these "freebies" in my circulation figures. Sometimes I can sell some of the donations to second-hand stores and use the money for RIF (Reading is Fundamental) projects. I save some of the donated books for the public library's book sales. When we catalog the donated books, I indicate they are gifts, in

case anyone asks why we have so many Louis L'Amour titles. English teachers appreciate donations for their classroom collections.

— *Anitra Gordon, Lincoln High School, Ypsilanti, Michigan*

Keeping Clean

Because middle school kids can be pretty grubby, I keep a pop-up box of moist wipes on my desk. The wipes are also useful in cleaning barcodes for scanning and in removing ink stains. I believe my exposure to germs has been reduced since I'm able to clean my hands frequently.

— *Anne Ozog, Waterloo (New York) Middle School*

Keeping Current

Book and software companies come and go, changing addresses or merging with other companies. To keep up, I use the readers' coupons in professional magazines. Quite often, this results in being placed on a mailing list. Yes, the mailings can be a nuisance, but I often discover new products that are of interest.

— *Anne Ozog, Waterloo (New York) Middle School*

Keeping in Touch with Yourself

I use my voice mail at school as a message system. When I'm at home and think of something I need to do or look up, I call myself and leave a message.

— *Anitra Gordon, Lincoln High School, Ypsilanti, Michigan*

Liven Up the Look of Computer Monitors

Liven up dull, gray computer monitors with handmade "screenies"-computer screen frames of heavy-duty laminated cardboard that measure 16 inches by 13-1/4 inches to fit 13-inch, 14-inch, and 15-inch monitors. The "screenies" are easy to mount with Velcro®. Make them out of gift wrap for special occasions or decorate them with clip art. Have students make their own personalized "screenies" using blank frames and experimenting with fanciful shapes. A brontosaurus shape, for example, could have an area in its center to accommodate the screen of the monitor.

— *Andrea Troisi, LaSalle Middle School, Niagara Falls, New York*

Looking Good at Test Time

We make use of the closed-circuit television system to deliver test directions to classrooms where students are taking standardized tests. This assures that each group gets the same instructions at the same time. It also means that we can keep the testing groups small. Students tend to score higher on these tests when they are tested in small groups. Since the media specialists set up the equipment, we get accolades for our technical expertise from the counseling department, the administration, and the parent proctors.

— *Caroline C Bennett, Creekside High School, Fairburn, Georgia*

Make Training a Priority

Training teachers to use the technology is too important and time-consuming to share billing with other activities. I highly recommend scheduling faculty meetings devoted exclusively to training. Beforehand, set up training stations of hardware and software as well as "training tables" of food to brighten the spirits of your faculty. Divide teachers into small groups and rotate them through each center to practice using a piece of equipment or software. Post a proficient faculty member at each station.

— *Sandy Nelson, Lee County Schools, Fort Myers, Florida*

Making Barcode Labels Stick

Do barcodes and their protective labels refuse to adhere to some books? Scrape the surface of the book with the open blade of your scissors. You'll get better adhesion.

— *Lu Richardson, Barnwell (South Carolina) High School*

Making Way for New Carpeting

Last summer I was faced with the task of moving the library collection so that a new carpet could be installed. Having had a bad experience earlier in moving the library to a new site, I knew I had to find a way for the custodians to keep the boxes in order. I purchased colored stickers and color coded the boxes to the stacks, a different color for each aisle. The boxes were also given numbers. When the stacks were put back, the correct boxes were placed beside them. The reshelving of the collection went smoothly, and the new carpet looks great.

— *Sheila Brooks, Ukiah (California) High School*

Messages on the Screen Saver

We like to change the screen saver message on the network frequently to catch the attention of students. In order to have some variety, we ask teachers and library aides for suggestions. Messages may publicize a book fair, a sports event, or an upcoming holiday. Just before Christmas we printed the phrase 'Joy to the World" in Spanish, French, Latin, and German.

— *Carol N. Kelly, St. Paul's School for Girls, Brooklandville, Maryland*

More Than Bulletin Board Lettering

The Ellison Letter Machine cutouts can be used for many projects besides bulletin boards. With the opaque projector, teachers often enlarge shapes and use them for set decorations. Spider and bat shapes are very effective for a haunted house.

— *Beverly Budzynski, Grand Blanc (Michigan) Middle School*

Morning Announcements

With the explosion of technology, it is commonplace to have TVs and VCRs in the classrooms. This luxury makes it possible to conduct morning announcements through a broadcast system. Each morning, announcements are quietly displayed on the television screen, allowing students plenty of time to write down important dates and times. Scanned pictures can be incorporated to liven the news and help capture students' attention. The announcements can flash across the screen for as long as a teacher feels is necessary. They also can remain on the cafeteria or media center monitor throughout the day so that students who are late to school will not miss important information. There are no more loud, rambling intercoms in the morning, and there is no more confusion about dates and deadlines. Everyone benefits from this valuable means of communication.

— *Nancy Wells, Pope High School, Marietta, Georgia*

Nail Polish Remover to the Rescue

Seemingly nothing in the custodian's cleaning supplies would remove the traces of adhesive tape on the windows of my office. Posters had once hung there. I tried nail polish remover and presto, no more mucky glass.

— *Elizabeth Hanelt, Don Julio Junior High School, North Highlands, California*

New Life for Card Catalogs

After automating the catalog and circulation, we looked around the school for someone who might be able to use the wood cabinets that had housed catalog cards. The vocational education classes were happy to take the cabinets and use them to store nails and other small items. In return, the woodworking students built three new bookshelves for the library.

— *Fran Feigert, Northwest High School, Justin, Texas*

New Uses for Old Catalog Cards

We use discarded catalog cards to "decorate" study carrels. The cards are glued to pieces of cardboard cut to fit the sides of the carrels. The cardboard panels are covered with plastic and taped inside the carrels for interesting decoration that discourages graffiti. We also make bookmarks from the cards by trimming off the hole-punched edge and adding a rubber-stamp design to the unprinted side.

— *Faye Griffith, Venice High School, Los Angeles, California*

Passes with Pizzazz

In our high school, students must have a pass to go to the restroom or their locker. To brighten everyone's day, I have designed my own passes on our computer using Print Shop. The pass has the essential information required by the office, but I also add little items such as "Have you read a good book lately?" or a favorite quotation. I have designed seasonal passes, motivational passes, and passes that build self-esteem. Some have comics or jokes on them. Students always comment on the unique hall passes they get in the library.

— *Patricia Kolencik, North Clarion High School, Tionesta, Pennsylvania*

Posters Delivered in Prime Condition

I attend one or more librarians' conferences yearly. I always take one or two empty mailing tubes along to carry back the posters distributed by book publishers and others. Then I distribute the unrumpled and unfolded posters to teachers.

— *Karen Sebesta, Highlands High School, San Antonio, Texas*

Practical Reasons to Tape

Videotape the lecture and demonstration portions of any workshops you conduct. You can use the tape later to review your presentation and to present information to new teachers or those who did not attend.

— *Sandy Pope, South Elementary School, Eldon, Missouri*

Preserving Book Jackets

We laminate book jackets, trim the covers, and tape them to the book. For us, laminating works better than using the jacket covers.

— *Karen Olson, Castle Heights Middle School, Rock Hill, South Carolina*

Professional Growth & Proficiency Tests

During the week of the statewide proficiency test, students who are not taking the test report to school later than usual. I make use of these mornings by taking the two library aides on visits to other libraries. We have toured school, public, business, and university libraries. It gives us a chance to meet with other professionals in the area and compare policies, resources, and equipment. It's sparked several ideas for both immediate improvements and future goals.

— *Karen George, Newark (Ohio) High School*

Puppets on the News

We videotape the school news approximately 10 minutes before it is aired to the classrooms. Since viewer interest seemed to lag, we added hand puppets to the production. Not only did our ratings go up, but shy students and teachers were less reluctant to go on camera. Taping is more fun too.

— *Nancy Bahr, East Middle School, Plymouth, Michigan*

Quicker Photocopying

Here's a simple but effective time-saver: always photocopy from the back of a chapter or article and work forward. The pages will stack up in numerical order.

— *John Royce, International School, Hamburg, Germany*

Raining Computer Cables

The cables (Ethernet, telephone, zip drive, modem) trailing off the back of my desk were easily unplugged when they were accidentally kicked or bumped. Twist ties and duct tape didn't help, and holders designed for cables weren't big enough. A maintenance worker, using a piece of rain gutter pipe, created a holder for us. It is attached to the back of the desk and holds all the cables and power strips neatly.

— *Mary Alice Anderson, Media Specialist, Winona (Minnesota) Middle School*

Reaching Out

Our Texas Education Network link to the Internet, known as the TENET station, in the library is busy all day because I actively encourage teachers to sign up for accounts. Often I offer "TENET Time" after school to encourage use of the Internet among teachers. I also use the Internet to pull up call numbers for cataloging, to teach information searches, and to share ideas with fellow librarians. Recently I "met" the librarian at the high school where my brother teaches art, and we're now sharing our stories online.

— *Joellen G. Cullison, Deer Park Senior High School, South Campus, Pasadena, Texas*

Recycle Catalog Cards

I gave an English teacher my discarded catalog cards to use for students' vocabulary review. Students use the backs to make their own vocabulary cards and love the fact that the cards have holes and can be stored in their ringed notebooks.

— *Evelyn Hammaren, Randolph (New Jersey) High School*

Recycling Catalog Cabinets

When we went online with our card catalog, we recycled the cabinets. The art teacher was delighted with one set for her art supplies. We use a second cabinet to store bulbs for the audiovisual equipment.

— *Doris Fox, Aldine Senior High School, Houston, Texas*

Recycling Extra Printer Paper

We put a "recycling box" near the computers to encourage students to collect the extra sheets of paper that invariably are produced by the printer. The box has cut down on floor mess, and students who need a piece of paper just visit the box.

— *Carol Burbridge, Jardine Middle School, Topeka, Kansas*

Recycling Laminating Film

A teacher in our school keeps the scraps of plastic from laminating projects for students to use as transparencies. She cuts the scraps into page-size rectangles and uses water-based overhead projection pens to write on them. Students can wash the ink from the film and use it over and over for their presentations. This saves our school the cost of write-on transparency sheets.

— *Phyllis Press, Manchester Township Middle School, Lakehurst, New Jersey*

Recycling Posters

The walls of our high school corridors are covered with posters advertising fund raisers, dances, and meetings. We noticed that when the events were over, the posters ended up in the trash. To encourage recycling, the library now offers a bounty of 25 cents for any poster turned in with an unused side. We always have a big supply of recycled posters on hand, which we sell to students for the same price. Saves money and trees.

— *David Burke, Weston (Connecticut) High School*

School Web Sites: Is Yours Snazzy or Snoozy?

To make your site a snooze, be sure to include a copy of the school handbook, rules and regulations, and minutes from every meeting held this year. To really put them to sleep, upload every official school publication. To make your school site snazzy, showcase students' work, post virtual tours or field trips with digital photos, and include launch pads (favorite educational links), information about famous local events, happenings, or disasters. You can even include school-sponsored chats, free via sites like chatplanet. Include e-mail addresses so visitors can interact. Remember that your site will be visited by children as well as adults. Does your site include content for children? And finally, does your Web team include students as well as adults?

— *Bill Jordan, International School, Stavanger, Norway*

Sharing Free Offers

I keep the disks/ CD-ROMs from online service companies offering free trial hours and give them to teachers and students who are interested in subscribing to a service.

— *Dahlia Werner, Rusch Junior High School, Portage, Wisconsin*

Sources of Vertical File Materials

Don't overlook government and nonprofit agencies' publications as a source of free material for your vertical file. I have received pamphlets and written materials from the American Cancer Society, the National AIDS Clearinghouse, the Environmental Protection Agency, and the National Clearinghouse on Child Abuse and Neglect. Addresses and phone numbers can be found in *The New York Public Library Desk Reference*, local telephone books, or via a search on the World Wide Web.

— *Arlene Kachka, Holy Trinity High School, Chicago, Illinois*

Special Mouse Pads

Some printing shops can transfer a photograph onto a mouse pad. Take a picture of the school, a composite picture of the staff, or a child's drawing and have unique mousepads created for your school's computer lab.

— *Sharron L. McElmeel*

Storytime for Older Children

At our school's annual "lock-in" event, the students stay at school from 9:30 P.M. to breakfast in the morning. They participate in activities such as "broomball" and basketball or watch movies. Usually midnight to 2 A.M. is a slow time, and students frequently come to the library for conversation or sleeping. This year I sponsored a storytime in the 12 to 2 A.M. slot. During the previous week, the students had been asked for the titles of children's books they'd like to have available. The lower school library lent us the requested books plus the pillows used for storytime. We provided a rocking chair and soft lighting to set the mood. This proved to be a popular activity with students staying to hear two or three stories read by me or by a student. The students loved hearing their old favorites again, and I liked having the library involved in a student event.

— *Margaret Tabar, St. Paul Academy & Summit School, St. Paul, Minnesota*

The Green Library: College Catalogs

Each year we ask seniors to recycle extra college catalogs, brochures, and admissions videotapes by bringing them to the library. Whatever the counselors don't need, we offer to interested underclassmen.

— *Gail Szeliga, Union Endicott High School, Endicott, New York*

Transparency Protection

Our home economics teacher shared this hint when I gave her some sheet protectors: Place all unframed transparencies for overhead projector use in clear sheet protectors. No need to remove the transparencies to use them, and they do not seem to get as hot while on the projector. The transparencies stay clean and may be stored in a ring binder since the protectors are hole punched. Also, anything that is used on the copy machine can be kept in binders in such protectors, eliminating the necessity to hole punch the originals. Originals are not lost in the copying process, they are kept neat and clean, and they are easily refiled.

— *Janet Hofstetter, California (Missouri) High School*

Waste Not Want Not

While trying to live with budget cuts, the library has adopted the "waste not want not" philosophy. When the graphic arts department donated hundreds of strips of card stock to the library to be used as bookmarks, we sponsored an art contest. We circulated 100 strips to interested students. A week later, the bookmarks were displayed in the library along with ballots for voting for favorites. The artists of the three most popular bookmarks received a cash prize. The real winner was the library, which had 100 original bookmarks to share with other students.

— *Sheila Moore Sorrells, Edward H. White High School, Jax, Florida*

Workstation Naming Ends Confusion

With our multiple, not-yet-networked workstations, students were often confused when I instructed them to "meet me at the third workstation on the left." We decided to name our workstations, and our Macintosh hard drives as well. After considering several themes, we decided on popular cartoon characters. Our stations now sport pictures of the cartoon characters, confusion has disappeared, and humor (occasionally) prevails.

— *Joyce Valenza, Wissahickon High School, Ambler, Pennsylvania*

SECTION 7

Public Relations

> **From the library point of view I have learned that she commits the cardinal sin who takes all the references on a given subject and then sends a class to the library to look that subject up!**
>
> *Isabella Austin, 1909*

Dealing with the misconceptions of what a library and librarian really can do is part the mission of any public relations efforts. For example, how does one deal with the instructor who checks out all the references on a topic and then expects her students to get the information from the library? Public relation initiatives not only strive to acquaint the users to the resources and services that are available in the library but also serve to help them have a positive image of the library media center. The entire topic of collaboration and curriculum involvement could be considered part of the library media center's public relations efforts. The same is true for every session of library skills that might be taught. Don't mistake public relations for advertising. Effective public relations is proactive, and having a strong program in place can alleviate the tendency to be reactive, instead allowing it to be responsive. But building a reputation through responsive action and letting others know that the library can deliver is all part of using public relations effectively. The line between pubic relations and advertising is very narrow. Both public relations efforts and advertising complement one another in creating an awareness of the role of the librarian and the place the resources of the library play in the educational program.

"Pull-the-Plug" Week

In conjunction with National Library Week, we celebrate "Pull the Plug" Week, during which families are encouraged to do without television and video games for seven days. Each day, students bring signed notes from home that they stayed away from the tube. We ask students what they did instead and publish this information as added encouragement. The notes make students eligible for prize drawings, and all students who abstain for the entire week are invited to an ice cream party. District officials and school board members attend.

— *Cathy Bonnell, Ironwood Elementary School, Phoenix, Arizona*

"Rebates" Win Friends for the Library

We must charge students 10 cents per sheet for photocopies and printouts. As a public relations gesture, I issue two coupons per semester to each student. The coupons can be redeemed for the paperwork or applied to fines. I also give five-cent coupons to students who do well on library instruction assignments.

— *Donna Grayson, Immaculate Conception Middle School, Traverse City, Michigan*

What's for Lunch?

The library staff was constantly being asked by students, "What's for lunch?" The cafeteria manager agreed to provide us with the lunch menu for two weeks at a time. We use Print Shop to produce a weekly menu that we post in various places in the school. This answers that daily question and strengthens the relationship between the library and cafeteria.

— *Elizabeth Deer, Pearl (Mississippi) High School*

A Basket That Saves Steps

You can save lots of steps if you fill a basket with the items that students are always asking for. I keep a basket close to the circulation desk with items such as pencils, scissors, pens, felt markers, rulers, a compass, tape, crayons, a hole puncher, and a stapler.

— *Vivian Glenn, Morgan High School, McConnelsville, Ohio*

A Fine Idea

As an incentive to get students to send their parents to an evening meeting on teenage sexuality, our media center offered "fine bucks" to those whose parents showed up. The fine bucks were green, of course, and could be redeemed for up to $1 off library fines on overdue books.

— *Deborah Young Maehs, Kingfisher (Oklahoma) Middle School*

A Shoe Bag of Supplies

To save the staff's time in loaning office supplies to students, we hung a plastic shoe bag on the wall near the circulation desk and filled the pockets with supplies. Each pocket is labeled. Some of the items available to students are staplers, pens, pencils, rulers, cal-culators, glue sticks, compasses, protractors, and scissors. The shoe bag has been a big hit with students.

— *Annette Thibodeaux & Kathy Klapatch, Archbishop Chapelle High School, Metairie, Louisiana*

Action Shots of Teachers and Students

In November, our parochial high school holds an open house for junior high students and their parents. During the first two months of school, I keep a disposable camera at my desk to capture action shots of teachers and students as they use the library and its resources. For the open house, I put the pictures on poster board with captions identifying the teacher, subject area, and project. This year I displayed the poster on an easel. Naturally I keep the poster up for several days because students and teachers love to see themselves on display.

— *Dottie Bobzin, Clearwater (Florida) Central Catholic High School*

An Invitation to County Officials

For Law Day in May, we invited the county attorney to speak on the legal system. Students also asked questions about becoming an attorney or county prosecutor. A news article about the visit appeared on the front page of the newspaper.

— *Madeleine M. Hoss, Metcalf Laboratory School, Illinois State University, Normal, Illinois*

Annotated Book Lists

Our high school library has always prepared new materials lists to inform faculty of recent book and nonprint purchases. To make the lists even more useful, we now include not only the standard author, title, and call number information but also a brief annotation. It is not difficult to come up with such an annotation. It can be copied from the new catalog cards or from the book. Add some catchy clip art to the heading on your new materials list, and staff members (and students as well) will notice your efforts.

— *Margaret Lincoln, Lakeview High School, Battle Creek, Michigan*

Annotations for New Tapes

I keep a file on my computer called New Materials. Whenever I tape something like a new Reading Rainbow or Bill Nye TV show, I add it to the list. I sometimes include a short description, especially if the title isn't descriptive, and I might add my own recommendation. I list the taped shows by category, and when I fill the page, I date it and send it to the teachers.

— *Margie Hall, Chapel Hill Elementary School, Douglasville, Georgia*

Automated Candy Bars

Our library's circulation system has an automatic backup feature. During National Library Week, we have it set to backup after every 25th transaction. Whoever is at the computer at the time of the automatic backup receives a candy bar. This is one of our most popular NLW activities.

— *Joy M. Harrison, Buffalo (Missouri) High School*

Banners & More Banners

At our high school, banners and posters congratulate, encourage, announce, instruct, remind, and maybe even inspire. Banner making is another way of drawing students into the library. In our workroom, we provide refillable markers, rolls and sheets of construction paper, and poster board (donated by a carton manufacturer). The markers come in a screw top pot with openings for each of the three marker sizes: 1/2 inch, 1 inch, and 2 inches. We bought four marker units four years ago and have recently added three more colors. The only problems have been minor irritations, like borrowed scissors and tape that never returns. The tape loss can be endured, but favored scissors are close to the heart. I'm considering welding them to something at least as burdensome as an oxen yoke. If there's a right-brained librarian out there who's perfected scissor security, I'd like to hear some solutions.

— *Jackie Tafoya, Harper Creek High School, Battle Creek, Michigan*

Birthday Cards for Teachers

Since teachers and staff do so much for the library, we try to do a little something for them by sending cards on their birthdays. We use Print Shop (Broderbund) to create the card and attach a candy bar. Those with summer birthdays get their cards on the last day of school.

— *Carolyn Deweese, Dacula (Georgia) High School*

Book Donations

What do you do when a "generous" book donor comes to the library with a box of old books and requests a receipt, complete with value of the books, for tax purposes? How can you pretend that a 20-year-old textbook has retained its original value? A speaker at a library conference made the following suggestion: give the donor a receipt listing the number of books, then sign and date the receipt. Tell the donor that he or she can insert the value of the books. If handling this type of situation is a continuing problem, be sure to make this solution part of your formal administrative policy statement.

— *Edna Boardman, Minot (North Dakota)*
  High School, Magic City Campus

Book Ordering Party

To involve teachers in the selection of books and other resources, I organized a "Book Ordering Party" during the early days of October. We served refreshments while teachers browsed catalogs and other selection aids. Many requests and recommendations were made, and teachers seemed to enjoy this opportunity to participate in selection.

— *Valerie Merritt, Wallace-Rose Hill High*
  School, Teachey, North Carolina

Editor's Note: If you have an independent book dealer in your area, you might ask if the dealer would let you select a multitude of books to bring into the library. Using this same concept, hold an "ordering book fair." Instructors who spot books that fit into their curriculum put a sticky note, with their name, on the book. When the fair is over, gather those with notes stuck on them and double-check your collection to help prioritize your final selections. Send back the books you don't wish to order and put in a purchase order for those you have put on your final selection list. smc

Bookmarks for Library Week

For National Library Week in April, we ran a bookmark art contest. The art teachers and our library staff judged the entries based on neatness, originality, and adherence to the specified shape and size. A winner was chosen for each grade, and the school print shop printed the winning designs on several bright colors of cover stock. The reverse side of the bookmarks listed next year's nominees for the Oklahoma Sequoyah young adult book award. Winners received a printed copy of their bookmark and a paperback of their choice.

— *Shirley Fitzpatrick, Ernest Childers Middle*
  School, Broken Arrow, Oklahoma

Brochure for New Students

Because our school is located in a rapidly growing area, dozens of new students enroll during the year. We created a brochure highlighting media center services and policies and an application form for a library card. The guidance office gives the brochure to new students as they register.

— *Barbara Weekley, Dacula (Georgia) High*
  School

Brown Baggers

To remedy the problem of our junior high students not coming into the library, we started a series of brown bag programs. Up to 25 students sign up to bring bag lunches to the library for each one-hour program. We have scheduled presentations on make-up and skin care, gun safety, and holiday crafts. For each program, we display appropriate books and pass out bibliographies. These brown bag lunch programs have made a real difference in the number of students who use the library.

— *Angela Eichhorn, Penderlea School, Willard,*
  North Carolina

Cake Walk for Books

At our school's fall festival, the library held a "cake walk" for books. Participants walked around 10 numbered chairs while music was played. When the music stopped, the players sat down and we drew a number from one to ten. The player whose number was drawn chose a book. We used free books from our book fair.

— *Sue Welch, Jane Long Middle School, Bryan, Texas*

Canned Food for Fines

To observe Canned Food Month in February, we sponsored a food drive in the library. The theme was "Have a Heart." I drew two large hearts on the carpet in chalk-one for the seventh grade and one for the eighth. Cans were used to outline the hearts and then to fill them. On a designated day, students could use cans of food to pay library fines of up to 50 cents. Competition between the grades helped to spur the collection. By the end of the month, we had collected hundreds of cans of food.

— *Patty Barr, Roosevelt Middle School, Decatur, Illinois*

Card Play

When our computerized system replaced the old card catalog, we generated some publicity and interest with a contest involving the old catalog cards. Library aides dumped drawers of cards in a corner while the school television crew filmed the event. We offered a magazine subscription to the closest guess at the number of cards. Cleanup was a project of the Ecology Club.

— *Gail A. Grill, Garden Spot High School, New Holland, Pennsylvania*

Celebrate Technology!

Celebrate your successes and showcase technology. Parent and community groups will become more supportive of technology budgets if they experience what the money obtains. Once a month, schedule a parents' or visitors' day in the classroom or library media center and have students ready to demonstrate the use of reference CD-ROMs, video cameras, Internet searches, and other technology being used in the school. For special activities, schedule more elaborate celebrations. Once our school's Web site was completed, we held the "Web Site Celebration." Among those invited were our state senators, school board members, administrators, and parents. We also put a notice in the newspaper. Classes involved in developing the site hosted during each hour of the day.

— *Sharron L. McElmeel*

Celebrating Dewey

At the beginning of December, I send out formal invitations for patrons to stop by the periodical desk for a peppermint patty in celebration of the birth of Melvil Dewey, December 10, 1851. My invitation includes this P.S.: "Those who correctly identify this unsung hero will receive two patties."

— *Lucy Ann Glover, E. A. Laney High School, Wilmington, North Carolina*

Celebrating School Library Media Month

To celebrate School Library Media Month (with no budget), we asked faculty members to share special talents, trips, hobbies, and collections with students in the library. The response was amazing! We had slide presentations from teachers who had traveled to Africa and the Far East, booktalks on the latest nonfiction about Vietnam, "Getting

Hooked on Books" discussions by our physical education teachers, and play readings by students and faculty members. A marquee-like bulletin board was set up near the library's entrance to announce "Faculty Features," and daily announcements were made over the PA system. Some teachers brought their classes in to hear the presentations, and many students arranged their lunch and free time around our schedule. Each presenting teacher received a certificate of appreciation for their efforts.

— *Tally Negroni, Stamford (Connecticut) High School*

Cheat Sheet for New Teachers

At the library orientation for new teachers, we hand out photocopies of pages from the most recent yearbook with photos of the faculty and staff. Because the newly hired teachers have so many new names to remember, they appreciate this gesture.

— *Peggy Fleming, Churchville-Chili Senior High School, Churchville, New York*

Christmas Book Fairs

When I first decided to try a high school book fair, I had difficulty finding a company that offered a good high school collection. Then when the books arrived, the company sent elementary books by mistake. Since the fair was scheduled the first week of December, we decided to keep those books and have the company quickly send the high school books. Our students bought presents for younger brothers and sisters, and teachers found great stocking stuffers for their younger children. Now, all our book fairs offer materials for all ages, and each fair is very successful. I think the key is to have the fair just before Christmas.

— *Pamela K. Childers, East Rutherford High School, Forest City, North Carolina*

Clip Art Calendars

Students enjoy making monthly calendars decorated with clip art. (I use THE BOOK REPORT'S Instant Art packages.) Students add birthdays, events, and observances by researching Chase's Annual Events. For example, on our May calendar page, we added National Be Kind to Animals Week, Visit Your Relatives Day, and Debra Winger's birthday.

— *Carol Smallwood, Pellston (Michigan) Public Schools*

College Video Collection

When we decided to build our college video-tape collection, we did some research to target our requests. The guidance counselor provided a list of all the colleges from which our students graduated. We asked those colleges for their free 10- to 20-minute promotional videotapes. Since I was able to say that our students had attended their particular school, response was terrific. Tapes are especially popular on weekends when both the student and their parents can see their prospective schools.

— *Lora Dixon, St. Pius X High School, Festus, Missouri*

Common Vision

For media specialists or technology coordinators, the best place to start expanding program ownership is with your building principal. Shared annual goals are the quickest and easiest way to create common visions and expectations between you and your boss. In our district, I schedule two meetings a year with individual media specialists and their principals. For the first 20-minute meeting in the fall, I ask the media specialists and principals each to bring a list of three things they would like to accomplish in the media center in the coming year. During the meeting, we establish three common goals. Progress on these goals forms the basis for the spring meeting. It is important to remember that by paying serious attention to our administrators' goals and finding ways to help meet them, we are improving the total school environment and strengthening our role within it.

— *Doug Johnson, Mankato (Minnesota) Public Schools*

Community Service from the Library

Our middle school library aides not only help shelve books and dust shelves but also work to promote reading throughout the community. So far, they have:

1. Donated children's books to doctors' waiting rooms and the pediatric wing of the hospital
2. Sent books to new babies born in the local hospital. A letter to parents explaining the importance of reading to young children was included.
3. Purchased magazine subscriptions for two nursing homes
4. Adopted senior citizens at a local nursing home. In addition to reading to them, the aides organized games and parties.
5. Sponsored monthly library contests, including a Book Exchange, Favorite Book Contest, and Stump the Librarian
6. Gave prizes to the student from each grade who read the most books
7. Wrote to 150 celebrities and politicians asking for words to encourage students to read more. The responses, which were displayed then kept in a scrapbook, have come from a wide variety of people— Oprah, Judy Blume, Willard Scott, and Presidents Clinton, Bush, Reagan, Carter, and Ford.

— *Donna Wilson Brown, Hammonton (New Jersey) Middle School*

Create Video Keepsakes

Here's a project students will love: Buy a videotape transfer box and help them videotape pictures from their family albums. To give each tape individual flair, allow each student to create or choose the computer graphics that introduce his or her tape. Students will be proud of their efforts, and parents will be pleased with the results.

— *Patti Smith, Howard Middle School, Orlando, Florida*

Creativity Center

With seasonal rubber stamps, colored stamp pads, and a variety of papers, we set up workstations at which students can make greeting cards and bookmarks. The paper is donated by a local paper supply company. Print shops could also be a source of paper. Teachers have also discovered our paper supply and use the papers of various colors, textures, and weights in their classrooms. Students have a great time making cards for their friends and families. The stations also attract many teachers and students to the library.

— *Susan Wright-Miller, Valleywood Middle School, Grand Rapids, Michigan*

Discard *DISCARD*

Some libraries stamp weeded books with the word *DISCARD*, and this can be bad PR. Budgets are tight, so administrators, parents, and trustees may find it paradoxical that we "discard" books and then ask for money to buy more. A less wasteful-sounding term is *WITHDRAWN*, which indicates that an outdated book has been carefully evaluated. It's amazing how much the term we use reflects on our images as stewards of public funds.

— *Ron McCracken, Sutton (Ontario) District High School, Canada*

Discarding Back Issues

During the last week of school, we discard magazines that are eight years old. Instead of putting them in the recycling bin, we pile the magazines on several library tables and invite the teachers and students to take them.

— *Edna Boardman, Minot (North Dakota) High School, Magic City Campus*

Faculty Paperback Collection

We recently had a large donation of paperback books to our school resource center. Many of them were not suitable for our collection, so we put them on a shelf in the faculty room where the teachers meet daily to work or to eat lunch. For the convenience of the staff, the books do not need to be officially checked out. The collection has been very popular, and the teachers have since brought in additional paperbacks to share.

— *Barbara Cucciarre, Magnificat High School, Rocky Rivet, Ohio*

Faculty Playday Starts the Year Off Right

On the Wednesday before school begins each fall, I open the high school library for a three-hour "faculty playday" and invite teachers to preview new materials and equipment. It's also a time for teachers to use the laminator, to get bulletin board paper, to check out overhead projectors, and to visit with one another.

— *Joellen G. Cullison, Deer Park Senior High School, South Campus, Pasadena, Texas*

Faculty Tapes

Classic books on tape are a favorite with our faculty, who like to listen to them while driving. Tapes are particularly popular with the hunters and fishers on the staff—favorite author: Jack London.

— *Karen Sebesta, Highlands High School, San Antonio, Texas*

Family Night in the Computer Lab

Our middle school library hosts several contests each year, and it was becoming difficult to find enticing low-cost prizes for the winners. Then we came up with the idea of making "Family Night in the Computer Lab" the prize for the top three winners. Hosted by our student library aides and the librarian, this prize has proven to be a big draw to the contests. The family nights themselves have been very successful. Our satisfied family members have ranged in age from 4 to 64. Some family members are familiar with computers, but many have never touched one before.

— *Connie Quirk, Brookings (South Dakota) Middle School*

Famous Author Portraits

For National Library Week, I found portraits of 15 famous authors and poets and arranged them on a display with a clue beneath each portrait. Teachers and students then were challenged to identify them. Some students spent all week during their study hall time looking through reference books to find the answers. Teachers were surprised by how few of these famous authors they could identify with their pictures. Prizes were awarded to students who found the correct answers and to those who were diligent enough to enter.

— *Jane A. Morner, Edison High School, Milan, Ohio*

Final Exam Party for Teachers

During finals week our library sponsors a "Marking Party" that begins when the students leave the school at mid-day. Teachers are invited to bring their papers to the library, where we serve coffee, tea, and cake and have mellow music playing. The Scantron machine is brought out to the library floor, and teachers are invited to take breaks to browse through our new books and "play around" with our databases.

— *Joyce Valenza, Wissahickon School District, Ambler, Pennsylvania*

Final Exam Party for Students

During final exams we offer an "Exam Coffee Break," which is scheduled during the 30-minute break between the two-hour exam periods. The library staff offers coffee and tea in a garden area across from the library. We have about 500 students, but not all join us. We purchase the drinks from the cafeteria, and their staff makes sure everything is hot and ready to go.

— *Bev Oliver, Indian Hill High School, Cincinnati, Ohio*

For Coupon Clippers

To lure teachers into the library to look over new books and materials, I create a "coupon" that appears in my monthly faculty newsletter. Coupons are good for food that will be available in the library workroom on a certain day. New library materials are then arranged invitingly next to the goody table so that teachers can look them over while they snack.

— *Thelma Seevers, Blair (Nebraska) Community High School*

Freebie Rack

Browsers in our high school library are drawn to the bookrack on the floor near the main circulation desk. Almost accidentally, I began to display free publications such as *Pet Press* and the classified ad sheets distributed weekly at the grocery store. I've added newspaper voters' guides or inserts such as bridal fair guides or time schedules for the Olympics. I also display magazines from local industries and colleges. The rack makes a lively display that is popular with students and staff.

— *Joellen G. Cullison, Deer Park Senior High School, South Campus, Pasadena, Texas*

Friend in an Emergency

From overdue fines, I maintain a box of supplies for student use. There, students can find scissors, rulers, and staplers for use in projects and an emergency supply of index cards, notebook paper, and cough drops. The cost is minimal for the amount of family spirit and goodwill the box generates.

— *Sister Marjorie Stumpf, St. Savior High School, Brooklyn, New York*

Games in the Teachers' Lunchroom

When we purchased "Photosearch," a set of pictures to be used for library research, we had so much fun trying to guess where and when the photos were taken that I took them to the lunchroom with me. The teachers enjoyed the photos, and someone jokingly remarked that every Wednesday should be game day. The next Wednesday, I took in "GeoSafari," which had been sitting around unused for months. Not only did the teachers have a game to play, but they discovered a new classroom aid, which several used that week. Now we are searching through our professional resources, audiovisuals, and computer software to continue game day in hopes that teachers will discover all the things we have in the library to make their jobs easier.

— *Susan Deardorff, Kankakee Valley Middle School, Wheatfield, Indiana*

Get Golf Pencils

Pencils were always in high demand but short supply in our library. Our inexpensive solution to this problem was to purchase "golf" pencils, which cost a dollar or two per box of 144. For a small fee, we can also get some good PR by having the school and library's name imprinted on the pencils.

— *Linda Cook, Cape Cod Academy, Osterville, Massachusetts*

Getting Them into the Library

To draw more attention to the library and its materials, we plan a week of high-interest activities rather than the everyday book fair or display. We invite music groups, hair designers, cosmeticians, artists, weavers, historians, and others whom students enjoy hearing. Such activities attract students who would not normally come to the library. We also set up a book display relevant to the subject being presented.

— *Sharon Newman, Rowan County Senior High School, Morehead, Kentucky*

Happy Birthday from the Library

To make the library a friendlier place, we distribute birthday treat packages to students who stop by on their birthdays. Using tin foil and colored plastic wrap, we make a package filled with wrapped candy that we buy half price after major holidays. Coming out of the top is a lollipop, colorful bookmark, and a

pencil with the school's name on it. We tie this up with curlicue ribbon and attach a personalized birthday card we designed using Print Shop. We announce the birthday treats several times during the year and have signs scattered around the school that read, "Stop by the library on your birthday for a special treat." When students come in, we have them sign the "Birthday Book." Even sophisticated high school students seem to enjoy the special attention.

— *Audrey Dunn, McArthur High School, Hollywood, Florida*

Happy Birthday to Our Network

When our computer network system turned one year old, we celebrated. We tied helium balloons to the computer stations and printed signs saying "Happy Birthday to Our Great Automation System." We also baked cupcakes for the faculty and staff and put a single birthday candle on each. The celebration focused recognition on our technology and showed everyone how proud we were of what we had achieved. Easy to organize, the day proved a big success.

— *Elisa Baker, Ursuline High School, Santa Rosa, California*

Holiday Fines

To pay a library fine before Thanksgiving or Christmas, students may bring a can of food. The collected cans are then taken to the city food bank. Students feel better about paying fines when they are also helping others.

— *Elizabeth Gunthorp, John Marshall High School, San Antonio, Texas*

Host an Internet Party

To promote the library media center and increase your list of curriculum-related Web sites, host an Internet party. As an admission ticket, have faculty members bring an index or Rolodex card that contains the Internet address of a curriculum-related Web site. Ask faculty members to include a brief description and suggestions for using the links on the Web site. Put the cards in a file for future reference. Serve refreshments and use the party to introduce the staff to the library's resources. At the end of the party, randomly select one of the Web site cards and present a door prize to the lucky contributor.

— *Andrea Troisi, LaSalle Middle School, Niagara Falls, New York*

In-House Bookmarks

Students in our junior high school prefer our library's unique bookmarks over the purchased kind. I enjoy designing bookmarks, but I also hold contests. Students are asked to make two versions of their bookmark design—one in color for display and judging and a black & white version for reproduction on our copy machine. We usually select a first, second, and third place as well as three honorable mentions from the colored designs. The reproducible versions of the winners are copied onto colored construction paper and made available at the check-out desk. Students like them so much, they take one of each design.

— *Linda Entrican, Ocean Springs (Mississippi) Junior High School*

Installation Information Helps Families

When students share the exciting news that their families are purchasing home computers, we give them copies of home computer installation articles and a form on which to list essential information, such as RAM capacity and memory size. We advise them to keep the completed fact sheets beside their computers for future reference. We also provide "how-to" information for new Internet users.

— *Janet Hofstetter, California (Missouri) High School*

Login Screens Feature Students' Designs

My students use IBM's *LinkWay* software to design login screens for our network. Using *LinkWay Paint*, the graphics program, they can create simple, colorful pictures with holiday greetings or reminders of special school events. I copy their work to a disk and then transfer them to our network using the "Update Login Screen" part of the sysop menu. It's a wonderful way to encourage creativity and build self-esteem, and the whole school enjoys the unique screens.

— *Beverly Sangermano, Quarry Hill Community School, Monson, Massachusetts*

Editor's Note: Even the youngest of elementary students can create graphics to be used as screen wallpaper. Macintosh users may wish to investigate a simple but very useful program Color It!™ *from Microfrontier. Visit their Website at <www.microfrontier.com>. smc*

Internet Training

We offered Internet training sessions during teachers' prep periods and after school. Faculty members signed up in advance for the basic introduction to online searching techniques. We then designed a certificate, signed by the principal and the librarian, for each participant. I was amazed at how happy people were to receive the certificates. Many have framed or posted the certificates in their offices or classrooms.

— *Elisa Baker, Ursuline High School, Santa Rosa, California*

Introducing New Teachers to the Library

To introduce ourselves to new teachers, we host a reception at the beginning of each school year. We share refreshments, tour the media center, and give each teacher a folder containing the media handbook, a supply of media center passes, and a bibliography of the videotapes in their subject area. We hope that teachers will add our monthly newsletter and other media information as they receive it.

— *Sheila Tanner, Dacula (Georgia) High School*

It's Textbook Woman!

When I came to our 1,200-student junior high, I found I was responsible for textbooks as well as the library materials. We have a 60% mobility rate, so "reading the rules" at the beginning of the year just didn't do much good. I wanted a fun way to remind students of the responsibilities that come with those expensive textbooks. The answer? "It's a bird, it's a plane, it's TEXTBOOK WOMAN!!!" TW, in appropriate costume complete with a famous red cape, visits our homerooms occasionally to reward students who have their textbooks covered, and she prints funny but pointed announcements once a week in our bulletin. Even though I don't like the idea of a librarian being responsible for textbooks, the TW gimmick has paid off in many ways. Students at junior high age love the corniness of the

character and have even drawn TW cartoons for the school newspaper. Textbook loss and damage have decreased markedly. Maybe your library needs a local super hero—and you too could have a staff member say, "I had no idea a librarian could be such fun!"

— *Lynn Shoff, Roosevelt Junior High, San Diego, California*

It's Time to Choose Careers & Colleges

During eighth-grade orientation, students are first introduced to books and software that can help them choose careers and colleges and find scholarships. When they reach their senior year, we have a brochure titled "Calling All Seniors" and illustrated with a clock reminding them "It's time to check out the career and college materials." We have been pleased by the number of students who respond to the brochure by coming to the media center.

— *Terri Morrel, Mitchell-Baker High School, Camilla, Georgia*

Library = Contest Clearinghouse

The school library is the perfect place for housing information on contests. In addition to my normal duties, I serve as the contest coordinator for our school (enrollment 350) and see that students and faculty are aware of contests, rules, and deadlines. Positive results stemming from these extra efforts include more interaction with faculty members, an increased circulation of materials related to competition topics, and many winners. Last year our students won nearly $2,000 worth of prize money and garnered positive publicity for our school.

— *Janice Deans, Father Lopez High School, Daytona Beach, Florida*

Library Announcements

I often send in items to be read on the announcements that are broadcast on the public address system each morning. I focus on new books, magazine articles, or newspaper items that might be of interest to students. Often, I make the announcement humorous or use vocabulary words that might be unfamiliar. Keeps students thinking about the media center.

— *Ed Nizalowski, Newark Valley, New York*

Library Brochure

Create interest in your library program by promoting it with an inexpensive two-fold brochure. You don't even need to buy a typesetting program. Many word processing programs will allow printing horizontally (landscape format) and in three equal columns. Once those selections are made, you will have created a template.

Your brochure will have four to five divisions for information printed front-to-back. Fold a piece of paper into thirds to study the layout. The first third is the title page. It will actually be the third column on the first page. You may want to include your name, names of assistants, library name, logo, school and district name, hours, address, and phone number.

Inside the pamphlet, use bold headings and bulleted short phrases to target key facts. Included here might be yearly statistics, available print and nonprint materials, check-out procedures, fines, special programs, author visits, book fairs, and new technology. You can purchase special brochure paper from office supply companies or use regular copy paper. Fluorescent colors, clip art, and graphics will make your product stand out.

— *Debbie Collier, Orange Grove Elementary School, Houston, Texas*

Library Fashions for Fall

At the teachers' meeting the day before school begins, the adult library aides model "library fashions": the Laminated Look (the model is wrapped in laminating film and we read the rules for laminating); the AV Look (the model is wrapped in extension cords, adapters, and plastic equipment covers while we explain the use and care of equipment); the Copyright Look (the model wears a prison uniform and handcuffs borrowed from the police force while we discuss copyright laws and illegal taping); and the Overdue Look (the model has taped overdue notices to a dress, and we present overdue policies). I end with humorous booktalks for titles that seem to match faculty members. This last year I recommended *The Frog Princess* to the science teacher who teaches dissection, *The Royal Wedding* to a teacher getting married, and *The Working Mother* to a teacher back from maternity leave.

— *Karen Hildebrand, Willis Intermediate School, Delaware, Ohio*

Library Outreach

Presenting library materials at club meetings can be a successful form of outreach. Many students do not realize that the library has materials for something other than term papers. At a meeting of a support group for minorities in our school, I showed books and magazines featuring celebrities from minority groups and described services for all students in the library. I brought books of poems and on poetry writing to the Poetry Club.

— *Laura J. Viau, McQuaid Jesuit High School, Rochester, New York*

Library PR through the Year

Here are some ideas I use to promote public relations all year long:

▶ Host department meetings during our workweek before school starts in the fall.

▶ Provide new teacher orientation.

▶ Set up a Parent Library Volunteer program.

▶ Attend monthly department meetings to encourage teachers to give suggestions on how the library can serve them better.

▶ Submit articles to the PTA newsletter and school district newsletter about happenings in the library.

▶ Prepare regular reports for the school principal and faculty.

▶ Work with the public library. I make sure that all sixth graders in our school have a public library card, and we take the whole sixth grade to the public library in November. I also encourage all students to become involved in the summer reading program at the public library.

▶ Ask teachers to bring toys from their childhood to display in December.

▶ Invite local celebrities to come in to the library to speak on how reading has been important in their lives. Our "celebrities" have included the superintendent, school board members, the mayor, city council members, ministers, and parents.

▶ Have a National Library Week Tea for faculty and staff.

— *Libby Cooper, John Sevier Middle School, Kingsport, Tennessee*

Library-Supplied Bags for Open House

At the annual school open house, I gave parents a plastic bag for carrying the handouts they received from teachers. A local book-store donated the attractive bags. The parents appreciate the gesture, and the library gained from good PR.

— *Peggy Fleming, Churchville-Chili High School, Churchville, New York*

Limelight on Library Patrons

Once a year, our Student of the Month recognition takes a bookish turn. I recognize a range of interests and abilities by selecting about 20 Library Students of the Month in these categories: Library User and Reader, Most Improved Library User, and Computer Whiz. The seventh and eighth graders receive a small pin, a fast-food restaurant coupon, and have their photos displayed in the school's main lobby. Later, Library Students of the Month and their parents are treated to an ice cream sundae party.

— *Diane C. Pozar, Wallkill (New York) Middle School*

Little-Known Facts about Your Teachers

To help high school students get to know their teachers, I put this request in teachers' mailboxes: "Please give a statement that shares something about you that the students and faculty don't know and would find interesting." I set a return date and got some wonderful and funny facts back. The facts were used in a display that asked, "How well do you know your teachers?" On one side, the teacher's names were numbered and on the other side, the statements were identified with letters. Students were to match numbers and letters.

— *Marilyn Yaggy, Pope High School, Marietta, Georgia*

Editor's Note: This idea would make a popular display in the library media center or article in the school newspaper. smc

Lounge Branch

Since it's not always convenient for teachers to come to the library to look at professional materials, we decided to go to the teachers. Our "Lounge Branch" consists of a single bookcase located in the teachers' lounge. A limited number of professional books and magazines are prominently displayed; the collection is changed monthly. Staff members check out the materials on their own. Teachers have been responsive, and professional materials are where they should be—in the hands of the teachers!

— *Barbara Britton, Malabar Middle School, Mansfield, Ohio*

Lunch in the Library

Students enjoy eating their cafeteria or brown-bag lunch in the library while listening to a guest speaker. Visitors have included a lawyer, a weight lifter, a live snake presentation, skateboard and surfing enthusiasts, a doll collector, craft demonstrations, and Topper, a drug-sniffing dog. Community members have been generous with their time, and students are enthusiastic. If too many students sign up for one lunch, we draw names, then maintain a list so everyone gets an opportunity to participate.

— *Elaine Smith, Hanahan (South Carolina) Middle School*

Lunch Time Learning

"Lunch in the Library" is a lunch time program to attract students who might not otherwise choose to come to the library. We feature topics and speakers of interest to teenagers. For example, after a local teenage girl was kidnapped, a deputy sheriff spoke on personal safety for young women. A recent program focused on finances and financial planning for teenagers.

— *Annette Thibodeaux, Archbishop Chapelle High School, Metairie, Louisiana*

Memories Are Made of This

Want to do something special for a departing colleague? All you need is a grapevine wreath and a spool of narrow ribbon. In advance, ask each attendee to bring a small object and to be prepared to relate it to an anecdote about the honoree. As guests share their anecdotes, give each a length of ribbon to tie his or her object onto the wreath. After everyone has spoken, the departing colleague will have a wreath full of wonderful memories to take home.

— *Carol Burbridge, Jardine Middle School, Topeka, Kansas*

Monthly Happenings Calendar

I use *Chase's Annual Events* and THE BOOK REPORT Library Planning Calendar to generate posters of important events and birthdays. I call these posters "Monthly Happenings" and liven them up with clip art reproductions. The students and staff seem to enjoy reading these each month.

— *Karen Zapasnik, Deerfield Beach (Florida) High School*

Monthly Workshops Promote Technology

Many teachers are unfamiliar with videodiscs, CD-ROM discs, and multimedia presentations. Media and technology specialists can work together to provide monthly workshops to show teachers what these technologies are, why they are useful, and how they can be incorporated into exciting, dynamic lessons for students.

— *Tia Esposito, Epiphany School, Miami, Florida*

Morning Wisdom

Most schools have morning announcements whether they are presented in a video format, read on the intercom, or distributed on a printed bulletin for teachers to read. Our library has started to provide a "Thought for the Day" at the end of our announcements, so I have been collecting quotable quotes, especially from current figures. Here are a couple: "Kind words can be short and easy to speak, but their echoes are truly endless." –Mother Theresa. "You're never a loser until you quit trying." –Mike Ditka.

— *Marsha Kibbey, Wilson Middle School, Wyandotte, Michigan*

New Books for Newborns

Our Student Council raised money to purchase a new book for each baby born in our community during Book Week. A local paper company donated baby-wrapping paper. Each new parent also received a tip sheet on the importance of reading to young children. This project was a positive PR move for our school and made students more aware of community concerns and the importance of reading.

— *Pat Milheiser, Madison Junior High, Appleton, Wisconsin*

Newsletter Gets the Word Out

Periodically (and irregularly), I send a one-page Notes from the Media Center newsletter to faculty to tell them about new software, CD-ROMs, and recently discovered Internet sites of interest. I write a brief description of each and intentionally avoid categorizing by subject area so that all teachers read each description. The newsletter always draws responses from people asking for more information or for a demonstration.

— *Shelley Glantz, Arlington (Massachusetts) High School*

Newsletter Ideas

The monthly newsletter I distribute actually collects itself in a pocket folder I keep on my desk. I include technology tidbits, announce new materials, and list upcoming PBS shows that support our curriculum. I particularly enjoy writing "teacher bouquets" that spotlight units being taught in the library. The newsletter is always so full that I have items to save for the next issue.

— *Joellen G. Cullison, Deer Park Senior High School, South Campus, Pasadena, Texas*

Nourish the Body and the Mind

Books supply food for thought, but they don't fill growling tummies. Our media center does three things to make coming to see us a treat—literally! First, we keep a supply of red licorice and other goodies to share in our textbook workroom. Second, we sponsor a "bread day" each year when our staff shares their baked goods and recipes. Finally, we compiled a Christmas cookbook, "Seasoned Greetings," of recipes and cooking hints based on food brought to our holiday potluck.

— *Media Staff, Wangenheim Middle School, San Diego, California*

Open House for OPAC

To celebrate our new online catalog, we held an open house in the library media center for faculty, central administration, public librarians, and school committees. We draped the card catalog in black crepe paper and put an RIP (rest in peace) sign on it. In addition to refreshments, everyone received a personalized remembrance-an appropriate card from the old catalog. A few of the faculty members are authors and were thrilled to get their catalog card. Others received a card for a favorite book or a subject card related to their teaching area.

— *Shelley Glantz, Arlington (Massachusetts) High School*

Editor's Note: If you are already automated, don't dismiss this celebration idea. Celebrate the online catalog's "anniversary" or celebrate a new upgrade in your computer system. Any excuse to showcase technology in your school will pay dividends in community support. smc

Overdue Book Rap

I was amazed at the positive response I got from a little piece of bad poetry. Kids stopped me in the hall and asked me to "do your rap":

> Well, my dear,
> It's that time of the year
> When "Library books are due," we hear.
> Day in, day out,
> Ms. Tope will shout,
> "Bring back your book, magazine, &
>   pamphlet,
> whatever it's about.
> Clean out your locker, your car, & your
>   room,
> Get that stuff back here soon!"
> May 18th is the final due date.
> Return those books. Don't wait."

I can't promise it will get your books in any faster, but it was a lot more fun than the usual end-of-the-year announcement to return library books "or else."

— *Barbara C. Tope, Madison Plains Schools, London, Ohio*

Overdue Coupons

I am always looking for ways to maintain good PR with the teachers in my school. This year when teachers attended my staff development session, I presented them with "official library coupons," ranging in value from 10 to 50 cents, for the teachers to give to their students to pay library fines. Each time a teacher participated in any way during the workshop, they received additional coupons. The workshop was a lot of fun, with everyone competing to get the most coupons. I was able to reward the teachers, and they in turn could reward their students. An added benefit for me was that a lot of overdue fines were cleared.

— *Wanda White, Pascagoula (Mississippi) High School*

Overdue Help from Teachers

We send weekly overdue notices to students through their English teachers. On weeks when a teacher has no students on the fine list, we reward the teacher by putting a small treat (candy bar, cookies) in his or her mailbox with a thank-you note. This has really motivated our teachers to encourage students to take care of fines and overdue books.

— *Elizabeth Deer, Pearl (Mississippi) High School*

Personalized Introduction to New E-mail Users

E-mail was new to our staff this fall. Before teachers attended a required workshop, I sent a message to every person who would have a local address. Writing 40-plus messages would have taken too much time. Instead, I e-mailed a message to myself. Then I replied to the message but changed the addressee and added a personal salutation. Occasionally I wrote an extra sentence about something new in the library. The teachers were surprised to discover a personal message already in their mailboxes when they practiced their skills in the workshop.

I also e-mail myself as a test occasionally to check how my e-mail address looks. I've been sent too many messages with addresses that needed corrections or had missing parts, so I check mine for peace of mind.

— *Janet Hofstetter, California (Missouri) High School*

Plasticized PR

The laminator can be a wonderful public relations tool. In our school, students come into the library to ask the staff to laminate personal items to hang in their lockers as well as school-related art projects and visuals for their oral reports.

— *Rosemary Sackleh, Lexington (Kentucky) Catholic High School*

PR and Morning Announcements

During Computer Learning Month in October, I place a computer word and its definition each day on the school's daily attendance and announcement sheet. In addition, during the daily television announcements, a student provides the word and its definition. It's great PR for the library.

— *Patricia Kolencik, North Clarion High School, Tionesta, Pennsylvania*

PR at the Mailbox

At the end of semester, I decorate the mailboxes of teachers who brought classes to the library or took books to the classroom. Sometimes I add a candy bar with a short thank-you note. I've used bows, ribbon, and even Christmas garland for decorations.

— *Rosemary Sackleh, Lexington (Kentucky) Catholic High School*

Preserving Masters

When photocopying, it's easy to mix the original in with the copies until eventually you are copying a copy of a copy of a copy. To flag my master forms and keep them in mint condition, I laminate them. This also prevents me from accidentally filling out the master form, only to find later that I have no blank form to make copies.

— *Nancy Keating, Sugar Loaf Union Free School, Chester, New York*

Professional Book Collection

To help teachers who take college courses for professional growth and to build our professional collection at the same time, our library offers to reimburse teachers for textbooks purchased for use in the courses. The following conditions and limitations have been published in our handbook:

▶ Books must be placed in the school library professional collection after the final exam of the course.

▶ Reimbursement will be 100% of the purchase price (not to exceed the published list price).

▶ Requests for reimbursement must be made within 45 days of purchase.

▶ Receipts must be included with the request.

▶ Offer is limited to two books per course per semester per person.

▶ Duplicate titles will be limited to two. It is the teacher's responsibility to check the library collection before purchasing books.

▶ Offer is limited to new textbooks.

▶ Total expenditures cannot exceed the budget allocated.

— *Sandra Johnson, McEachern High School, Powder Springs, Georgia*

Professional Reading Update

Each month as new issues of professional journals arrive, I photocopy the table of contents for each teacher. With a quick glance, they can spot articles of interest that they might otherwise miss. An added plus: teachers come to the library for the journals.

— *Frances Vanish, Southern Middle School, Lusby, Maryland*

Promoting Hard Cover Fiction

Our students prefer paperback books to the hard cover fiction. To promote circulation of hard cover books, I created bookmarks for genres such as mystery, romance, horror, science fiction, and fantasy. One side of the bookmark has a design appropriate to the genre; the other side lists authors of hard cover books in that genre that we have in our collection. These bookmarks are popular, and our circulation of hard cover fiction has increased.

— *Linda Rosendahl, Lynn (Massachusetts) English High School*

Public Library Connections

To help improve communication between the public library and school libraries in our area, the young adult services librarian attends meetings of the secondary school media association. When new editions of Books in Print arrive, she collects copies of the previous edition and distributes them to school libraries that can use them. Be sure to contact your public library to see what connections you can make.

— *Diane Tuccillo, Mesa (Arizona) Public Library*

Publishing Brochures

Often students want to make a three-column flier. But while formatting is easy with *PageMaker* or *Microsoft Publisher*, it's time consuming to teach these programs to students. There is a simple solution: Set up *Microsoft Works*, or a similar program, with columns suitable for brochures. Here are the directions for *Microsoft Works*:

1. Open program.
2. Select new document.
3. Select format; then select columns. (Type three columns with a half inch between.)
4. Go to Page Setup in the File Menu to adjust the margins and paper orientation. (These measurements work well: 0.5 for top and bottom, 0.25 for right and left. Choose landscape from Page Setup.)
5. Select location for pictures.
6. Select Clip Art from the Insert Menu. Choose picture and press Insert.
7. Go to Format and select Picture/Object if you want to use the Text Wrap feature.

— *Kathy Sells, Lincoln High School, Ypsilanti, Michigan*

Quick Response

Even though you may not be the district level person responsible for repair and maintenance, it seems inevitable that you will be called for low-level, spur-of-the-moment trouble shooting. These are often of the "Help! My program just locked up" or "The printer has gone berserk" variety and are delivered by a student. Just as often, you cannot leave the media center. However, it is important to respond. A short note, sent back with the student, should include the time you can check on the problem and a brief instruction or stop-gap measure for the teacher to try. Be sure to follow up on the situation at the time you indicated. This may save both you and the teacher frustration later.

— *Sandy Pope, South Elementary School, Eldon, Missouri*

Reading Motivation for Teachers

I keep about 10 new books on a rack in the teachers' lunchroom. The books may be checked out by simply signing the card and leaving it in my mailbox in the office. I include leisure reading as well as curriculum-related books. This has proven popular and brought teachers into the library. Teachers who find themselves alone in the lunchroom appreciate a book to read.

— *Laura J. Viau, McQuaid Jesuit High School, Rochester, New York*

Recognizing Library Aides

Just before our spring Open House, we take photos of each of our student library aides and ask each of them to write a brief biography. The photos and writings are arranged on a bulletin board at the entrance to the media center, where it makes a big hit with visiting parents and friends.

— *Jean Litchfield, Wangenheim Junior High School, San Diego, California*

Recycling Outdated CD-ROMs

In addition to our popular Stump the Librarian Contest and Amnesty Day during National Library Week, we held a daily drawing for outdated CD-ROM encyclopedias. Teachers were happy to win a CD-ROM for their classroom computers.

— *Bobbie Zimmerman, Bill Reed Middle School, Loveland, Colorado*

Reviewer/Media Celebrity

The TOM magazine indexing system (Information Access) indexes the names of reviewers as well as titles and authors of books reviewed. A student typed my name on the computer and found me listed as a reviewer in this magazine. He called his friends over to see the screen. "If you can get published in THE BOOK REPORT, what are you doing teaching in a little school like this?" one student asked. I explained it was all in a day's work, but the students are impressed. They enjoy looking me up on the computer and noting the books I've reviewed.

— *Robert L. Otte, South Christian High School, Grand Rapids, Michigan*

Saving Time Online

The daily volume of e-mail from LM_NET had me ready to unsubscribe until I decided to read only the first line of messages. If the first line sparks my interest, I scan further. If the message would be of interest to one of my colleagues, I forward the message with a personal note. Since local e-mail is set up for departments to receive the same message, I can forward a message to an entire department in the time it takes to forward one message. Several of our teachers have made some interesting contacts. And, getting some mail is exciting for those teachers who have not found a good listserv yet.

— *Janet Hofstetter, California (Missouri) High School*

School & Public Library Cooperation

We find the biggest deterrent to students using the public library is the lack of a borrower's card, so we make it painless for them to get cards. Each September, with the blessings of our public librarians, I visit the ninth-grade classes with library card application forms. I deliver the completed forms to the public library and after they are processed, I pick the cards up for the social studies teachers to distribute. One girl filled out a form despite current fines of about $20 in lost book charges. The public library's computer caught this, and the girl's class ran a "Free the Books" bake sale that paid for her fine. Our efforts are also seen in the year's first newsletter to parents. Our superintendent proclaims September "Library Card Month" and encourages parents to get their children cards and take them to the library. We are now planning to print the public library's hours in our school district calendar.

— *Carolyn Gierke, Sweet Home Central High School, Amherst, New York*

School and Public Library Cooperation

Once every two months, a committee of librarians from our school district's 18 elementary, middle, and high schools meets with a group of staff members from our town's public library. The public librarians inform us of their activities and summarize public library use by students from the schools. We in turn try to give them advance notice of school assignments before hundreds of students inundate the public library for additional sources. Our public library has also established a dial-up access system that provides a shared database with several local public libraries. This has been made available to our schools since the collection is available online. The regular meetings have enhanced the relationship between the public and school libraries to the great benefit of the students.

— *Renee Naughton, Walnut Springs Middle School, Westerville, Ohio*

School and Public Library Cooperation

In our community, school and public library cooperation often seems to flow in one direction, from the public library to the schools. We have found a way to repay our public library. Every summer the public library stages a large used-book sale (20,000 to 30,000 books). The school administration provides warehouse storage for the skids of books and the ideal site for the sale itself—the high school cafeteria. Over the years, the library tried different sites, such as tents and garages, but none was truly satisfactory. Since school isn't in session during the summer sale dates, there's ample space for customer parking, many tables for displaying the books, and time for volunteers to sort and price the books. The high school library loans book trucks, spare bookends, ladders, dollies, and other equipment.

— *Mary Hauge, Head Librarian, West Aurora (Illinois) High School*

Scouts to the Rescue

In a new high school library with a limited budget, we have looked for ways to build our collection inexpensively. Donations of books by the community have helped, but some of our largest donations came from the Boy Scout's Eagle troops. We have received hundreds of dollars in cash from fund raisers sponsored by the Eagle Scouts. They also collected books, back issues of magazines, old calendars (used for their pictures), posters, and pamphlets. Follett's *Circulation/Catalog Plus* networked with their MARC records on the *Alliance Plus* CD-ROM made cataloging these donations a breeze.

— *Suzanne Couch, Hunter High School, West Valley City, Utah*

Senior Center

We converted one of the library conference rooms into a "Senior Center," complete with all our college catalogs and videotapes, books on the SAT and ACT, college applications, and books on succeeding in college. The walls are decorated with college pennants and motivational posters. When the center opened, we sent notes to seniors' parents so they could encourage their children to use the room or even come in themselves to check out the materials.

— *Diane Crowe & Virginia Holcombe, Nimitz High School, Houston, Texas*

Sharing Free Offers

I get a lot of "free" subscription CDs for online service companies. I keep the disks and offer them to my faculty, staff, or students who come to me interested in subscribing to an online service company.

— *Dahlia Werner, Rusch Junior High School, Portage, Wisconsin*

Sharing LM_NET Gleanings

When reading LM_NET mail, I find many items that will interest members of our staff or me. I open the word processing program and drop in all the tips or ideas that interest me. Then I print the items and pass many along to the staff. If the item is a long bibliography, I print the bibliography as a separate document.

— *Anitra Gordon, Lincoln High School, Ypsilanti, Michigan*

Something New for Everyone

When I distribute our list of recent acquisitions, I personalize a copy for every staff member by highlighting books or videotapes that relate to their professional or personal interests. This is a time-consuming effort since we have nearly 200 teachers, administrators, and secretaries. The payback in positive PR is more than worth the effort.

— *Kathleen McBroom, Fordson High School, Dearborn, Michigan*

Special Tree

Last spring the library council and the science club collected money to plant a redbud tree on our campus in memory of the victims of the bombing of the federal building in Oklahoma City. The library canceled the end-of-school amnesty week for overdue fines and instead donated the collected fines to the tree purchase.

— *Leigh Ann Jones, Carroll Middle School, Southlake, Texas*

Starry, Starry Night

During National Library Week, we invite our faculty and students to participate in our own version of the "Night of a Thousand Stars." Our aspiring authors are eager to read their original poetry or short stories, and the performance displays our school's talents to the community. Best of all, new patrons come to our library. Be sure to publicize with fliers and announcements in the school bulletin. Another way to arouse interest is to include students on the planning committee for the event.

— *Brenda Watson, North Carolina School of Science and Mathematics, Durham, North Carolina*

Student Clips

When students are recognized in our local newspaper, I clip the photos and articles, attach them to a colorful flier, and send them to the students. Parents have told me how much this meant to their children.

— *Margaret Bird, Garber High School, Essexville, Michigan*

Students 'Pig Out on Books'

To encourage after-school use of the library, I organized a month-long "Pig Out on Books" campaign in conjunction with a restaurant chain and local businesses. To generate interest among our 400 students, I created pig bulletin boards, pig mobiles, and pig bookmarks. I put plush pigs on bookshelves. Also, with no explanation, I slapped pig stickers on students' shirts. Those wearing pig stickers were surprised to receive free ice cream at lunch. Students were then invited to enter one of the following contests: pie-eating, pig trivia, hamburger-eating, or sculpting a pig from ice cream. The prizes were stuffed animals (pigs!) sewed by home economics students; each pig held a $5 bill. At our hilarious grand finale, 50 students worked in pairs to carve 25 gallons of donated ice cream into pig sculptures. No one went away hungry and more important, students learned the library was a fun place to visit.

— *Donna Brown, Hammonton (New Jersey) Middle School*

Summer Reading for Teachers

A few weeks before the end of school, I filled a revolving bookrack with summer reading for teachers. I labeled the display 'Beach Blanket Books' and included mysteries, books by popular novelists, and other light reading. Teachers who did not have time to browse the shelves were able to run in and find several titles within a few minutes. The display was popular with teachers and will be an annual event.

— *Shelley Glantz, Arlington (Massachusetts) High School*

Tea and the Library

For Library Week, I sponsor a faculty/staff tea. I provide coffee, tea, and sweet treats and invite everyone on the staff, including the cafeteria and custodial workers, to stop by after school for the celebration. New books are displayed, and books I plan to discard are available to anyone who wants them.

— *Connie Wright, Southwestern High School, Jamestown, New York*

Teen Advisory Board

In an effort to promote the library to middle school students, our public library started a Young Adult Advisory Board for students' grades 4-8. They meet once a month on a Saturday to create a newsletter for other teens. They also make posters for upcoming library events.

— *Mayre Jo George, Fossil Ridge Public Library, Braidwood, Illinois*

Test Taking in the Library

We encourage teachers to have students take make-up tests in the library. The students leave their completed tests with the library staff, and this leaves no question as to where the tests were taken or with what help. Students with a lot of make-up work are potential dropouts, and we find that this policy brings rare visitors to the library who may benefit from this extra exposure.

— *Eleanor Essman, Wellston High School*

Testing Help for Teachers

After years of being a classroom teacher, I know how difficult it is to schedule students to take make-up tests. But as a new librarian, I was having a problem getting teachers into the library to review the collection, request materials, or discuss the library's involvement in the curriculum. To solve both problems, I offered teachers a test administration service. I have two sets of folders in the library; each teacher has a folder in both sets. When students miss a test, the teacher comes to the library and places the test papers in the "to do" set of folders. Students come in from study hall, and I supervise their taking the make-up test in a restricted area. The finished test goes into the "done" set of folders for teachers to pick up at their convenience. As teachers pop in to drop off or collect tests, I get a chance to discuss library business with them. In addition to helping the teachers and me, students benefit because they can take make-up tests any time without needing to fit into their teacher's schedule.

— *Judy Shockey, Clintwood (Virginia) High School*

Thankful for Overdues

To motivate students to return overdue library books and to help needy families at holiday time, we instituted a new kind of overdue amnesty policy. Instead of paying library fines with money, students are encouraged to bring in cans of food. Posters and daily announcements remind everyone of the overdue book/food drive. Some students even calculated the number of cans needed to equal the fine even though we did not require it.

— *Sandy Barron, Tomball (Texas) High School*

The Remarkable Library

In the Houston area, a grocery chain runs a campaign billing itself as "Your Remarkable Store." Unabashedly, I stole their successful marketing strategy to turn our high school library into "Your Remarkable Library." Our students sing the jingle and constantly refer to the library as "The Remarkable Library." The chairman of the board of the grocery chain responded to my invitation to visit the library. He toured and visited with students and made "The Remarkable Library" seem truly special. Our students and staff believe we are "Remarkable," and we work hard to justify their confidence.

— *Joellen G. Cullison, Deer Park Senior High School, South Campus, Pasadena, Texas*

Trivia for Teachers

Trivia contests are often staged to attract students to library resources. The idea works as well for teachers. For the past two years, we have held a contest for teachers only. Teachers who never used the library came in during their conference period to look for answers. Sometimes their students helped them use the reference materials.

— *Elizabeth Guntharp, John Marshall High School, San Antonio, Texas*

Trivia for Teens

High school students love trivia! Our library continually sponsors trivia contests on topics ranging from music (50s, 60s, 70s) to NCAA basketball. We have an electronic sign that posts the questions. As students provide the correct answer, their names are placed in a drawing for a prize. We give them posters, music certificates, T-shirts, or cans of pop.

— *Marian Sweany, St. Mary's (Kansas) High School*

Weekly Column

To better publicize the library and especially the Internet, I offered to write a weekly column for our school newspaper. Some of the topics have been how to get on board the Internet, how to buy a modem, online services, e-mail, and plagiarism. I also include a Web Site of the Week in each column, and ask students to submit new sites they have discovered for possible publication. Although it is a lot of work, more students have become aware of the library (and the librarian!) and its resources.

— *Elisa Baker, Ursuline High School, Santa Rosa, California*

Welcome Back Bags

As the teachers come back to school in the fall, we have a goody bag ready for each. In addition to the teacher's guide to our library, a bookmark, and some candy, bags are personalized with a book from our collection that fits that teacher's subject area or other interest. When teachers stop by to thank us, we invite them to sign up for library projects.

— *Kathy Fredrick, Chamberlin High School, Twinsburg, Ohio*

Welcome to Student Teachers

As soon as I have the names of student teachers who will be working in our school, I prepare a welcoming packet of materials explaining and publicizing the library facilities and services. Included are a library map, calendar, orientation sheet, and a candy bar. The student teachers tend to gravitate to us since they need a temporary home as they settle in. In return, we learn about new trends and books.

— *Joellen G. Cullison, Deer Park Senior High School, South Campus, Pasadena, Texas*

Welcoming ESL Students

Our school has a growing number of students for whom English is a second language. To make them welcome in the library, we displayed their pictures with flags and maps of their country of origin. We purchased English dictionaries for each student's primary language and located books that would be easy for them to read. When we weed, we give the ESL students first choice of the easy-to-read discards, especially biographies. We also subscribe to magazines in Spanish and plan to add other languages.

— *Winifred Sihon, Issaquah (Washington) High School*

While-U-Wait Book Displays

I display new books for the professional collection near the copy machine. It doesn't take long for them to get checked out.

— *Elaine Brunswick, St. Henry Local School*

Whole Hearts

For Valentine's Day we printed small pink notes with a border of hearts and half of a heart in the middle. We used Broderbund's Print Shop. The note stated: "We want to help you Wholeheartedly! Bring this half of your heart to the circulation desk. We will have a surprise for you!" We put the notes in teachers' mailboxes and asked students to pass them out to students in the hall during lunch hour. At the circulation desk, we collected the notes and gave out lollipops with each note collected. We saw a few faces we don't usually see in the library.

— *Karen Zapasnik, Deerfield Beach (Florida) High School*

Worth It: A Prolific Copy Machine

We have a one-year-old copy machine in our library that does wondrous magic. In addition to normal copying functions, it can make transparencies for class use and enlargements for bulletin boards—features that come in handy for students and teachers alike. This machine has brought many into the library who might otherwise never use its services.

— *Joan Lundgard, Bellarmine College Preparatory, San Jose, California*

SECTION 8

Read, Read, and Read

> ## The man who does not read good books
> ## has not advantage over the man who can't read them.
> *Mark Twain*

The National Academy of Education's Commission on Reading, in 1986, issued a highly publicized report. That report, *Becoming a Nation of Readers*, said very clearly that access to interesting and informative books is one of the keys to building a nation of readers. Equally important is a librarian who encourages wide reading and helps match books to readers. Here are some tips to help you bring readers to books and to match books to readers.

"What Are You Reading?" Bulletin Board

When students check out a novel, I ask them if they would like to fill out a "What are you reading?" certificate to be posted on a special bulletin board. Students check this board regularly, looking for their names as well as names of other students. If I forget to give a certificate, students will remind me because they love to see their names and opinions on display.

— *Patricia Kolencik, North Clarion High School, Tionesta, Pennsylvania*

Annotated Bookmarks

At the beginning of a booktalking session for tenth and eleventh graders, I pass out bookmarks and ask students to turn them over and jot down titles of at least three books that they would like to read. Most students note titles during the booktalks and keep the bookmarks in the first book they read. Then, when they return that book, they have a list of titles they want to read next.

— *Evelyn Hammaren, Randolph (New Jersey) High School*

Award Ceremony for Recognized Readers

As part of our celebration of National Library Week and New York's statewide Read Aloud Day, the high school library held an awards ceremony to recognize student readers. We asked English teachers to nominate students.

Each nominee was photographed and asked to write a description of a favorite book. Parents, the nominating teachers, and administrators were invited to the ceremony, where certificates and library mementos were presented. Several students read aloud from their favorite books.

— *Anita Weisenfeld, Tottenville High School, Staten Island, New York*

Blue Light Special

When new books are ready for circulation, we promote them by borrowing from the "blue light special" gimmick used by a department store chain. Books are arranged on a table under a blue spotlight borrowed from the stage. The Blue Light Special is then announced on the speaker system and in the daily bulletin. This very simple technique got a great response.

— *Evelyn Hammaren, Randolph (New Jersey) High School*

Book Annotation Database

To motivate high school students to read, I write brief, inviting annotations for all new fiction books. In the past, these have been read on the announcements or printed in the student newspaper with few results. More successful has been a loose-leaf binder that holds all the annotations. This is kept at the circulation desk, where students can browse at their leisure. To compile the contents of the binder, my student assistants and I use the computer program *Apple Works* to create a database that includes the author's name, book title, call number, subject heading, and annotation. The only limitation is that the annotation has to fit into the space allotted. The printouts are placed in the binder, two pages to a piastic sheet, in alphabetical order by author's last name. Students can select

books without pressure. As an added benefit, the binder is a good resource for me when I need to give booktalks to classes at short notice.

— *Ellen Walsten, Snow Hill (Maryland) High School*

Book Fair Coupons Encourage Reading

Before our latest school book fair, I gave English, special education, and bilingual education students a coupon to select the free paperback of their choice. Parent volunteers at the fair recorded the price on the back of each coupon. Then I deducted the amounts from the value of the free books I get from the book fair company.

— *Cindy Dobrez, West Ottawa Middle School, Holland, Michigan*

Book Jacket Notebook

A book jacket notebook helps students make reading selections better than they can by gazing at the spines of the books on the shelves. To make the notebook, I purchased clear sheet protectors that have the three-hole punch on the side. Book jackets are slipped into the protectors, which are placed in loose-leaf notebooks stored near the books. An added benefit to keeping the jackets in the notebooks is that the students are not tempted to plagiarize the blurb when writing their book reports.

— *Mable A. West, Breckenridge (Texas) Junior High*

Book Ratings

The reading teachers and I have cooperatively developed a reading incentive program. Upon reading books, students fill out a short evaluation form: "stupendous," "good," "so-so," or "forget it," and report the plot conflict-fiction, or a previously unknown fact-nonfiction. After the reading teachers initial the slips, I group the titles by ratings and type a weekly list of books and readers' names. These lists are placed outside the library, and every student who participates receives a certificate. We pull names from the slips turned in each week, awarding winners local book store gift certificates. Students who accrue a certain number of points receive a paperback book, and the girl and boy who read the most books during the program receive trophies.

— *Peggy Dillner, George Read Middle School, New Castle, Delaware*

Book Review Wall

Following the lead of bookstores, we have set up a "book review wall." Cards are available in the fiction section, where students can write a three- or four-sentence review. We post these reviews on the wall.

— *Fran Feigert, Northwest High School, Justin, Texas*

Book Swapping

Right before spring vacation each year, we hold an after-school book swap. Parents especially appreciate the opportunity to recycle items from home bookshelves, students love taking "new" books home, and teachers and parents enjoy meeting over coffee and free books. Our student council sells doughnuts and hot chocolate to raise money for community charities.

— *JoAnn Mitchell, Derby Academy, Hingham, Massachusetts*

Bookmarks Help Publicize New Books

Before displaying new books, I first use Print Shop to make a bookmark for each that lists the title, author, and a brief summary. I then run off several copies of each bookmark and leave them at the circulation desk, teachers' lounge, and student store. I also use the bookmarks for library passes and sometimes post them on the bulletin board outside the library's main entrance. It's always a pleasure when a student or teacher brings back the bookmark and requests the book!

— *Patricia Kolenick, North Clarion High School, Tionesta, Pennsylvania*

Books for Activities

I find that attending the school's annual activities fair in September is an excellent way to promote the library. Last year I displayed a table of books on speech and debate, chess, skiing, bowling, drama, and other interests of student clubs. This year, I placed the books on the clubs' tables. Since we are not automated, students could check out the books on the spot. It is not unusual for students to come to the library during the year looking for books they saw at the September fair.

— *Laura J. Viau, McQuaid Jesuit High School, Rochester, New York*

Booktalk Collection

To encourage further student interest in books that I have booktalked, I compiled a Booktalk Folder that contains a printed version of the talks. The talks are arranged alphabetically by author, and the word processor makes it easy to keep an updated list of the talks in the front of the folder. Students frequently use the folder to urge other students to read a book they liked. Teachers can use the folder to help students make book selections.

— *Susan Couvillon, North Vermilion High School, Maurice, Louisiana*

Booktalking Nonfiction

As a way to introduce the idea that nonfiction books can be as entertaining as fiction, I worked with the English department to booktalk an assortment of nonfiction. Books on the supernatural, sports, pet care, and other popular topics were highlighted and followed up with a class activity. The circulation of nonfiction has increased.

— *Esther Andrle, Hampton Middle School, Allison Park, Pennsylvania*

Browsing Books

Popular books such as the *Garfield* and *Calvin and Hobbes* comics and the *Guinness World Record* series are featured on our browsing table. Students are aware that these books cannot be checked out but can be enjoyed in bits and pieces during a few minutes free time before school or at lunchtime. Other colorful, high interest books from the circulating collection are placed on the browsing table on a rotating basis.

— *Christine Van Hamersveld, Teague Middle School, Humble, Texas*

Celebrating Literature

I sponsor lunchtime readings in the media center to celebrate special occasions, such as Black History Month and National Library Week. Students sign up to be readers or members of the audience so I will know how many refreshments to provide. I also ask students to list what they will be reading so I can prepare programs. English teachers give extra credit to participants, and sometimes the teachers are readers. This has become a special time when students and teachers celebrate the beauty and variety of literature together.

— *Frances Gass, Camden County (North Carolina) High School*

Celebrating, School Library-Style—Annual Reading Incentive Programs

During School Library Media Month and National Library Week, we sponsored activities in the library. One event was a trivia contest with a twist: "Stump the Librarian." Students submitted questions, and the library staff had to find correct answers using only school resources. If we could not answer a question by the end of the week, the student who asked it received a certificate for a free ice cream from the cafeteria. With over 50 questions submitted, we gave away only a couple of ice creams, but the contest was a fun challenge for students and staff alike! The students were also impressed that there is so much information about popular subjects— including rock stars—in the library. We also made posters showing both state- and school-wide results of The Connecticut Educational Media Association's annual favorite books poll. Students enjoyed looking for books their classmates recommended. A third activity encouraged students to clear overdues and fines, since National Library Week coincides with the end of the third marking quarter. We rewarded each student having no accounts outstanding on the day we sent out overdue notices with free ice cream. Food, we've discovered, is the kids' favorite incentive. Students wanted these programs to continue— we promised them that they'll enjoy next year's activities just as much!

— *Catherine M Andronik, Bedford Middle School, Westport, Connecticut*

Classroom Booktalks

I struggled with booktalks for English classes until I tried giving them in the classroom on the day before the group comes to the library to choose books. I prepare a written book list with a blurb about each book and take the books with me on a cart.

— *Cheryl Read, Meridian High School, Bellingham, Washington*

Color-Coded Dots

I put yellow dots on books that teachers want students to read for book reports. I use bright apple-green dots for high-low books designated for "pleasure reading only." Since green dots are for pleasure reading, students feel no embarrassment about checking out high-low books.

— *Liz Snead, Park View Middle School, South Hill, Virginia*

Feuding Sixth Graders

Our special version of Family Feud allows us to welcome new sixth graders to our school and to find out about the new kids on the block at the same time. The first time the reading teachers bring sixth-grade classes to the library, I have them fill out a survey asking their favorite authors, kind of book, athlete, role model, food, color, car, and so on. I compile the answers for the game and also use the information to order books the students will like. When classes return to the library, I put them into "families" at the library tables. Family heads are chosen randomly. Families get to discuss each question and the head of the family selects the answer. The winning team from each class participates in a playoff, where winners get paperback books and their photo displayed on the bulletin board.

— *Bonnie Rice, Salado Middle School, San Antonio, Texas*

Fiction by Genre

Many of the English teachers in our building like to assign book reports by genre, but having students lined up to use the card catalog was frustrating for them. Also, pulling all fiction books of a certain genre off the shelves for each assignment was time consuming for the library staff. My solution: rearrange our fiction collection by genre. I began by rearranging the shelf list cards by the genres most often requested: mystery, science fiction/fantasy, animals, sports, historical, westerns. I ordered subject labels to stick on the books to help keep them correctly categorized. At the end of the year, student aides pulled more than 3,000 hard cover fiction books from the shelves. We worked from the reorganized shelf list cards to label the books and reshelve them by genre. Teachers and students both like the new system. I plan on adding adventure, classics, and romance categories soon.

— *Esther Sinofsky, Frost Junior High School, Granada Hills, California*

First Come, First Served

I was frustrated after presenting booktalks because students who reserved the books didn't come to get them when their turns came. Now, after booktalks, I display the books' covers on a bulletin board with flashing lights like a movie marquee. The books themselves go out on Fridays with my admonition, "First come, first served." It's amazing how many students now line up on Friday mornings to check out the featured volumes. Even students who missed the booktalks will ask for the "Friday books."

— *Mimi Malis, Covington Middle School, Austin, Texas*

For Sports Fans Only

Beckett's *Sports Card Price Guides* are so popular in our junior high library that I've established a sports card center at a reading table for six. Back issues are in Princeton Files at the end of the table, and students often consult the guides while perusing their collections. It's amazing how quickly students build research skills when the topic is one that interests them!

— *Roxanne Morris, Punxsutawney (Pennsylvania) Junior High School*

Glorifying Great Reads

I've found the most effective way to "advertise" good books to students is also the easiest—I simply read the first couple of paragraphs aloud on the public address system as part of Monday morning's bulletin. My gig, "Great Beginnings," is quite popular with students. Children's authors—especially those who write for young adults—are masters at writing in styles that lure young readers. Two "Great Beginnings" that have been very successful at my school are deFelice's *Weasel* and Shusterman's *Shadow Club*.

— *Susan Gibb, Santiago Middle School, Orange, California*

Halloween Reading Lottery

During the month of October, we sponsor a Halloween reading lottery that stimulates lots of student excitement. After students finish reading a mystery, ghost story, or other scary book, they fill out a lottery ticket with their name, grade, and other pertinent information on one side and a short summary of the book on the other. Students can enter as often as they wish. Thanks to the generosity of local merchants, we were able to give away 99 prizes on Halloween day. Winners were drawn from more than 200 entries; we also gave prizes to the boy and girl who had read the most books.

— *Libby Cooper, Sevier Middle School, Kingsport, Tennessee*

If It's Purple, It Must Be Funny

We color code the fiction in our library so finding specific genres will be easier for patrons. We use half-inch, brightly colored adhesive dots and affix them to the spine just above the call number. Yellow indicates historical fiction, green is adventure, and blue is science fiction. Our newest code is for humor, which now has a bright purple dot. For the middle school level, unfortunately, there are few humorous novels.

— *LaDuska Adriance, Cooper Middle School, McLean, Virginia*

InterDistrict Author Visits

So that our students can meet well-known, highly respected young adult authors, we have pooled resources with neighboring school districts to share author visits. Dividing airfare and hotel bills among four or five schools makes the event affordable. We have found that it is best for one librarian to serve as coordinator or contact person. This person pays all the bills (except speaking fees, for which each school is responsible) with a check from her school, then bills each participating school its share. Librarians involved coordinate transportation to and from the airport and to the different schools. Meals, teas, and so forth are combined with faculty gatherings, Honor Society socials, and book autographing sessions. This is a great way not only to cut expenses but also to get to know neighboring teachers and librarians, sharing ideas, materials, and success.

— *Sherry Gatewood, Spring, Texas*

Introduction to Young Adult Fiction

To promote fiction reading among freshmen and sophomores, I initiated a project with English teachers. First I booktalk 15-20 novels. Students then read a book from our collection and complete a report form, which I evaluate and return to the teacher for recording. There are several benefits: students and teachers are introduced to young-adult literature, the teachers get a break from grading, and I become familiar with many books in the collection by reading the reports.

— *Susan Schanerman, Corona Del Sol High School, Tempe, Arizona*

Involving the Public Library in Reading Incentives

When we started the Accelerated Reader program (Advantage Learning Systems), I gave the public library a list of the books included. This promoted community interest in the reading incentive program and increased the number of copies of the featured books available to students. Now our students can look forward to beginning a school year with rewards after a summer of "accelerated reading."

— *Sheila A. Acosta, Rhodes Middle School, San Antonio, Texas*

Keeping Book Reviews by Students

The ninth-grade speech students write reviews of books they read, rating them with stars—the same system used with movie reviews. The photography students then take color pictures of the book jackets. We laminate the pictures and reviews onto tag board, and we keep these in a box on the circulation desk.

— *Ruth Hadzar, Hillside Junior High School, Boise, Idaho*

Kids Reading to Kids

During reading contests, I always give credit to students who read to younger children. It is a wonderful way to get two kids into books instead of one. Middle schoolers get 100 pages of credit for every 10 picture books they read aloud while babysitting or entertaining younger members of their families.

— *Katharine Keeble, B. Sherman Middle School, Holly, Michigan*

Library Lions Contest

One of our most successful contests was very easy. I purchased the Library Lions Poster (ALA Graphics), reproduced from *Animalia* by Graeme Base (Abrams). This is a beautiful alphabet book for all ages and great for teaching alliteration. Beside the framed poster, I put these directions for submitting answers: "The picture is taken from a book in our library. Locate the book and write down the title, author, and page number." There were several clues: the picture was a large one so it had to be in an oversize book. The "L" alliteration gave a clue that it was an alphabet book. And, the illustration was so distinctive that it was a clue to the striking cover of the book. Middle school students enthusiastically set out to find the book. I think this was a great way to introduce them to a fine example of book illustration.

— *Diane C Pozar, Wallkill (New York) Middle School*

Literary Pumpkins

Each year we stage the Great (Literary) Pumpkin Contest. Students carve or decorate a pumpkin as their favorite literary characters. Any character is fine as long as he or she has appeared in a book. Some favorites have been the Cat in the Hat, Captain Hook, Huckleberry Finn, and Forrest Gump. We award gift certificates from a bookstore for the three prizes. Students pick the winning pumpkins by ballot. On "election" day, over half of the student body comes to the library to vote.

— *J'Aime L. Foust, Queensbury (New York) High School*

Local Celebrities Promote Reading

During National Library Week, we invited 25 "celebrities" from our community to talk to our language arts classes about their favorite books and the role of reading in their success. One speaker read a portion of her favorite book aloud and then gave it to one of the students to read and pass on to a friend. Another speaker told students he avoided television so he would have time to read. Student comments included: "Our celebrity read aloud parts from *The Wizard of Oz*. I thought it was funny that this was the favorite book of an older woman. I also realized that the book was not the same as the movie." "Last night I went to the mall and bought three of the books that our speaker talked about."

— *Libby Cooper, Sevier Middle School, Kingsport, Tennessee*

More Book Selection Help

To encourage students to read our contemporary fiction collection, we put together a notebook of pages from publisher catalogs that describe the books. The clippings are arranged in alphabetical order by author and glued to the notebook pages, which are then laminated. Students enjoy paging through the notebook and choosing books independently.

— *Paula Cline, Genoa (Ohio) Area High School*

MTV for Books

Students in our high school library class plan and put together booktalks on videotape to "sell" favorite books to their friends. The rules are simple: they cannot tell the story line, they cannot use the blurb on the book, and they must use good taste. Otherwise, they plan their talks, add music, and become the star of their own videotapes filmed anywhere on the school grounds and using any props or other students they wish. The process of putting together an interesting "commercial" for the book usually inspires extra creativity and confidence, which makes the books more intriguing for their friends.

— *Kathy McCurry, Fair Grove (Missouri) High School*

Nonfiction Specials

Although students normally approach the nonfiction shelves only when they have a class assignment, our collection does contain nonfiction paperbacks with great reader appeal such as Joyce Vedral's *Boyfriends* or *The Autobiography of Malcolm X*. To keep these from collecting dust in the nonfiction shelves, I have a special shelf in the paperback section marked "Paperback Specials." It works-students do find and borrow them.

— *Sister Marjorie Stumpf, St. Savior High School, Brooklyn, New York*

Notes for Booktalks

I sometimes take six or seven books to a classroom for booktalks. When I am promoting several books in one session, I have found "notes" to be very helpful. A 4" x 6" index card, with a few keywords on it, can be taped to the back of most books. Since I hold the book with the cover facing the students, they don't see the index card on the back. I can take a quick glance at notes on the card when necessary. I also write the date the booktalk was done and save the cards for future book talks.

— *Mary Kaschak, Roosevelt Middle School, Newark, Ohio*

Novel Feast

Have you ever read a novel that was simply delicious? Do you devour good literature? Do you long to have your students savor the taste of fine writing? That is exactly what happened when I planned a party at which novels would not only provide the conversation but also the food. Students were asked to bring their novels along with a snack food that was either eaten in the story or that illustrated a topic or character in the book. Before the party, we brainstormed for ideas, and the students soon got the concept. Jake, who was reading Stephen King's *It*, brought clown-shaped fruit snacks. Stephen, who read *Journey to the Center of the Earth*, brought cinnamon red hots to symbolize the earth's core. Kim brought red Kool Aid because she had read *Dark Angel*, a story about vampires. Naomi brought marshmallows because of the nickname of a Paul Zindel character. I brought matzah crackers in honor of Jane Yolen's *The Devil's Arithmetic*. We had such a good time munching treats and chatting about our books that our readers asked, "When are we going to do this again?"

— *Lynn Presley-Clark, Liberty Middle-Magnet School, Madison, Alabama*

Novel Idea for New Books

To advertise new books, we print the title of a new book and a brief annotation on the back of restroom passes. It's amazing to see how many students return from the restroom and check out a new book.

— *Patricia Kolencik, North Clarion High School, Tionesta, Pennsylvania*

Of Candy Bars and Reading Lists

I watched our students buy fund raising candy over the year, wondering how to work this to my advantage. Then the ALA Best Books for Young Adults list arrived and I thought of an idea: Students can read a book from this list, fill out an information card on the book, and earn a candy bar. I have had success with this program, which exposes students to better literature than they normally read. To my surprise, the nonfiction titles move even faster than the fiction ones.

— *Virginia Mikhelsen, Hudson (Iowa) Community Junior-Senior High School*

Personal Recommendations

Junior high schoolers like to have their pictures taken, and they like to read what someone else has read. To add interest to our library, I take Polaroid snapshots of students who are willing to write a two- or three-sentence review of a book they liked. The pictures and reviews are posted all over the library. Students enjoy looking at pictures of themselves and their friends, and that gets them to read the reviews and check out books.

— *Marsha Saucier, Westview Middle School, Austin, Texas*

Postcard Pals

We established a Postcard Pals program to motivate students to read during the summer months. The first step was to develop a pamphlet of recommended authors and titles. Near the end of the school year, all students in the developmental reading program receive a copy of the pamphlet, a letter explaining the summer reading program, and three postcards already addressed to the teacher. As students read books over the summer, they write the name of the book they read and any comments on the back of the postcard. They mail it to the teacher, who responds with a postcard to the student. In the fall, postcards from the students are displayed in the library. This program is most successful when you get parents involved.

— *Renee Brenon & Nellie Mae Schauer, Indian River Middle School, Philadelphia, New York*

Postcards Home

To promote the library and reading, I send a postcard to parents informing them when their child has been a frequent library patron or frequent reader.

— *Patricia Kolencik, North Clarion High School, Tionesta, Pennsylvania*

Pulitzer Prize Winners in the Classroom

An English teacher in our school required ninth-grade honors students to read prize winners. I bought more than 35 titles for 30 students. I took the 35 books to the classroom, where the teacher and I discussed them. The students picked numbers to determine the order in which they would select a book. The students could change their book for another if they didn't like their choice. At the end of their reading, the students gave oral reports on the book and its author. Most students enjoyed the books, the challenge, and the knowledge that they were reading outstanding books. Several students asked for other titles by the same author. I keep the students supplied with information on new titles by their authors, especially those who make the bestseller lists. This unit works well with older students too.

— *Anitra Gordon, Lincoln High School, Ypsilanti, Michigan*

Race into Reading

Here's a way to display books about racecars and other types of automobiles. On a round table, place an old auto tire (we got one from the auto shop teacher). Add some miniature cars around the top of the tire as if they are racing. Books may be placed around the outside of the tire. Construction paper letters spelling "Race into Reading" can be attached to the tread of the tire with straight pins.

— *Rosamund Douglass, Nathan B. Forrest Senior High School, Jacksonville, Florida*

Reader Advice on Tag Board

For those times when we can't individually recommend books to students for reports or recreational reading, we keep a file of book synopses at the circulation desk. These are taken from sources such as review journals or guides to literature for teenagers. The summaries are laminated to tag board so they can withstand repeated use.

— *Connie Weber, Churubusco (Indiana) Middle/High School*

Reading Recommendation Notebook

When preparing an oral and written book review, one of our senior students decided to rate the book using a 1 to 10 system along with brief critical comment about the book. His idea was so enthusiastically adopted by other students that we decided to collect the ratings in a special book review notebook. Arranged in alphabetical order by title, all book reviews have the number rating and comment. The notebook is kept on the check-out counter, easily available to students looking for books recommended by their peers.

— *Helen Haw, St. Helena Central High School, Greensburg, Louisiana*

Recognizing Readers

At the end of the year, we run a printout of student and faculty checkouts. Then we note the students and teachers who have checked out 10 or more books. Using the software programs *Certificate Maker* (Springboard) or *Library Magic* (MC 2), we create certificates for each student and staff member who checked out 10 or more books, 20 or more, and so on. We use different paper colors for each category, and each certificate is personalized with the individual's name and the signatures of the librarians. Last year we gave lollipops with the 10-plus and 20-plus certificates. Recipients of the 30-plus certificates also received an "I Love to Read" button. Readers of 40-plus books received "Book Lover" mugs. We gave the student who read 225 books a T-shirt. The library staff personally delivers the certificates during homeroom. This project is always the talk of the school for days. Many of the students and teachers are surprised when they learn how many books they checked out. Last year we issued over 200 certificates. It was great PR and we had fun!

— *Karen Zapasnik, Deerfield Beach (Florida) High School*

Recreational Furniture for Reading

Last year I decided to set up a recreational reading area in the library. When I discovered the cost of lounge furniture, I had to come up with an alternative. I purchased a set of lawn furniture (wood) from a discount store. The set included a love seat, two side chairs, and a coffee table. The love seat and chairs had small folding tables on each arm. These tables are perfect for students to use as desks. To make the set more attractive and comfortable, I stapled bath rugs to the seat backs. Because the set was on an end-of-the-season sale, the total cost was under $150.

— *Joy M. Harrison, Buffalo (Missouri) High School*

Recycle the Card Catalog, Drawers and All

Recycle the old card catalog. Convert the drawers to planters. You can buy plastic liners to fit the drawers so that you can fill them with plants, real or artificial. The cabinet itself can be recycled for a display area by removing the drawer dividers, painting the interior, and adding a stick light. We added a hinged door with glass. The industrial arts teachers may be willing to help with this project. And finally, for the cards themselves, we send appropriate cards to authors and ask the authors to autograph the catalog card and return it to us.

— *Barbara Bluestein, Princeton High School, Cincinnati, Ohio*

Editor's Note: Consider sending two cards to each author and then donate one of the cards from each author to your local professional reading or library associations for a fund raiser to benefit the organization. smc

Redwall Rewards

The favorite fantasy book in our library is *Redwall* by Brian Jacques, but its length is intimidating to some middle school students. To motivate more students to try this book, I have printed buttons that read "I Made It Through The Wall—Redwall—351 pages." As students read the book, they are awarded a button, and on the daily announcements, we proclaim: "Ten more students have made it through The Wall. Look for the students wearing buttons and ask them about it." When students are asked about their buttons, they tell others about the story and encourage them to read it, also. This project has brought recognition to our middle school fantasy readers and has enticed many others to read *Redwall*. We have seven copies, and there is a waiting list. Students are also standing in line to read the rest of the series.

— *Louise Kehoe, Hemlock (Michigan) Middle School*

Review the Books & Hold the Anchovies

In response to our administration's call for an emphasis on literacy, we conducted a voluntary program of inviting students to become book reviewers for the school. With each simple review form completed, students received a chance to win a prize drawing. Students who completed three reviews were invited to a pizza party. Over 40 students participated, and by the end of the program, we needed pizza for 10 ravenous teens. We will definitely do this again.

— *Janet Wagner, Oak Park (Illinois) & River Forest High School*

Reviews Are for Reading

After reading the books of their choice, all seventh graders in my library science class write their book reviews on 5 x 8 cards. When they turn in their reviews, I take a picture of each student. Then I display the reviews and the photos in the library for one year. The young reviewers are proud to see their work—and their faces—on display.

— *Margaret Heydrick, Rocky Grove High School, Franklin, Pennsylvania*

Rewarding Readers

Each month we recognize students who have accumulated 15 points in the computerized reading program *Electronic Bookshelf*. Students are invited to the library during the school's activity period. We serve soft drinks and popcorn.

— *Pat Donahue, Van (Texas) Independent School District*

Sensitive Topics

Many students want to read about a certain problem that may be bothering them, but are hesitant to ask for a book about the problem. To generate a list of problem books in our collection, I include a fiction reading assignment in my library skills course for ninth graders. After reading a novel, students prepare a 3 x 5 card that includes title, author, and the theme of the book—adoption, alcoholism, stepfamily, teen pregnancy, and so forth. Cards can be used to generate a list for distribution so students can make their choice privately.

— *Sister Francis Marita, Hallahan High School, Philadelphia, Pennsylvania*

Serving Reluctant Readers

To encourage remedial reading and ESL students to choose books in the library, we have replaced "Easy Reading" labels on the appropriate books with labels that say "Quick Reading." The labels are in neon red, which makes the books easy for students to find. Students who need these books are no longer embarrassed to carry them around as they were with the previous labels.

— *Barbara Resnick, Queens Vocational High School, Long Island City, New York*

Shopping for Books

To give students "ownership" in their library and to promote our paperback collection, I take groups of students, three or four each time, to a local bookstore to select paperbacks for our annual Book Fair or for our paperback collection. The students are given guidelines on cost, appropriateness for high school, variety of topics/genres/interest level, and so forth. The students have fun browsing through the store. If some books must be eliminated because of over-expenditure, students must be able to defend their choices. The shoppers are allowed to be the first to check out the new books. Also, as a special thank-you, I treat them to dinner as part of our outing.

— *Mary Stallings, Poquoson (Virginia) High School*

Spirits of Lonely Books

During my "traveling" booktalks in October, I dress in black with a hood and gloves to present myself as the spirit of a dead book. I feature books that have seldom or never been checked out while begging in a ghostly voice, "Please read me."

— *Osurian Clark, McNair Middle School, Decatur, Georgia*

Sports Under Glass

Sports pages of our daily newspaper had a way of disappearing before we came up with the idea of "sports under glass." We cut a piece of Plexiglas the size of our tabletop and each day place the sports page underneath. No more missing pages.

— *Gail Szeliga, Union Endicott High School, Endicott, New York*

Student Book Reviewers

We printed up 4 x 6 cards so English teachers can ask students to write a mini-review of books they like. In addition to a space for a short summary, we have check boxes for the genre—horror, romance, science fiction—as well as recommendation levels. When cards are turned in to us, we add the student reviews to the summary field on our automated card catalog. Students can also search for their names using the keyword feature on our system. We also keep the original cards at the desk for students to browse through when they're looking for a good novel.

— *Andrew Fowler, Lake Park High School, Roselle, Illinois*

Student-Written Reading Tests

We use *Accelerated Reader* in our media center. Many books used in the classrooms or read independently by students are not on the test disks or are on disks we are not interested in purchasing. I developed criteria for writing book tests, and now students themselves write tests. I proofread the students' writing, make some changes, and enter the tests into the computer program. Students are good at choosing important facts and writing concise questions.

— *Lynn N. Morrow, Chesterfield (South Carolina) Middle School*

Students' Choice

To involve students in book selection, we take library club students on an annual tour of a large bookstore, where they select one paperback for our collection. Before the tour, the club has spent some meetings in discussion of the collection, interests of the student body, popular authors, and book reviews. When the books are processed, we put a label in each stating that it was selected by the club. These books are also put on display. They have proved to be popular with other students.

— *Elizabeth Garbarino, Riverhead (New York) Middle School*

Teasing Readers

To promote new novels, once a week we write a short teaser to be printed in the daily announcements. An example of our teasers is: "CyberWorld is a virtual reality amusement park where you can live out your wildest dreams. But, the line between fantasy and reality is growing razor-thin. If you like suspense, read *Death Dream* by Ben Bova, available in the Kickapoo High School Library."

— *Deborah Dick & Deborah Davis, Kickapoo High School, Springfield, Missouri*

Teen Recommended

This year, I made yellow cardboard markers that fit into book pockets and carry the words "Teen Recommended." The markers were placed in books that had been recommended by a young reader. The response to books that contained the marker was overwhelming. Many books that had previously languished on our shelves are now hot items!

— *Greer Mulholland, Brentwood Junior-Senior High School, Pittsburgh, Pennsylvania*

Teen S-O-S Section Is a Success

In order to accommodate student interest in the growing number of books on teenage problems, lifestyles, changing bodies, and so forth, I began a special collection of fiction and nonfiction titles called "Teen S-O-S." About 250 books have been placed on three bookcases arranged in a triangle section of the library. The books are color-coded with yellow stickers, and a portable Teen S-O-S bulletin board display is arranged on top of the bookcases. The displays include hot line numbers, articles, and other information. Using *Bibliography Writer* software, I compiled an annotated bibliography that is kept near this special collection. The subject headings are AIDS, abuse, adolescence, alcoholism, coping, crime, death, developing sexuality, dropouts, drugs, family relationships, homosexuality, mental/emotional problems, physical handicaps, pregnancy, relationships, and runaways. The response has been fantastic! Other librarians have picked up the idea from in-service meetings, and our city's Rotary Club awarded a grant to add additional resources to the collection. The most enthusiastic response has come from the students themselves, who benefit from being able to find such information on their own.

— *Millicent Cade Hoskin, Central High School, Memphis, Tennessee*

The Novel Reading Zone

To encourage reading for fun, we have set aside a small area near the fiction books called the Novel Reading Zone. The space is furnished with comfortable chairs, a love seat, and a coffee table filled with novels. Green plants and artwork add to the atmosphere. No homework, class work, or reading of magazines or newspapers is allowed in this area—it is just for novel reading. The Zone is a hit. We have more people than space, and there is usually someone reading every hour of every day.

— *Delores Neumueller, Lourdes Academy Senior High, Oshkosh, Wisconsin*

Unwrapping Excitement

Instead of unpacking new books in the back room, I open them in the library while students are there. The effect is like opening presents. The students gather around the book carts, and many select books they want to read. We process those immediately, getting the latest acquisitions into eager hands. During a recent unpacking, 26 books went out. The process takes a little extra time, but it's rewarding to see this excitement over books.

— *Diane C Pozar, Wallkill (New York) Middle School*

What's for Lunch?

Why, "Lunchbox Literature," of course. At least that's the case at my school each Wednesday when I broadcast a 15-minute read-aloud program each day during lunch. Student volunteers join me in reading favorite selections on this in-house program, which has become a hit with students.

— *Liz Snead, Park View Middle School, South Hill, Virginia*

Young Adult Authors on File

Whenever I come across a magazine article about a young adult author, I place a copy in the vertical file. If we have a class set of books by the author, I also place the article in an envelope with the teacher's guide.

— *Carole Bell, Brown Middle School, McAllen, Texas*

SECTION 9

Volunteers – Students and Community

> ## The work of the librarian is very hazily defined in the minds of the average layman.
>
> *Lucile F. Fargo, 1936*

In addition to providing valuable assistance in the library media center, student volunteers and volunteers from the school community have an inside track on being able to observe the role of the librarian. They are able to assist with the clerical tasks, providing some of the routine services, and enable the library media specialist to focus on being proactive rather than only responsive. One would not want to "hire" a volunteer that one would not "hire" if she or he were going to be paid. But that doesn't mean that all volunteers have to be hired to do all jobs. The clerical/secretarial help we hire as part of staff are usually hired for their abilities in many areas. When community volunteers or student volunteers are interviewed and hired, so to speak, we must, I feel, hold them to the same standards with one exception. Each volunteer might have a specific talent or interest in a task—that volunteer may be "hired" with that task in mind. Volunteers have signed on to shelve books an hour a week, put up bulletin boards, bake cookies for LMC gatherings, respond to requests for items from closed stacks (such as back issues of periodicals), clip vertical file articles, run errands, make new spine labels, or keep the center tidy. The list could be endless. But one of the most important roles is the impression each volunteer takes away from the center. It is this image that will get conveyed to their fellow students and fellow community members. Many library media specialists recognize that volunteers are their best public relations messengers and their best secret weapon. Their help in all aspects of operating the library media center will be invaluable.

"Hit the Box"

Eighth-grade assistants are usually more enthusiastic than accurate when it comes to stapling the numerous library skills booklets, booklists, and PR materials we distribute. I solved the problem by drawing a small box in the corner of the cover sheet before duplicating. Now the only instructions my avid stapling students need is to "hit the box."

— *Linda Kochinski, Albion (Michigan) Junior High School*

Adopt-A-Shelf

An "Adopt-A-Highway" sign gave me an idea that keeps the library shelves neat even though I have no staff. After recruiting a small group of enthusiastic student helpers, I made a sign using Print Shop and posted this message on various shelves: "This section adopted and maintained by (student's name), Friend of the Library." The students are responsible for maintaining their "adopted" section, shelving returned books, reading the shelves, and keeping the section neat and clean. Students schedule their own time in the library for this school service. Once the system got started, other students asked if they could adopt a section. Not only is the library neater, but the students are getting recognition for their efforts.

— *Jane Dyke, Birchwood High School, Columbia, South Carolina*

Advisees Become Aides

Our school has a daily 25-minute advisor period. The problem was I was assigned a group of "advisees," but teachers also wanted to send students to the library during the adviser period, held at the beginning of the school day. The first year I struggled with 20 or so seventh graders assigned to me plus students on passes and teachers requesting materials and equipment. About midterm I began to use my advisees as "book police" by sending them after overdues. Some were cooperative, some weren't. In the spring I went to the seventh-grade teachers and promised to schedule visiting days for each grade level if they would let me select my group of advisees. I gave applications to the sixth graders and chose a balanced group with diverse interests. They are trained and rotate through four groups—desk, displays, technology, and recycling—plus stints as book police. Because they applied for the job and were chosen, the students are helpful and enthusiastic. I always have many more applicants than I can choose. Last year we exported the idea to eighth grade and formed a computer assistance group.

— *Danelle Jentges, Test Middle School, Richmond, Indiana*

Bored with Vacation

At the end of the school year, I post a sign-up sheet for student aides who are willing to work in the library during the last few days of summer vacation. In August, I get in touch with these volunteers and ask them to come in for a few hours. By the end of the summer many students have become bored with vacation time. There are always a number of eager helpers. Among other things, the aides process summer magazines and new books and decorate bulletin boards.

— *Mary Kaschak, Roosevelt Middle School, Newark, Ohio*

Clip-On Hall Passes

Clip-on name badges work well as hall passes for library aides who are delivering equipment or running errands. The badges can be color-coded and personalized as well as updated frequently. Students feel important wearing the badges.

— *Judy O'Connor, Owen Valley High School, Spencer, Indiana*

Editor's Note: Community volunteers should also be provided with an official badge. A badge identifies the volunteer as an adult in the school who has a legitimate reason for being there. Not all members of a faculty can be expected to recognize volunteers from a specific department. smc

Consumable Picture File

When I was librarian in a junior high school, I maintained a cut-up picture file that was used heavily. I decided to try it at the high school, and it has proved popular there as well. I use flat boxes that the pop for our vending machine comes in. Each box is labeled with subjects of pictures. Popular pictures in my school include Rocky Mountain wildlife, scenery, sports, and flowers. Periodically, I ask for magazine and calendar donations from staff, students, and the community. Student aides clip and sort the pictures. All are "consumable"–that is, the students may keep them for their projects. A fringe benefit is that the file prevents pictures from being cut out of books and research magazines.

— *Cathy Smyers, Laurel (Montana) High School*

Dewey Numbers for Library Club Members

Each member of the library club has an assigned Dewey number or a designation like paperbacks or fiction A-M. They read the shelves for their numbers to find misplaced books and shelve returned books. Many hands make light work.

— *Georganna Krumlinde, Troy (Missouri) Buchanan High School*

Dual-Purpose Flyers

To help parents of library aides understand what their students do, I prepared a flier. In it, I listed their jobs, how they help the library, and what they learn from the experience. The flier was sent home with report cards. The fliers also serve as a reminder and a checklist for the aides themselves.

— *Anitra Gordon, Lincoln High School, Ypsilanti, Michigan*

Editor's Note: A similar brochure could serve as a public relations piece and a call for community volunteers. Parents, grandparents, and other community people might volunteer more readily if they realized what the job involved. Distribute the brochures at your school's Parent-Teacher Organizational meetings and during school-wide open houses. smc

Gifts for Student Volunteers

To give our many student volunteers a small holiday gift without spending more than we could afford, we designed a special certificate of appreciation. The top three-fourths of the page was the certificate, while the bottom fourth was divided into two coupons: one worth $2 off a book purchase at our upcoming book fair and one worth a free replacement for a lost library card. The award was rolled and adorned with a curly red ribbon; a red pencil was secured inside the ribbon. A pass to the library during lunch period was also included.

— *Joyce Bryan, Pine Forest High School, Pensacola, Florida*

Hello-grams

For our Library Club fund raiser this year, we sold Hellograms at Christmas time. We made greeting cards in the shape of red construction paper stockings. Students paid 25 cents to write a message to a friend on a Hellogram, which we would then deliver to the friend's homeroom. The student library workers really got involved, and we raised $250.

— *Vicki Bell, Eupora (Mississippi) High School*

Information File

Keeping abreast of articles for the information file was a time-consuming task and one that always seemed to be last on the list of things to do. Turning the project over to student aides solved the problem. The list of subject headings in the information file was divided among the aides. During each nine-week grading period, each aide is responsible for obtaining and labeling at least 20 appropriate newspaper articles for the subjects assigned. I check the aides' work and give them a letter grade before they file the articles. Students are reading the newspapers that we subscribe to as well as their family newspapers and newsmagazines.

— *Myra Riddle Parker, Reid Ross Junior High School, Fayetteville, North Carolina*

Job Boards & Monthly Reports

I created "job boards" by laminating a piece of poster board (11 x 16) and gluing rows of book pockets to it. I have four boards on my

office wall, labeled for the current week, next week, next month, and the summer. I write reminders of jobs on old catalog cards (cut in half) and file the cards in the appropriate pocket. When the jobs are finished, I toss the cards in a basket and use them to compile monthly reports.

— *Bev Oliver, Indian Hill High School, Cincinnati, Ohio*

Library = Homeroom

At our school the day opens with a 17-minute homeroom period. Every year I choose two students to serve as homeroom library aides. These students report to the library instead of going to their scheduled homerooms. They are an invaluable help to me in the mornings—delivering equipment to teachers, turning on computers, answering the telephone, and staffing the circulation desk.

— *Mary Kaschak, Roosevelt Middle School, Newark, Ohio*

Library Aides' ID Cards

Our school requires hall passes for students at all times. Giving a pass to aides every time they went on library errands got to be a problem. Since the school also requires that all students have a picture ID, I took an additional photo of the aides at the beginning of the school year. In the information section of the ID card, I typed the periods they were assigned to the library. I put each ID card in a holder with a clip. The cards are stored in a drawer at the circulation desk. When the aides need to leave the library they clip on the ID and are easily identified in the hallways.

— *Lydia Gutierrez, Lincoln Middle School, McAllen, Texas*

Library Helper Sign-In

To help organize the Library Helpers Club, I have introduced a sign-in card system. In September and again when second semester starts in January, each volunteer fills out a 3 x 5 card with last name, first name, home-room, and days usually available for assisting in the library. Each card is interfiled with those of the other volunteers, and the file box is left in an accessible spot on the sign-out desk. When students report to volunteer, they must pull their card and make a notation of the date and a short description of what help they will give. For example, "9/16/91-sort paperbacks." Students who want credit for community service hours for Scouts or another organization are insured of an up-to-date record of hours. I like this method of signing-in since it is a preview of the experience students will have keeping track of their hours in entry-level jobs.

— *Margaret H. Addor, Titusville Middle School, Poughkeepsie, New York*

Library TAs

We have designed a course that gives students a class credit for working as a Library Teaching Assistant (TA). This year we have eight TAs assigned to different blocks of time with no more than two students per block. TAs are each given areas they are responsible for keeping in order, shelving, and doing shelf check-in. A TA may be responsible for a row of books, several rows of periodicals, and several vertical file drawers. TAs are trained for additional tasks, such as writing letters to request free information. So TAs can begin work independently, their daily assignments are written on cards placed in pockets in the workroom.

— *C. Hilland, Southgate School, Campbell River, British Columbia, Canada*

Library/AV Club

Members of the Library/AV Club in our school receive certain privileges: they pay no library overdue fines, and they receive free photocopying and other perks. Recently we have added the "Library/AV Award" for a graduating senior who has worked as a dependable library volunteer for a minimum of three years. This award is given only when there is a candidate who meets all of the requirements.

— *Susan Yallaly, St. Joseph-Ogden High School, St. Joseph, Illinois*

Looking for Ten Good Techies

To encourage the use of technology in the classroom, I advertise for "student techies." The middle school students compete for the position by filling out an application for just 10 openings. Those chosen may come to the media center any time to use the Xap-Shot camera or prepare a *Power Point* presentation. Usually only two or three techies are free at the same time, so there's enough equipment to go around. These students quickly mastered the equipment and were off and running. Teachers who happened to see the techies at work in the media center began asking to see their presentations and were soon scheduling these students to give demonstrations. The eighth-grade teachers even gave the techies information to include in a presentation on an upcoming class trip. Students and teachers are coming to realize that technology can be used in the classroom effectively.

— *Connie Weber, Churubusco (Indiana) Middle/High School*

Markers Help Check Student Shelving

I found a simple way to help middle school aides shelve books. Each one selected a different color and made 30 construction paper markers that they initialized. These markers were stored in book card pockets attached to stiff cardboard placed near the check-out desk. As they shelved, the students inserted their markers in the books. I could check reshelved books quickly, removing the markers as I did so. This was an especially helpful procedure, since my student assistants changed with each semester.

— *Virginia Lee Schanz, Retired Librarian, Marshall, Missouri*

Moving Fun with Student Volunteers

Moving day for our junior high school library was a great success thanks to the efforts of 30 student volunteers. Moving more than 16,000 books in one day was mind-boggling but fun when we decided each student helper would have his or her own book cart (borrowed from various local libraries), which they could name and decorate. Before the big day, students came in before and after school to work on their masterpieces. One student had a Michael Jordan motif with white, red, and black streamers festooning her cart. Another made a Moose Mobile, antlers and all, with brown construction paper. One unique cart was replete with trash recycled from the library trash can. The students felt a real sense of ownership to the whole process, and we celebrated the move with a pizza party at the end of the day. What could have been a nightmare turned into one of my happiest memories as a librarian.

— *Susan Bridson, Santa Fe Trail Junior High School, Olathe, Kansas*

One Library Pass

I make one "pass" for library aides and avoid the problem of lost passes. On one sheet of paper, I list the names of all aides by the hours they work. The paper is pasted on cardboard and then laminated or covered with contact paper. This pass is used by all aides but only during their library hour.

— *Anitra Gordon, Lincoln High School, Ypsilanti, Michigan*

Parent Volunteers

Parent volunteers in our school prefer not to have a regularly scheduled time to work in the library. Instead, they are notified when special projects are needed. A volunteer may come in one or two days per week for two or three hours until the project is done. Some of the tasks handled in this manner have included book barcoding, typing catalog cards for the paperback collection, placing detection tags in books, rearranging the periodical room, and clipping materials for the vertical file.

— *Jackie Foster, D. W. Daniel High School, Central, South Carolina*

Recognizing Library Aides

Student library aides deserve special recognition at the end of the school year. For the May bulletin board, which is in the hallway outside the library, I take photographs of the aides and mount them on tagboard cutouts of open books. The aide's name and the period worked in the library are printed on the cutouts. I use a picture of a magician with the caption "Presenting the Best." On another book-shaped cutout, I print the words "Library Aides" and the year. The aides are pleased by the recognition, and the bulletin board is always an attention-getter.

— *Lydia Gutierrez, Lincoln Middle School, McAllen, Texas*

Recruiting Coupon Cutters

To increase the number of travel materials in the vertical file, recruit a parent to fill out reader response cards in automobile or travel magazines. The parent may need to have the materials sent to a home address.

— *Carol Burbridge, Jardine Middle School, Topeka, Kansas*

Senior Citizens & Book Fairs

The community senior citizens' organization provided the perfect solution to our search for book fair volunteers. The senior citizens were so personable and enthusiastic that the fair was our best ever. Volunteers also read to groups of children for special occasions.

— *Bonnie Rice, Poth (Texas) K-12 Library*

Student Aides' Reference

We keep a quick reference manual at the circulation desk listing procedures for all jobs that library assistants perform. This way, when both media specialists are busy, the assistants can still perform their duties.

— *Kathleen Varner, Tate High School, Gonzalez, Florida*

Student Assistant Name Tags

We made permanent name tags for our student library assistants to wear when they are on duty. The tags let other students know the assistants are official members of the library staff, and the identification can serve as a hall pass when the assistants run errands.

— *Peggy Mahaffey, Rock Hill (South Carolina) High School*

Student Assistant Notebooks

We provide individual notebooks for each student library assistant. In the notebook, which remains in the library, we supply a copy of our guidelines and procedures and the student's "Weekly Jobs" sheet. The jobs sheet outlines responsibilities for each day. Students check off jobs as they are completed and turn in the sheets at the end of the week.

— *Rosemary Knapp, Camas (Washington) High School*

Subjects for Artists

A picture file can be useful in a high school with an art program. Our art students use photographs as references for their drawings and paintings. Landscapes, seascapes, flowers, animals, sports, and faces are among the most popular subjects. Student aides can easily find these pictures in old magazines, especially in copies of *National Geographic*. The aides paste the pictures on construction paper and file them. The aides like the work because they can talk with friends while working. The library benefits too. When books were checked out by students for reference photographs, the books often came back with smudges of paint or pastels.

— *Anitra Gordon, Lincoln High School, Ypsilanti, Michigan*

Training Parent Volunteers in Technology

Our Internet lab is located in a confined space that requires adult supervision. Because we have a small staff, we recruited volunteers from among parents. The volunteers attend a four-hour course, which is similar to the introduction offered to teachers by the media specialists. When teachers bring classes to the lab, there is another adult available for supervision, enabling teachers to work with students on a specific project.

— *Winifred F. Durand, Pope High School, Marietta, Georgia*

Use for Catalog Cards after Conversion

After doing our online conversion, I dismantled the card catalog. Even though we had sent the shelf list for conversion, many of the new MARC records for books in the 520s lacked summaries. I organized students to sort through the old cards and throw away any without summaries. Then, adult volunteers and aides used the remaining cards to copy the summaries into each title record that lacked a summary. There has been a tremendous increase in the number of hits generated by keyword searches.

— *Barbara Yaney, Waubonsie Valley High School, Aurora, Illinois*